A PRACTITIONER'S GUIDE
TO THE
EDWARDS PERSONAL
PREFERENCE SCHEDULE

A PRACTITIONER'S GUIDE
—— TO THE ——
EDWARDS PERSONAL
PREFERENCE SCHEDULE

By

JANET E. HELMS, Ph.D.

Assistant Professor
Department of Psychology
University of Maryland
College Park, Maryland

Formerly, Southern Illinois University
Carbondale, Illinois

CHARLES C THOMAS • PUBLISHER
Springfield • Illinois • U.S.A.

Published and Distributed Throughout the World by

CHARLES C THOMAS • PUBLISHER

2600 South First Street

Springfield, Illinois, 62717, U.S.A.

© *1983 by* CHARLES C THOMAS • PUBLISHER

ISBN 0-398-04740-5

Library of Congress Catalog Card Number: 82-10548

With THOMAS BOOKS *careful attention is given to all details of manufacturing and
design. It is the Publisher's desire to present books that are satisfactory as to their physical
qualities and artistic possibilities and appropriate for their particular use.* THOMAS
BOOKS *will be true to those laws of quality that assure a good name and good will.*

Printed in the United States of America
CU-R-1

Library of Congress Cataloging in Publication Data

Helms, Janet E.
   A practitioner's guide to the Edwards personal
preference schedule.

   Bibliography: p.
   Includes index.
   1. Edwards personal preference schedule. I. Title.
BF698.8.E3H44 1983   155.2'83   82-10548
ISBN 0-398-04740-5

Dedicated to
    my parents, Brown and Elteser;
    my friend, Tedla;
    the graduate psychology faculty at Iowa State University
    (1970-1974) — for different reasons.

PREFACE

THE seeds of the idea for *The Practitioner's Guide to the Edwards Personal Preference Schedule* began to take root when I was a graduate student and was first introduced to the inventory. I was intrigued by the prospect of having a measure at my disposal that allowed me to communicate the results to test takers without subterfuge, but I was perplexed to find that there were few definite guidelines and even less readily accessible information about the instrument in spite of the fact that it had been around for almost two decades.

Although I eventually evolved some strategies of my own for using the Edwards in my counseling interventions, my interest in the scholarly aspects of the scale lay dormant until I began trying to communicate to my own graduate students how to use the inventory. To their credit, many of them wanted to know the whys and wherefores of what they were doing, and I began writing position papers to explain why I used the scales as I did. The *Guide* represents an elaboration and extension of these papers. In writing them, I have tried to present information in a way that would be useful to practitioners, but would be based on existing literature. I have tried also to avoid the esoteric statistical debates that have surrounded the EPPS, while presenting enough information about relevant resources so that those who wish to indulge in such investigations will have access to relevant resources in one place.

In completing my manuscript, I had the assistance of several talented and creative secretaries: Sandra Thompson, Patricia Loadman, Joyce Bodkin, Karen Rains, Mary Hewitt, and Josephine Shaffer. I would like to thank each of them for their unique contributions in translating my scribbles into legible script. I would also like to thank my Southern Illinois neighbors, the Garavaglias, who kept my grass from reaching the sky and supplied my typewriter with their electricity when the tornadic winds of summer stole mine. The computer science centers at Southern Illinois and University of Maryland contributed the funds necessary for computer analyses. Finally, I would like to thank all of the writers cited herein who made the effort and took the time to publish their work. Without them, there would be no practitioner's guide.

CONTENTS

SECTION I: OVERVIEW

Chapter

SECTION II: VALIDITY ISSUES

Chapter

SECTION III: PERSONALITY CHARACTERISTICS

Chapter

SECTION IV: VOCATIONAL/EDUCATIONAL USAGE

Chapter

SECTION V: BEHAVIOR CORRELATES

SECTION VI: APPENDICES

FIGURES

TABLES

A PRACTITIONER'S GUIDE
TO THE
EDWARDS PERSONAL
PREFERENCE SCHEDULE

SECTION I

OVERVIEW

Chapter 1

INTRODUCTION

W HEN the Edwards Personal Preference Schedule[1] (1959) first entered the personality testing arena, it was both hailed and harangued by test reviewers because of its relatively unique approaches to personality assessment, e.g. Wittenborn, 1956; Gustad, 1956. Special features of the inventory included (a) the author's attempt to measure several normal personality characteristics concurrently, (b) personality scales that were based on a personality theory, and (c) the forced choice format to control for a social desirability response set. At one time or another, most of these features have been discussed in the literature as will become apparent in subsequent chapters.

DESCRIPTION OF THE SCALES. The EPPS consists of fifteen personality scales, which measure personality needs, and two validity scales, one of which must be calculated by the test user. The content of the fifteen need scales, Achievement (Ach), Deference (Def), Order (Ord), Exhibition (Exh), Autonomy (Aut), Affiliation (Aff), Intraception (Int), Succorance (Suc), Dominance (Dom), Abasement (Aba), Nurturance (Nur), Change (Chg), Endurance (End), Heterosexuality (Het), and Aggression (Agg), are summarized in Table 1-I. Edwards (1959) reports that Murray's (1938) personality theory was used to name the needs, but that the actual needs assessed had been discussed by others as well as Murray.

Score Profiles

The maximum score that a person can receive on a scale is 28 and the minimum score is 0. It is, however, impossible to obtain a score of 0 or 28 on all fifteen scales simultaneously unless the test scorer has made a major scoring error too serious to contemplate. This is because the 225 inventory items are presented in forced-choice dyads containing items representing two different needs so that endorsement of one item automatically reduces one's score on one or another of the other fourteen need scales. This scoring procedure makes the EPPS an ipsative measure and, as such, interpretation of the scores to a client can be somewhat confusing since the need levels are not independent, but rather occur relative to one another. Although the EPPS manual does present T scores and percentiles (the latter of which can be displayed on a profile chart as shown in Figure 1-1) for college and adult samples, these group comparisons are largely inadequate for portraying the relative nature of their needs to test takers.

---

[1]The abbreviation EPPS or simply the Edwards will be used to refer to the inventory from henceforth.

Table 1 - I

THE MANIFEST NEEDS ASSOCIATED WITH
EACH OF THE 15 EPPS VARIABLES ARE:

1. ach Achievement: To do one's best to be successful, to accomplish tasks requiring skill and effort, to be a recognized authority, to accomplish something of great significance, to do a difficult job well, to solve difficult problems and puzzles, to be able to do things better than others, to write a great novel or play.

2. def Deference: To get suggestions from others, to find out what others think, to follow instructions and do what is expected, to praise others, to tell others that they have done a good job, to accept the leadership of others, to read about great men, to conform to custom and avoid the unconventional, to let others make decisions.

3. ord Order: To have written work neat and organized, to make plans before starting on a difficult task, to have things organized, to keep things neat and orderly, to make advance plans when taking a trip, to organize details of work, to keep letters and files according to some system, to have meals organized and a definite time for eating, to have things arranged so that they run smoothly without change.

4. exh Exhibition: To say witty and clever things, to tell amusing jokes and stories, to talk about personal adventures and experiences, to have others notice and comment upon one's appearance, to say things just to see what effect it will have on others, to talk about personal achievements, to be the center of attention, to use words that others do not know the meaning of, to ask questions others cannot answer.

5. aut Autonomy: To be able to come and go as desire, to say what one thinks about things, to be independent of others in making decisions, to feel free to do what one wants, to do things that are

Table 1 - I (continued)

unconventional, to avoid situations where one is expected to conform, to do things without regard to what others may think, to criticize those in positions of authority, to avoid responsibilities and obligations.

6. aff Affiliation: To be loyal to friends, to participate in friendly groups, to do things for friends, to form new friendships, to make as many friends as possible, to share things with friends, to do things with friends rather than alone, to form strong attachments, to write letters to friends.

7. int Intraception: To analyze one's motives and feelings, to observe others, to understand how others feel about problems, to put one's self in another's place, to judge people by why they do things rather than by what they do, to analyze the behavior of others, to analyze the motives of others, to predict how others will act.

8. suc Succorance: To have others provide help when in trouble, to seek encouragement from others, to have others be kind, to have others be sympathetic and understanding about personal problems, to receive a great deal of affection from others, to have others do favors cheerfully, to be helped by others when depressed, to have others feel sorry when one is sick, to have a fuss made over one when hurt.

9. dom Dominance: To argue for one's point of view, to be a leader in groups to which one belongs, to be regarded by others as a leader, to be elected or appointed chairman of committees, to make group decisions, to settle arguments and disputes between others, to persuade and influence others to do what one wants, to supervise and direct the actions of others, to tell others how to do their jobs.

10. aba Abasement: To feel guilty when one does something wrong, to accept blame when things do not go right, to feel that personal pain and misery suffered does more good than harm, to feel the need for

Table 1 - I (continued)

punishment for wrong doing, to feel better when giving in and avoiding
a fight than when having one's own way, to feel the need for confession
of errors, to feel depressed by inability to handle situations, to feel
timid in the presence of superiors, to feel inferior to others in most
respects.

11. nur Nurturance: To help friends when they are in trouble,
to assist others less fortunate, to treat others with kindness and sympathy,
to forgive others, to do small favors for others, to be generous with
others, to sympathize with others who are hurt or sick, to show a great
deal of affection toward others, to have others confide in one about
personal problems.

12. chg Change: To do new and different things, to travel, to
meet new people, to experience novelty and change in daily routine,
to experiment and try new things, to eat in new and different places,
to try new and different jobs, to move about the country and live in
different places, to participate in new fads and fashions.

13. end Endurance: To keep at a job until it is finished, to
complete any job undertaken, to work hard at a task, to keep at a puzzle
or problem until it is solved, to work at a single job before taking
on others, to stay up late working in order to get a job done, to put
in long hours of work without distraction, to stick at a problem even
though it may seem as if no progress is being made, to avoid being in-
terrupted while at work.

14. het Heterosexuality: To go out with members of the opposite
sex, to engage in social activities with the opposite sex, to be in love
with someone of the opposite sex, to kiss those of the opposite sex,
to be regarded as physically attractive by those of the opposite sex,
to participate in discussions about sex, to read books and plays involving

Table 1 - I (continued)

sex, to listen to or to tell jokes involving sex, to become sexually

excited.

15. agg Aggression: To attack contrary points of view, to tell

others what one thinks about them, to criticize others publicly, to

make fun of others, to tell others off when disagreeing with them, to

get revenge for insults, to become angry, to blame others when things

go wrong, to read newspaper accounts of violence.

Reproduced from Edwards, A. L. Edwards Personal Preference

Schedule: Revised Manual, 1959, by permission of The Psycho-

logical Corporation.

Rather than using the group norms, it is more useful to discuss the person's own rank ordering of needs with her or him. However, since test takers seem to be captivated by "pictures" of their needs, the author has found that individual profiles similar to the one shown in Figure 1-2 are particularly useful in encouraging the client to consider which needs are particularly important for her or him personally.

Reliability

INTERNAL CONSISTENCY. Edwards reported internal consistency estimates of his scales ranging from .60 to .87. The Deference Scale was the least reliable scale, and the Heterosexuality Scale was the most reliable. No one else has reported internal consistency data for all of the scales though Levonian, Comrey, Levy, and Proctor (1959) presented scale analyses that bear on the issue. In their separate analyses of the fifteen scales, they found small positive correlations among the items of each of the scales that were not necessarily significant. Their factor analyses did not reveal general factors for the scales, which would have been expected had the scales contained items reflecting a common underlying theme. Their results would argue against scale high internal consistency and suggest the need for further investigation of this aspect of the scales. On the other hand, Lipetz (1961), who was interested in the reliability of the Autonomy Scale as it related to female respondents, found reliability estimates of .28, .67, and .75 using three successive samples and two methods of computing the reliabilities. By way of constrast for the single male sample that he investigated, he reported a reliability estimate of .76 (as did Edwards

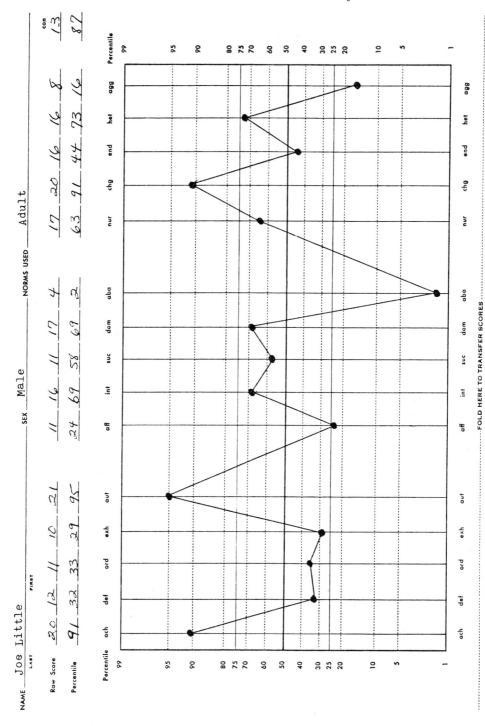

Figure 1-1. EDWARDS PERSONAL PREFERENCE SCHEDULE. Reproduced from *Edwards Personal Preference Schedule Manual* by permission. Copyright© 1959 by The Psychological Corporation, New York, N.Y. All rights reserved.

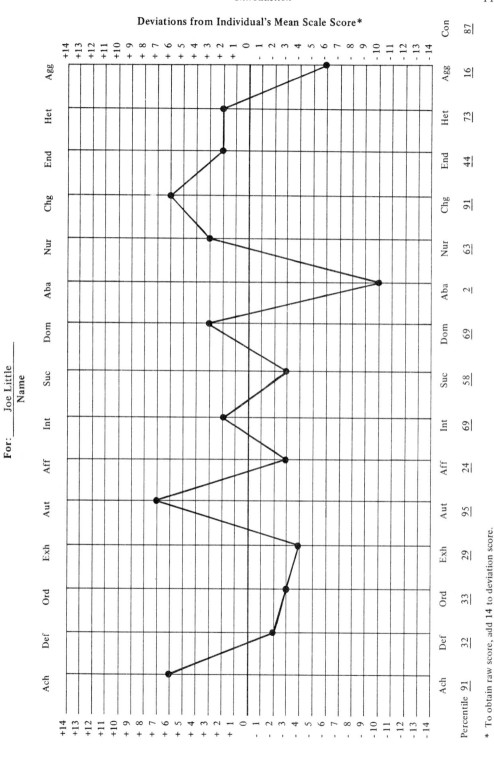

Figure 1-2. SUMMARY OF EPPS TEST SCORES

for his mixed sex sample). He concluded that the scale may be equally reliable for both sexes, but reliability may differ from sample to sample.

TEST-RETEST RELIABILITY. To determine the short-term stability of EPPS scale scores, Edwards tested a sample of college students on two occasions separated by one week. His original test-retest correlations for the individual scales plus those reported by subsequent investigators are summarized in Table I-II. Horst and Wright's (1959) reliability study in which a combined sample of forty-four men and forty-eight women undergraduates were tested at a one-week interval essentially replicated Edwards's original findings. Only one scale coefficient, that for endurance, was significantly lower than the ones reported by Edwards, and that one difference could have occurred by chance conceivably. At a three-week retest interval, nine scales (60 percent excluding the consistency scale which was not reported) had reliability coefficients that were not significantly lower than those reported by Edwards (Mann, 1958). In only two need scales, Affiliation and Nurturance, were the coefficients less than .60.

The reliability coefficients for a sample of 148 naval flight candidates retested at a seven-week interval were significantly lower for all of the scales including the consistency scale (Waters, 1968). Waters reported that the mean scores on the Achievement, Exhibition, and Dominance scales had increased whereas those for Abasement, Nurturance, Change, and Aggression had decreased. Caputo, Psathas, and Plapp (1966) retested a sample of fifty-two nursing students after fifteen months. They reported that eleven of the fifteen correlations that they found were significantly lower than Edwards's. The ones that did not differ were the Exhibition, Affiliation, Nurturance, and Change scales. The only two that were not significantly lower than Mann's (1958) were the Nurturance and Affiliation scales. In addition, the correlation for affiliation for the fifteen-month sample was significantly higher than that reported for Waters's seven-week sample, and the correlation for intraception was significantly lower.

Overall, the studies in which combined male and female subject samples have been used (i.e. Edwards, 1959; Mann, 1958; Horst and Wright, 1959) indicate that the scales have adequate stability up to a one-week period. At a three-week interval, considerable stability is still evident, but not to the level reported by Edwards for six of the scales: Order, Affiliation, Intraception, Dominance, Abasement, and Nurturance. At seven weeks and beyond, the stability for most of the scales is significantly less than what Edwards reported, but because Waters (1969) used a presumably all-male sample and Caputo et al. (1966) used a presumably all-female sample, then it is possible that the drop-off in reliability represents a sex effect of some sort.

It is also possible to argue that a stability coefficient at seven weeks (or beyond) no longer measures the stability of the instrument but instead measures the stability of the individuals' traits. In that case, it would appear that change was the most stable trait and intraception was the least stable trait

Table 1 - II

COEFFICIENTS OF STABILITY FOR
EPPS VARIABLES
STABILITY COEFFICIENTS FOR NEED SCALES[1]

		One Week	One Week	Three Weeks	Seven Weeks	Fifteen Months
1.	Achievement	.74	.83	.64	.53**	.47**
2.	Deference	.78	.67	.87	.47**	.45**
3.	Order	.87	.81	.77*	.57**	.59**
4.	Exhibition	.74	.64	.71	.53**	.60
5.	Autonomy	.83	.76	.76	.64**	.65*
6.	Affiliation	.77	.80	.55**	.37**	.64
7.	Intraception	.86	.84	.67**	.67**	.41**
8.	Succorance	.78	.78	.72	.51**	.46**
9.	Dominance	.87	.82	.73**	.56**	.60**
10.	Abasement	.88	.84	.69**	.67**	.59**
11.	Nurturance	.79	.81	.59**	.61**	.65
12.	Change	.83	.80	.86	.58**	.73
13.	Endurance	.86	.76*	.77	.62**	.61**
14.	Heterosexuality	.85	.76	.85	.62**	.45**
15.	Aggression	.78	.72	.80	.60**	.50**
Consistency Score		.78	---	---	.37**	---
N		89	92	96	148	52

[1]Sources of cited coefficients in order of citation are:

Edwards, 1959; Horst & Wright, 1959; Mann, 1958; Waters, 1968; Caputo et al., 1966.

*Correlation significantly smaller than Edwards' correlation for the same need at the .05 level of confidence

**Correlation significantly smaller than Edwards' correlation for the same need at or beyond the .01 level of confidence

for Caputo et al.'s (1966) female sample and intraception and abasement were the most stable and affiliation and consistency were the least stable traits for Waters's (1968) male sample.

PROFILE RETEST RELIABILITY. Another method that has been used to explore the reliability of the EPPS has been to intercorrelate the entire profiles of individuals who were retested after specified intervals. Stability coefficients reported in three such studies are shown in Table 1-III. Borislow's (1958) correlations which were obtained after a one-week interval, were generally higher than Caputo et al.'s (1966), which were obtained after a fifteen-month interval. Caputo et al. reported that all but one of their fifty-one profiles had correlations that exceeded 0, while the one that did not had a consistency score of 9 at the second testing. Waters (1968) reported that sixty-four of his total sample of

Table 1 - III

SUMMARY OF PROFILE RETEST STABILITY STUDIES

Stability Coefficient Intervals	Individual Study Frequencies Per Interval		
	Borislow (1958)	Caputo et al. (1966)	Waters (1968)
-.40 - -.30			1
-.30 - -.20			1
-.20 - -.10			
-.10 - -.00			
.00 - .10		1	
.10 - .20			1
.20 - .30			
.30 - .40		2	2
.40 - .50		7	4
.50 - .60		7	2
.60 - .70	1	13	15
.70 - .80	2	10	19
.80 - .90	2	9	23
.90 - 1.00	1	3	6
N	6	52	64

seventy-four profiles had correlations that were significantly different from 0. Of the ten that were not significant, six had consistency scores that were no higher than 9; only ten of the stable profiles had consistency scores less than or equal to 9. The profile retest stability studies provide evidence that individuals' patterns of scores have been found to be stable over one-week, seven-week, and fifteen-month testing intervals.

Validity Scales

CONSISTENCY SCORE. The main validity scale, consistency (con), is used to judge whether or not the test taker responded randomly to the inventory items. A maximum consistency score of 15 is possible. A person receives a point toward the consistency score by choosing the same alternative each time fifteen identical items are presented to her or him for a second time. Edwards recommends a consistency score of 11 or more as being indicative of a valid profile. Subsequent investigators have tended to violate this recommendation, though little empirical investigation indicates that such action is warranted. In her discussion of the consistency score, Heathers (writing for the EPPS manual) reported some confusion regarding the meaning of low consistency scores.

Three studies suggest that respondents with low consistency scores may differ from their more consistent counterparts. In the first such study, Medley (1961) divided ninety-one female student teachers into groups of consistent and inconsistent responders using Edwards's criterion. For the teachers with low scores, he found significant positive correlations between abasement, aggression, achievement, intraception, and their students' evaluation of their rapport and a negative correlation between heterosexuality and rapport. For the consistent teachers, none of the needs correlated significantly with rapport. Although Medley does not present data comparing the two groups, it is probable that the inconsistent responders differed from their peers in their level of the aforementioned needs.

Heilbrun (1963) used a self-devised consistency scale based on the percentage of times a person selected a self-descriptive statement having a higher social desirability value. He found that for a combined sample of sixty-four males and sixty-four female undergraduates, those with low consistency scores as compared to those with high scores had higher Psychasthenia (Pt) and Social Introversion (Si) scores and a higher anxiety index on the MMPI. His results suggest that inconsistent responders may be obsessive and prone to worry.

Finally, for this chapter, Helms used five scales of Holland's (1965) Vocational Preference Inventory to test the hypothesis that eleven women business and communications majors [2] with consistency scores of ten or less would differ from eleven women in the same majors with consistency scores that exceeded

---

[2] Dr. Mela Puig-Casaranc donated the profiles used in this analysis.

10. Scores on three of the scales, Infrequency, Masculinity, and Self-control, did not differ significantly between the two groups. Holland conceptualizes the Infrequency Scale "as a personal effectiveness scale with high scores indicative of incompetency and low scores indicative of personal effectiveness" (p. 25); high Masculinity Scale scores are characterized as indicating masculine interests and possible conflicts about one's identification with males or females; high Self-control Scale scores may indicate tendencies toward overcontrol of impulses.

For the high consistency group, their mean Infrequency and Self-control Scale scores would have located them at the 33rd percentile and their mean Masculinity Scale score would have located them at the 68th percentile. For the low consistency group, their mean score would have located them at the 81st, 25th, and 44th percentiles for the Masculinity, Self-control, and Infrequency scales, respectively. Thus, when their scores deviated from normal, they tended to vary in the same direction and at comparable levels.

On the other hand, the consistent EPPS scorers did differ significantly from the inconsistent EPPS scorers on the Acquiescence and the Status Scales. Consistent women scored higher on both scales. Their average score on the former would have located them at the 53rd percentile, and their score on the latter would have located them at the 63rd percentile. Respective percentiles for the low consistency scorers were 9th and 28th. Since Holland suggests that moderately high scores on the Acquiescence Scale may be indicative of self-confidence and that the Status Scale is perhaps an estimate of the person's self-esteem, then it appears that for the groups of women investigated, consistent women revealed scale levels that were suggestive of better self-confidence and self-esteem.

PROFILE STABILITY. The second validity score, profile stability, is computed by correlating half a person's score for each need with the other half of her or his scores. Edwards suggests that a profile stability coefficient of .44 should indicate a stable profile for most people, although the average correlation for his sample was a much higher value of .74.

For his six subjects, Borislow found profile stability coefficients all but one of which exceeded the .44 level over a one-week period. Fiske, Howard, and Rechenberg (1960) subsequently investigated the characteristics of the profile stability indicant. They found an average stability coefficient virtually identical to that reported by Edwards. In addition, they reported positive correlations between the stability coefficient and needs for Autonomy ($r = .37$), Exhibition ($r = .30$), Achievement ($r = .17$), Dominance ($r = .17$), and Consistency ($r = .23$). Abasement ($r = -.28$), Order ($r = -.27$), and Deference ($r = -.21$) correlated negatively with profile stability. They also found that the Dominant and Active scales of the Thurstone Temperament Schedule correlated positively with stability. Fiske et al. concluded that "consistency of a need profile on two groups of items appears to be related to active strivings for superior and controlling status" (p. 370).

Instrument Modifications

INSTRUCTIONS. Several methods have been used to search for factors that might contribute to the reliability and validity of the EPPS scales. Weigel and Frazier (1968) thought that the EPPS instructions might activate an implicit response set to respond either (1) "in terms of his [sic] 'conceptualized' likes and feelings, or (2) in terms of his [sic] likes and feelings as he [sic] sees them reflected in his [sic] typical behavior" (p. 337).

They administered the Dominance and Order scales, allegedly the most transparent scales (Korman and Coltharp, 1962) to a group of eighty-nine male and 100 female undergraduate students. Half of the sample received instructions to answer the items in terms of the way they felt and the other half received instructions to respond in terms of how they actually behaved. For neither sex did they find significant differences between the instruction groups.

Richardson (1969) replicated the study but presented both sets of instructions to each subject with each type of instruction being separated by a four-week interval. His results confirmed Weigel and Frazier's. Both sets of investigators concluded that the standard EPPS instructions did not activate a feeling versus behavior response set.

ALTERNATIVE SCORING FORMATS. Several efforts to discover better methods of administering and/or of scoring the EPPS have been initiated because of various authors' disgruntlement with the forced-choice format, which is characteristic of the EPPS items. *Better* is usually defined in terms of greater reliability or economy of administration time. In their study in which they compared the test-retest reliability of an ipsatized rating scale form of the EPPS to the standard form, Horst and Wright (1959) were seeking information relevant to both issues. In their ipsatized version of the scale, forty males and forty-eight female undergraduate students responded to the 135 unique items of the EPPS by using a 9-point rating scale to indicate how descriptive of them the items were. Standard scores for the group were computed, and then each person's scores were computed by calculating the deviations from his or her mean standard score for each scale. The deviation scores were then restandardized across persons. Horst and Wright refer to this process as *arithmetical ipsatization*.

The authors reported an average retest reliability of .87 for the ipsatized version of the EPPS and a retest reliability of .78 for the standard EPPS. They also stated that the time necessary for test takers to take the ipsatized version of the inventory was approximately forty minutes less than the hour required to complete the standard EPPS.

Lanyon (1966) devised an EPPS checklist version, which he called the free-choice EPPS. The nine times which were unique to each of the fifteen scales (total of 135 items) were identified and eighty-five males and forty-six females were asked to check the sixty-seven items that best described them. The retest reliability for the females (males were not retested) ranged from .65 (Achievement Scale) to .87 (Endurance Scale) with a median of .76 when the free-choice EPPS was used. Edwards had found reliabilities ranging from .74 (Achievement and Exhibition Scales) to .88 (Abasement Scale) with a median of .83. The authors contended that the free-choice EPPS would exhibit greater reliability than the regular EPPS were they to lengthen the scales to twenty-eight items each as are the regular scales.

Regarding the validity of his instrument, Lanyon (1966) only found a mean correlation of .63 between the male subjects' rank-ordered needs on the EPPS and the free-choice EPPS; correlations ranged from .19 to .94. These results suggest that the modified version of the EPPS yielded a pattern of needs that was only moderately similar to the EPPS pattern. Other validity indicants showed two small but significant correlations for the EPPS and one for the free-choice EPPS. Lanyon's measure reportedly took only about twenty minutes to administer.

Following a different tack, Santee (1975) proposed that inherent in the EPPS were items that sought information about how people regarded themselves as well as information about how they regarded others. He contended that people's preferences for themselves and others were different and constituted a serious confound in the scales. Therefore, he developed thirty separate scales that contained fourteen items that people could use to describe themselves and fourteen that they could use to describe what they preferred of others.

For his version of the EPPS, Santee reported that 89.2 percent of spouses who completed the inventory obtained individual consistency scores of eleven or higher as compared to 74.6 percent for Edward's original sample. Respondents' preferences for themselves did tend to differ from their preferences for others. Scales on which both sexes revealed significant self-other differences were Heterosexuality, Achievement, Exhibition, Affiliation, and Nurturance. Males also indicated self-other differences regarding the Autonomy, Dominance, Aggression, and Order Scales.

Instead of changing the response format or the item content as previous EPPS revisers had done, Navran (1977) recommended an alternative method of scoring the original items, which is summarized in Table 1-IV. His basic argument is that each of the EPPS scales contains several components or clusters that measure different aspects of the particular need. Although his method of rescoring the items has not been investigated empirically, Navran reports that interpretation of scores using the component analysis has proved to be useful and effective in his work with clients.

DERIVED SCORES. Trehub (1959) proposed an idea that certain combinations of the EPPS scales could be used diagnostically. In particular, he felt that level of intrapsychic conflict, which he calls *ego disjunction,* could be assessed by determining a person's score on pairs of needs that seemed to imply incompatible goals. The pairs that he selected were aggression-deference, succorance-nurturance, autonomy-abasement, and order-change. A person's disjunction score was computed by adding together standard scores for each need within a pair, subtracting 100 from the sum, and adding together the positive residuals. The higher the total of the residuals, the more ego disjunction was assumed to exist. In comparing samples of male college students, adolescents, neurotics,

Table 1 - IV

THE CONSTITUENT COMPONENTS OF THE EPPS VARIABLES

EPPS Variable	Components	No. of Items
1. Achievement:		
A.	Outstanding achievement per se:	10
B.	Competitive ambition	6
C.	Desire for recognition by others:	6
D.	High standards for self	6
2. Deference:		
A.	Following others' directions:	10
B.	Conforming to others' expectations:	3
C.	Seeking respected others' help:	3
D.	Praising others one admires:	3
E.	Praising one's superiors for doing well	3
F.	Admiring and being guided by great men	6
3. Order:		
A.	Planning prior to acting	12
B.	Scheduled, predictable routine	7
C.	Neatness, order in filing	6
D.	Being noticed by others	3
4. Exhibition:		
A.	Talking about oneself	9
B.	Relating to others in superior way	7
C.	Verbal wittiness:	6
D.	Being noticed by others:	6

Table 1 - IV (continued)

EPPS Variable	Components	No. of Items
5. Autonomy:		
A.	Avoiding conventionality, others' expectations............	13
B.	Being self-directing, valuing personal freedom...........	9
C.	Saying what one thinks, criticizing authority............	6
6. Affiliation:		
A.	Loyalty and strong attachments...........................	10
B.	Making many friendships..................................	6
C.	Doing things with friends................................	6
D.	Giving to and doing for friends..........................	6
7. Intraception:		
A.	Analyzing friend's feelings, personality, behavior........	10
B.	Analyzing others' feelings...............................	6
C.	Analyzing others' behavior...............................	6
D.	Analyzing own motives and feelings.......................	6
8. Succorance:		
A.	Having friends be kind, affectionate, giving.............	9
B.	(Physical) Having friends' support when hurt or sick......	7
C.	(Behavior) Having friends' support when one fails or is in trouble.......................................	6
D.	(Emotional) Having friends' support when one has problems or is depressed...........................	6
9. Dominance:		
A.	Directing others, making decisions.......................	10
B.	Wanting an actual leadership position....................	6
C.	Having others relate as if one is a leader..............	6
D.	Defending one's views, persuading others................	6

Table 1 - IV (continued)

EPPS Variable	Components	No. of Items
10.	Abasement:	
	A. Strongly punitive conscience..............................	12
	B. Poor self image; low self-esteem.........................	7
	C. Non-assertiveness, timidity..............................	6
	D. Masochism..	3
11.	Nurturance:	
	A. Helping troubled or sick friends.........................	9
	B. Being generous, affectionate, accommodating to friends..	10
	C. Being kind, generous, sympathetic to others.............	6
	D. Being forgiving to friend who may hurt you..............	3
12.	Change:	
	A. Travel, living and eating in different places, meeting new people..	13
	B. Welcoming the new, different, or experimental...........	9
	C. Variation in daily routine..............................	3
	D. Occupational variety....................................	3
13.	Endurance:	
	A. Need for completing any task begun......................	15
	B. Being persistent, hard worker...........................	7
	C. Disliking interruptions, distractions..................	6
14.	Heterosexuality:	
	A. Active sexual behavior, being in love, being seen as physically attractive..................................	12
	B. Dating, socializing with the opposite sex..............	6
	C. Talking and reading about sex, sexual humor............	10

Table 1 - IV (continued)

EPPS Variable	Components	No. of Items
15. Aggression:		
	A. Actually speaking aggressively.............................	7
	B. Feeling like speaking aggressively........................	9
	C. Projecting blame, feeling extreme anger or vengefulness...	9
	D. Vicarious aggression......................................	3

TABLE IV is reprinted from Navran, L., The Common Import Component Scoring of the Edwards Personal Preference Schedule. *Journal of Personality Assessment*, 1977, 41, 285-290 by permission of the publisher.

character disorders, and schizophrenics, Trehub found that character disorders, neurotics, and adolescents showed statistically equivalent levels of disjunction, college students showed the lowest level, and schizophrenics showed the highest level. Scores ranged from a low of twenty for college students to a high of about forty-five for the schizophrenics.

When Fordyce and Crow (1960) used the Ego Disjunction Scale score in an effort to discriminate male neurotics, character disorders, acute schizophrenics, and chronic schizophrenics from one another, they were successful. It is not clear from their presentation whether their samples were similar in age to Trehub's original test sample, but it is clear that their samples resided in a different region of the country. The authors suggest that regional variables may interact with patient characteristics.

Gocka and Rozynko (1961) warned against using the Ego Disjunction Scale scores as an uncontaminated measure of intrapsychic conflict without investigating further the role that demographic factors play in influencing such scores. In their study, for instance, they found the Ego Disjunction Scale scores for men and women under forty were significantly lower than the scores for men and women over forty.

Kamano (1963), using a sample of male undergraduates, found that the combination of high ego disjunction and high manifest anxiety was characteristic of subjects who experienced more approach-approach and avoidance-avoidance conflict and required more time to resolve conflict problems than subjects exhibiting different combinations of anxiety and ego disjunction. Neither consideration of ego disjunction alone nor of anxiety alone revealed significant conflict differences between high and low scorers. His results suggest that a combination of the Ego Disjunction Scale score and a measure expressly designed to measure psychopathology might be predictive of behavioral concomitants.

Summary

Most of the EPPS scales appear to have adequate test-retest reliability for testing intervals extending up to and including three weeks. Only one study of the internal consistency of any of the scales exists, and that study suggests that the internal consistency of the Autonomy Scale is probably adequate though it may differ from sample to sample. Investigations of the consistency scale and profile stability correlates suggest that low scores on either of these indicants may have clinical implications. More practitioner oriented studies of these aspects of the EPPS are needed.

Various alternative methods of scoring and/or administering the EPPS have been proposed, and for the most part these methods promise greater reliability and shorter administration time in the long run without great loss of scale meaningfulness. Nevertheless, before such scale alternations can be of benefit to the test user, it is necessary to develop norms for the populations on which the instrument is to be used and to conduct further validational studies.

Only one derived scale, Ego Disjunction, has appeared with any regularity in the literature. So far, it has been used almost exclusively with males. Current evidence suggests that Ego Disjunction Scale scores may be susceptible to demographic influences.

References

Borislow, B.: The Edwards Personal Preference Schedule (EPPS) and fakability. *Journal of Applied Psychology, 42:*22-27, 1958.

Caputo, D.V., Psathas, G., and Plapp, J.M.: Test-retest reliability of the EPPS. *Educational and Psychological Measurement, 26:*883-886, 1966.

Fiske, D.W., Howard, K., and Rechenberg, W.: The EPPS profile stability coefficient. *Journal of Consulting Psychology, 24:*370-374, 1960.

Fordyce, W.W., and Crow, W.R.: Ego disjunction: A failure to replicate Trehub's results. *Journal of Abnormal and Social Psychology, 60:*446-448, 1960.

Gocka, E.F., and Rozynko, V.: Some comments on the EPPS Ego Disjunction Score. *Journal of Abnormal Social Psychology, 62:* 458-460, 1961.

Gustad, J.W.: A review of the Edwards Personal Preference Schedule. *Journal of Consulting Psychology, 20:*322-324, 1956.

Heilbrun, A.B.: Social value: social behavior inconsistency and early signs of psychopathology in adolescence. *Child Development, 34:*187-194, 1963.

Holland, J.L.: *Vocational Preference Inventory Manual.* California, Consulting Psychologists Press, 1965.

Horst, P., and Wright, C.E.: Comparative reliability of two techniques of personality appraisal. *Journal of Clinical Psychology, 15:*388-391, 1959.

Kamano, D.K.: Relationship of ego disjunction and manifest anxiety to conflict resolution. *Journal of Abnormal Social Psychology, 66:*281-284, 1963.

Korman, M., and Coltharp, F.: Transparency in the Edwards Personal Preference Schedule. *Journal of Consulting Psychology, 26:*379-382, 1962.

Lanyon, R.I.: A free-choice version of the EPPS. *Journal of Clinical Psychology, 22:*202-205, 1966.

Levonian, E., Comrey, A., Levy, W., and Proctor, D.: A statistical evaluation of Edwards Personal Schedule. *Journal of Applied Psychology, 43:*353-359, 1959.

Lipetz, M.: Reliability of EPPS autonomy for males and females. *Psychological Reports, 8:*456, 1961.

Mann, J.H.: Self-ratings and the EPPS. *Journal of Applied Psychology, 42:*267-268, 1958.

Medley, D.M.: Teacher personality and teacher-pupil rapport. *Journal of Teacher Education, 12:* 152-156, 1961.

Murray, H.A.: *Explorations in personality. A clinical and experimental study of fifty men of college age.* New York, Oxford University Press, 1938.

Navran, L.: The common import component scoring of the EPPS. *Journal of Personality Assessment, 41:*285-290, 1977.

Richardson, F.C.: Effects of "feeling" and "behavior" instructions on responses to the EPPS: A replication. *Journal of Educational Research 62:*399, 1969.

Santee, R.T.: Self-other orientations and the Edwards Personal Preference Schedule. *Journal of Personality Assessment, 39:* 293-296, 1975.

Trehub, A.: Ego disjunction and psychopathology. *Journal of Abnormal Social Psychology, 58:*191-198, 1959.

Waters, L.K.: Stability of EPPS need scale scores and profiles over a seven-week interval. *Educational and Psychological Measurement, 28:*615-618, 1968.

Weigel, R.G., and Frazier, J.E.: The effects of "feeling and behavior" instructions on responses to the Edwards Personal Preference Schedule. *Journal of Educational Measurement, 5:*337-338, 1968.

Wittenborn, J.R.: A review of the Edwards Personal Preference Schedule. *Journal of Consulting Psychology, 20:*321-322, 1956.

Chapter 2

DEMOGRAPHIC EFFECTS ON THE EPPS SCALES

T HE original EPPS norms were developed using women and men representing a wide range of ages, different marital statuses, and various
regions of the country. However, with the exception of sex differences, no data
were presented concerning how demographic characteristics of respondents
could be expected to contribute to scale fluctuations. In this section, research
relevant to demographic influences is summarized.

Sex Differences

BETWEEN SEXES. Differences between the sexes on the EPPS scales have
tended to imitate the patterns initially reported by Edwards. Where sex differences have occurred, women have tended to score higher on the expressive
or social needs while men have tended to score higher on the instrumental or
goal-directed needs. Thus, for the most part, highest female needs have continued to be deference, affiliation, succorance, abasement, nurturance, intraception, and change, whereas highest male needs have continued to be
achievement, autonomy, dominance, heterosexuality, and aggression. Interestingly enough, although there have been some changes in the absolute
level of a few of these needs over the years (see Table 2-I), the direction of the
needs differences has remained relatively unchanged. Yet, when the level of a
need for both men and women of a particular sample has deviated from that exhibited by the norm groups, the tendency has been for both sexes to have
changed in the same direction, suggesting that some environmental factors
may impact the sexes similarly.

WITHIN SEX DIFFERENCES. The samples of women shown in Table 2-I consisting primarily of college student populations suggest that the levels of EPPS
needs reported in 1957 (Jackson and Guba, 1957; Grossack, 1957; Klett, 1957;
Allen and Dallek, 1957) tended to be about the same as those of the norm
groups in 1954. In those few instances where there were differences, nonminority women tended to have a greater need for deference, order, endurance, and aggression and a lesser need for dominance and heterosexuality
than did the norm group. Autonomy, intraception, succorance, and nurturance did not differ. Thus, the picture of women in the late 1950s was consistent with a traditional female sex-role identification.

The samples available in the years 1961 through 1969 (Kinnick and Nelson,
1970; Gauron, 1965; Boose and Boose, 1967; Satz and Allen, 1961; Fuster,
1962; Hamachek and Mori, 1964; Spangler and Thomas, 1962; Koons and

Table 2 - I

SUMMARY OF SEX DIFFERENCES ON THE EPPS SCALES

POPULATION	Females	Males	Ach[M]	Def[F]	Ord	Exh	Aut[M]	Aff[F]	Int[F]	Suc[F]	Dom[M]	Aba[F]	Nur[F]	Chg[F]	End	Het[M]	Agg[M]
1. EPPS college sample (1959)	749	760	L	H	0	0	L	H	H	H	L	H	H	H	0	L	L
2. High school students (Klett, 1957)	834	799	L[1,2]	0[1]	0	L[1,2]	L	H[1]	H[1,2]	H	L[1,2]	H[1,2]	H[1]	H[1,2]	L[1,2]	L	L[1,2]
3. Disabled patients (Spangler, et al., 1962)	40	40	0[3]	0	0	0	0	H	0	H	L	0	H	0	0	0	L
4. College freshmen (Koons, et al., 1964)	200	100	L[1,2]	0[1,2]	0	0	0[2]	H[1]	H[1,2]	H	0[1,2]	H[1,2]	H	0	0[1]	L[2]	L[1,2]
5. Midwest college freshmen (Tisdale, 1965)	132	160	L	0	0	0	L	H	H	H	L[2]	H[2]	H	H	0	L[2]	L
6. New York college students (Murgatroyd, et al., 1975)	163	83	L	0[1,2]	0[2]	L[1]	L[1]	H[1,2]	0[2]	H[1]	L[1,2]	H	H[1]	0	0	0[1]	L[1,2]
7. Black college students (Grossack 1957)	108	63	0[1]	0[1,2]	0[1,2]	L[1,2]	0[1,2]	0[1,2]	0	0[1]	0[1,2]	H[1,2]	0	H[1]	0	L[1,2]	L[1]

NEEDS

Table 2 - I (continued)

NEEDS

POPULATION	Females	Males	Ach[M]	Def[F]	Ord[F]	Exh	Aut[M]	Aff[F]	Int[F]	Suc[F]	Dom[M]	Aba[F]	Nur[F]	Chg[F]	End	Het[M]	Agg[M]
8. Indian college students (Fuster, 1962)	141	147	L^1	0^2	$L^{1,2}$	0^1	0^2	$H^{1,2}$	H^2	H	L^1	$H^{1,2}$	$H^{1,2}$	H	L^2	$L^{1,2}$	$L^{1,2}$
9. Miami college students (Satz, et al., 1961)	79	157	$L^{1,2}$	0	0	0	0	$H^{1,2}$	0	H	L	$0^{1,2}$	H	0	0	L	L^1
10. Culturally disadvantaged [sic] (Boose, et al., 1967)	187	119	L^1	$H^{1,2}$	$0^{1,2}$	$L^{1,2}$	$L^{1,2}$	0^1	H	H	$L^{1,2}$	$H^{1,2}$	H^2	$H^{1,2}$	$H^{1,2}$	$L^{1,2}$	$L^{1,2}$
11. EPPS adults (1959)	4,932	4,031	L	H	H	L	L	H	H	H	L	H	H	H	L	L	L
12. Psychiatric patients (Gauron, 1965)	163	159	L	0^1	$H^{1,2}$	$0^{1,2}$	L^1	H^1	0^2	H^2	L^2	H^2	H^2	H	$0^{1,2}$	0^1	L^2
13. College students (Kinnick, et al., 1970)	1,077	743	$L^{1,2}$	H^2	0^1	0	$L^{1,2}$	H	H^2	H	$L^{1,2}$	$H^{1,2}$	H	H	$0^{1,2}$	L^2	L
14. High school teachers (Jackson, et al, 1957)	52	91	L	$0^{1,2}$	$0^{1,2}$	$0^{1,2}$	L	H	0^2	H^2	L^1	H	H	0^1	$0^{1,2}$	$L^{1,2}$	L
15. Elementary teachers (Jackson et al., 1957)	196	27	L	$H^{1,2}$	0^1	0^1	L	H	0	H	L^1	H	H	H	0^1	$L^{1,2}$	L
16. Miami college students (Allen, et al., 1957)	42	82	0^1	0	0	0	0	0^1	0^2	H	0	$0^{1,2}$	H	0	0	L^1	L

Table 2 - I (continued)

NEEDS

POPULATION	Females	Males	Ach[M]	Def[F]	Ord	Exh	Aut[M]	Aff[F]	Int[F]	Suc[F]	Dom[M]	Aba[F]	Nur[F]	Chg[F]	End	Het[M]	Agg[M]
17. College students (Murgatroyd, et al., 1969)	87	46	0[1]	0[1,2]	0	0[1]	L[1,2]	H[1,2]	H[1]	H[1]	L[1,2]	0[1]	H	0	0[1,2]	0[1,2]	0
18. Secondary education majors (Hamachek & Mori, 1964)	70	99	0	0[1]	0	0	1	H[1]	0[2]	H	L	0	H	H	0	0[1]	L
19. Upper South black college students (Brazziel, 1964b)	62	60	0[3]	0	0	0	0	0	0	0	L	0	0	0	0	L	0
20. Lower South black college students (Brazziel, 1964b)	80	60	H[3]	L	0	0	L	0	H	0	0	0	0	0	H	L	0

1 – female subgroup differs from female norms;   2 – male subgroup differs from male norms;

3 – information not available.

L – female < male;   H – female > male;   0 – no significant difference;   M – high needs for males according

F – high needs for females.

to EPPS norms;

Birch, 1964; Tisdale, 1965; Murgatroyd and Gavurin, 1975; Adams, Blood, and Taylor, 1974) did not detract from this socially oriented picture of women. Autonomy, Dominance, Abasement, and Heterosexuality were the only scales on which as many as half of the comparison samples deviated from the norms. Women consistently displayed a lower need on the Dominance Scale, but they varied in both directions for the other three scales. No more than two samples differed from the norms on needs succorance, nurturance, and change. Other needs showed variations for less than half of the samples and in both directions. Only two samples were tested in the 1970s (Murgatroyd and Gavurin, 1975; Sharpe and Peterson, 1972). Murgatroyd and Gavurin's group did not differ from the norms on needs for order, intraception, abasement, or change. They had a greater need for autonomy, succorance, nurturance, heterosexuality, and aggression and a lesser need for deference, exhibition, affiliation, endurance, and dominance. Sharpe and Peterson found that there was a positive association between being female and needs for affiliation, nurturance, change, and abasement, but a negative correlation between being female and needs for dominance and autonomy. In general, it appears that the passage of time possibly has caused women to become more assertive and self-directive even though they have maintained an essentially social orientation.

As for male samples compared to male norms, Table 2-I shows that less than half of the available samples in 1957 and in 1961 through 1969 differed from the norms. For the 1957 samples, exhibition, deference, intraception, and heterosexuality differed for as many as three of the five samples. In the 1960s, there was more variability for certain of the scales; better than half of the samples showed differences in needs autonomy, dominance, abasement, and heterosexuality. Most of those male samples who differed from the norms demonstrated a lower level of these needs. As many as four of nine possible samples differed on needs for deference, order, intraception, endurance, and aggression. Most of the samples displayed higher needs for deference, endurance, and aggression, but lower needs for intraception; directions for differences in need for order were contradictory. Change and succorance continued to be similar to the norms for all but one sample as they had been for respondents in 1957.

The one sample tested in the 1970s (Murgatroyd and Gavurin, 1975) showed lower needs for deference, order, affiliation, dominance, and abasement and higher needs for intraception, endurance, and aggression when compared to norms. The direction of needs for affiliation, dominance, endurance, and aggression were consistent with those reported in most of the previous years and suggests that men may have moved somewhat away from external sources of goal attainment to internal ones.

Education and Training

Efforts to determine how education and training influence the EPPS scales have followed two tracks: (a) identification of scales that distinguish students from nonstudents and (b) identification of those EPPS variables that distinguish students within a particular academic setting from one another. In a study comparing the need levels of high school students who attended college the year succeeding their high school graduation with those who did not, George and Marshall (1971) found that students had higher needs for achievement, succorance, and dominance whereas nonstudents had higher needs for abasement and endurance. Likewise, Gunderson (1969) found positive correlations between college attendance and achievement and dominance and a negative correlation between college attendance and abasement for enlisted navy personnel.

The type of college one chooses to attend may reflect different need levels. Minkevich, George, and Marshall (1972) found that men (n = 32) and women (n = 30) commuters attending a two-year college had a higher need for deference during their freshman year, while men (n = 40) and women (n = 49) commuters attending a four-year college had a higher need for affiliation. These differences held regardless of the sex or socioeconomic status of the respondents. When compared to the means for the combined sample of men and women college students, two-year students exhibited lower needs for achievement, deference, affiliation, succorance, dominance, and abasement and a higher need for aggression. The four-year students also had lower needs for affiliation and deference.

Looking more closely at the characteristics of community college students, George, Marshall, Hoemann, and Minkevich (1972) found that freshmen had higher needs for dominance and endurance than did sophomores. Whether one was enrolled in a career (one- or two-year terminal programs) or transfer (college parallel programs leading to further education) programs apparently influenced or was influenced by certain needs; college sophomores enrolled in transfer programs had higher consistency scores than did freshmen who were enrolled in career programs. In addition, transfer students exhibited higher needs for dominance and aggression, whereas career students showed higher needs for change and endurance.

In a further analysis of these same subjects, George, Minkevich, and Hoemann (1973) reported that "students planning to transfer to a four-year college or university had higher scores in dominance, change, heterosexuality, and aggression than did those students planning to terminate their college education following the completion of their two-year career programs. On the other hand, career students had a significantly higher score on change than did transfer students" (p. 417). In addition, George et al. (1973) found that female career students had a higher need for deference than did female transfer students. Significant sex differences were found for needs affiliation, intraception, succorance, abasement, nurturance, change, heterosexuality, aggression, and consistency, apparently in a direction consistent with the EPPS norms.

Within a four-year college setting, Garrison and Scott (1962) found that a different set of needs was related to class level for women preparing to teach. Sophomores and juniors expressed a greater need for abasement than did seniors, while seniors showed a higher need for change than did either of the other two classes. Sophomores had a higher need for nurturance than seniors, and juniors had a higher need for heterosexuality. Surprisingly, seniors exhibited a higher need for deference than did juniors.

Garrison and Scott's (1962) data suggest that a person's reason for attending college as well as future plans may be reflected in her or his need level. Women who intended *to teach* evidenced a greater need for nurturance than did those who wanted to *be informed* or the miscellaneous group and a greater need for endurance than the miscellaneous group. The miscellaneous group, those who came to college for a variety of reasons, expressed greater need for autonomy, heterosexuality, and aggression and a lesser need for nurturance and endurance. Women who planned to teach for only a short time (one to four years) showed a higher need for succorance and less of a need for dominance, intraception, and endurance than did respondents who anticipated that they would teach a longer period of time. Women planning to teach ten or more years manifested lower needs for heterosexuality and succorance than did the short-term teachers.

There is little evidence that indicates that one's major or area of specialization may contribute to different need levels. Ozehosky, McCarthy, and Clark (1970) found that ROTC university graduates had a lower need for intraception and a higher need for heterosexuality than a random sample of non-ROTC undergraduates. Among community college students, George et al. (1973) found that freshmen business majors had higher needs for achievement, intraception, dominance, and endurance than did sophomores, but that sophomores had higher needs for affiliation, succorance, and nurturance. Freshmen enrolled in career programs had higher needs for achievement and exhibition than sophomores enrolled in the transfer program. For their part, sophomore career students expressed higher need for aggression than did freshmen transfer students. Career students as compared to transfer students enrolled in business courses also expressed higher needs for intraception and lower needs for dominance and aggression.

As for engineering majors, George et al. (1973) found that transfer students had higher dominance and consistency scores than did career students. Class level comparisons indicated that freshmen had higher dominance and consistency scores than sophomores; freshmen transfer students had a higher order need than did sophomore career students, but sophomore transfer students had a higher consistency score than did freshmen transfer students. The consistency score is the validity check for EPPS profiles. The mean score for freshmen career students was less than the minimum level recommended by Edwards and causes one to question the appropriateness of using the EPPS with this particular subsample of subjects.

Izard's (1962) longitudinal study carries the question of the effects of area of specialization into a four-year college setting and extends it to the area of how need levels change over time. An entering class of nursing and engineering students and male and female arts and science majors were tested in 1957 and retested four years later. Izard found that nursing students had decreased their needs for deference, abasement, order, affiliation, and endurance; however, they had increased their needs for autonomy, heterosexuality, and aggression. Needs for deference, abasement, and endurance were also decreased for engineering and female arts and science students while heterosexuality and autonomy were increased for both majors.

In addition, engineers had decreased needs for succorance and increased needs for dominance and aggression. Arts and science women exhibited decreased needs for dominance. The arts and science men decreased their needs for abasement and nurturance, but increased their need for achievement, aggression, and heterosexuality. In general, it appears that students became more individualistic and assertive and less conventional regardless of academic major.

Whereas Izard (1962) examined the influence of time on changes in need levels using the same subjects tested on two occasions, Adams, Blood, and Taylor asked the same question using a sample of education majors tested in 1958 and another which was tested in 1970. They found that males in 1970 had lower needs for order and higher needs for succorance and aggression. As compared to the earlier group of women, women in 1970 had less need for deference, order, affiliation, dominance, and endurance and more need for autonomy, succorance, change, heterosexuality, and aggression. Thus, women education majors appear to have changed more, and again the direction of the change was toward greater self-assertion and less social conformity.

Religion

Elevations on scales characteristic of people who prefer an orderly, disciplined life approve of authority, are dependent, and sacrifice personal ambitions in the service of others are characteristic of people who have committed themselves to a religious life. For example, Murgatroyd and Gavurin (1975) reported that Catholic sisters tested in 1973 had higher needs for deference, order, affiliation, succorance, abasement, nurturance, and endurance and lower needs for achievement, exhibition, autonomy, change, and heterosexuality than urban college women tested in the same year. The two groups did not differ in their needs for intraception, dominance, or aggression. Compared to the EPPS college norm group, the sisters had higher needs for deference, affiliation, succorance, abasement, and nurturance and lower needs for achievement, exhibition, dominance and heterosexuality. Thus, Catholic sisters appear to have low needs for personal gain or active self-expression except as expressed through close social relationships.

McClain's (1970) results provide indirect confirmation of many of the same scale variation. In a study in which he asked women (n = 189) and men (n = 103) how often they attended church and compared EPPS scales for varying frequencies of church attendance, he found that people who attended church at least once a week (frequent church attenders) were similar to the norm group with respect to their expressed needs. However, men and women who attended church less than once a week had higher needs for autonomy, heterosexuality, and change and lower needs for deference, abasement, endurance, and order than the norm group or than the frequent church attenders. Using a sample of male navy enlistees, Gunderson (1969) found small but significant negative correlations between frequency of worship and heterosexuality, being Catholic and the need for affiliation, and being neither Protestant nor Catholic and need for order. She found positive correlations between frequency of worship and need abasement and being Catholic and need aggression.

Byers, Forrest, and Zaccaria (1968) compared EPPS needs of three male ministerial groups, junior and senior theology students and clergymen to the norm group. They found that compared to the norm group the religious groups had significantly higher needs for affiliation, intraception, and change and a lower need for order and endurance. Interestingly, two of the religious groups also had lower needs for autonomy and deference, but higher needs for heterosexuality and nurturance.

Simon and Primavera's (1972) comparison of students enrolled in a women's Catholic college with the EPPS college women norms provides a discordant pattern of needs. They found that the women enrolled in a Catholic school had higher needs for autonomy, succorance, nurturance, heterosexuality, and aggression and lower needs for achievement, deference, order, dominance, and endurance than the norm group. The two groups had similar levels of needs for exhibition, affiliation, intraception, abasement, and change. Thus, the Catholic college women were characterized by a greater need for independence, self-assertion, and association with the opposite sex than their peers in other types of colleges and more closely resembled McClain's (1970) infrequent church attenders. The most obvious explanation for their resemblance to the nonreligious people is that women who attend a religious school may be deprived of certain social experiences that are available to women in other settings. As a consequence, they may use their college years to rebel against these restraints. This hypothesis is somewhat supported by the observation that the two groups of male theology students in Byers et al.'s (1968) study also had a high need for heterosexuality and a low need for deference.

A small cluster of studies present the idea that what one believes or one's style of beliefs may be influenced by (or influence) one's needs. Taking the position that extrinsic religious values, acceptance of religion as a form of power to be used to fulfill self-interests, would be related to college students needs, Tisdale (1966) intercorrelated the EPPS responses of 132 women and 160 men (primarily Protestants) with their responses to an extrinsic religious value inventory. Disregarding sex of respondents, he found that deference, affiliation, succorance, and abasement were positively related to extrinsic values and autonomy, intraception, aggression, and consistency were negatively related.

Examining the sexes separately, Tisdale (1966) found that order, succorance, and abasement were positively correlated and intraception, dominance, autonomy, and aggression were negatively correlated for women; for men, affiliation and abasement were positively related whereas autonomy, aggression, and consistency were negatively related. Church membership was also significantly related to religious values for men, but not for women. Tisdale interpreted his results to suggest that extrinsic values may have represented a general affiliative need for men and a manner of bringing order to their lives for women.

Tennison and Snyder (1968) used an attitude measure designed to assess positive attitudes toward religion. Their correlational analysis of 132 male and 167 female Protestant undergraduates revealed positive correlations between attitudes and deference, affiliation, abasement, and nurturance and negative correlations between attitudes and achievement, autonomy, intraception, dominance, and aggression. Thus, his results were quite similar to Tisdale's (1966) combined sex analysis.

Meredith (1968) searched for the relationship between attitudes toward organized religion and content of one's religious beliefs and the EPPS scales using a sample of 117 male and 165 female primarily Asian-American students. He found that the best EPPS predictor of males' favorable attitudes toward organized religion was endurance ($r = .37$); for women, heterosexuality ($r = -.16$) and change ($r = -.24$) predicted attitudes toward organized religion, but in an inverse direction. Regarding actual beliefs, Meredith reported that heterosexuality ($r = -.24$) was predictive for men and achievement was inversely related ($r = -.25$) for women.

Which scales are likely to be influenced by religious factors may be related to the sex of the person who is being considered. When mixed sex samples have been used to probe the issue, then it appears that elevated deference, abasement, and affiliation and depressed autonomy, aggression, and intraception are typical. When female samples are examined, then it appears that elevated succorance, order, abasement, nurturance and depressed achievement, dominance, autonomy, heterosexuality, and change are likely to be characteristic. For males, affiliation will be elevated more than likely, and autonomy will be depressed.

Age

The three scales that have been shown to vary most often with age are deference, order, and heterosexuality (Gunderson, 1969; Spangler and Thomas, 1962; Gauron, 1965). The older one is the higher one's scores are likely to be on the deference and order scales and the lower one's scores are likely to be on the heterosexuality scale. In addition, the situation in which the individual finds herself or himself or the role he or she plays in life may interact with age. Spangler and Thomas (1962), for instance, in a hospital setting found that disabled men and women aged sixty to sixty-nine and seventy to seventy-nine had higher needs for affiliation than people in the age range from forty to forty-nine years, and those people in the age ranges of sixty to sixty-nine, seventy to seventy-nine, and fifty to fifty-nine years had a higher need for succorance than forty to forty-nine year-olds. The age ranges that were significantly different in their need for deference were those disabled persons aged forty to forty-nine years; those respondents aged forty to forty-nine and fifty to fifty-nine years had higher needs for heterosexuality than those older than sixty. The shift with age toward a desire for more social contacts and personal care may reflect a greater loss of mobility if one is disabled and elderly as well.

Also, hospitalized psychiatric patients have shown age-related changes in scales in addition to the triad previously mentioned (Gauron, 1965). Women aged forty to fifty-nine years scored higher on endurance than women aged fifteen to nineteen; the older group of men scored higher on the Endurance and Abasement scales than the younger group of men. These two scales, particularly the Abasement Scale, are often associated with psychopathology and may mirror their long-term status as mental patients. On the other hand, the younger group of women showed higher needs for exhibition, abasement, and aggression; besides heterosexuality, younger men had higher need levels for the same group of needs as younger women with the exception of abasement. Gauron suggested that the cluster of needs characteristic of the younger women and men psychiatric patients might be indicative of the acting out or impulsive behavior characteristic of many adolescent psychiatric patients.

Hoffman and Nelson (1971) compared three age groups of hospitalized alcoholics: eighteen to forty-four, forty-five to fifty-four, and fifty-five to sixty-seven years. They found that the oldest group had higher needs for deference, order, and endurance than the youngest group and lower needs for heterosexuality than either of the two younger groups. The older group also had a lower need for dominance and change and a higher need for nurturance than at least one of the younger groups.

George and Stephens's (1968) sample of public health nurses had deference and order included among their top five needs regardless of whether they were in the age groups from twenty-three to thirty-one years or thirty-two to fifty-nine years. High needs for intraception were included in the top five needs of the younger women; endurance, achievement, and intraception were included in the top five needs of the older nurses. A concern for others seems to be a relatively constant characteristic of the role of nurses regardless of the person's age, but the way in which she (in this case) expresses herself may change from verbal expression in her earlier years to personal accomplishment in her later years. Using a male and female sample ranging in age from nineteen to seventy-four years (median was twenty-eight years), Sharpe and Peterson (1972) also found that aging was positively related to achievement need, but unlike the nursing sample, dominance and change were also positively associated with age, whereas age was negatively associated with intraception.

Eberlein (1970) investigated the effects of aging on in-service women elementary teachers' need levels. He found that deference was positively related to aging, whereas the exhibition and heterosexuality needs decreased with age. Trends that Eberlein noted were (a) the need for heterosexuality stabilized around age thirty years and then dropped precipitiously after age fifty; (b) teachers who were around forty years old showed increased, but stable, needs for order and endurance; (c) around the age of fifty years, teachers exhibited an increased need for abasement which also stabilized at the increased level.

Although they did not set out to investigate the effects of aging on the level of EPPS needs, Jackson and Guba (1957) found patterns of need changes for teachers that appeared to be consistent with Eberlein's (1970) age-related conclusions. They divided male and female teachers into groups representing three teaching experience levels: novice (zero to three years), intermediate (four to nine years), and veteran (ten or more years). Mean ages for these groups were not reported, but it seems reasonable to assume that increasing experience was positively correlated with age. Therefore, Jackson and Guba's findings that female teachers' needs for order, deference, and endurance increased and their needs for heterosexuality, exhibition, and affiliation decreased, which the authors attributed to increased experience, were as likely to have been due to increased age. The same can be said of male teachers' increase in need for deference and decrease in need for heterosexuality with increasing experience.

Thorpe (1958) compared need scale scores of physical education teachers, graduate students, and senior undergraduates. Presumably, these groups also represented different age ranges with the teachers being oldest and the seniors youngest on the average. She found that as compared to either seniors or the college norms, teachers had higher needs for deference, order, and dominance and lower needs for exhibition, succorance, change, and heterosexuality. Teachers apparently become more conventional, but less socially and self-involved, with increased age.

In summary then, although it is not easily discernable from the data at hand *when* age begins to impact the EPPS needs, it is reasonably clear that certain needs are altered. Deference and endurance consistently and order and dominance slightly less consistently are likely to show an increase with age; heterosexuality and exhibition usually decrease. At some time during the age span from nineteen to seventy-four years, achievement and abasement probably increase and then decrease again. The point(s) at which these changes occur, however, require additional investigation, although one author suggests that age fifty might be the crucial age for need abasement.

Cultural Influences

Surprisingly few studies exist in which minorities in the United States (or any other country for that matter) have been compared to the EPPS norms or a representative sample of nonminority respondents. Those studies that do exist (Fujita, 1957; Brazziel, 1964; Fenz and Arkoff, 1962; Arkoff, 1959) generally support Fujita's findings that minority women are more similar to nonminority respondents than are minority men. Rank order correlations computed between the EPPS means and the ranked means for various minority groups ranged from a low of .44 to a high of .75 for women and from .04 to .73 for men (see Table 2-II). In most instances the sexes of the same culture group were more similar to each other than they were to the norms.

Mean responses of different culture groups or nationalities are presented in Table 2-III. The greatest number of scale differences among women occurred for blacks (Grossack, 1957) and culturally disadvantaged women of unspecified race (Boose and Boose, 1967), each of whom differed from the norms on twelve scales; the group of American women showing the second highest number of scale differences, eight, were second and third generation Japanese American (Arkoff, 1959). All other groups, Hawaiian American women of Chinese, Filipino, Hawaiian, and Japanese descent (Fenz and Arkoff, 1962) differed on no more than four scales.

The various groups of male subjects differed on a minimum of eight and a maximum of eleven scales. The most "deviant" respondents were Japanese Americans and Hawaiians (Fenz and Arkoff, 1962), who differed on eleven scales, and culturally disadvantaged men (Boose and Boose, 1967), who differed on ten.

Four studies exist in which all fifteen EPPS needs were compared to the norms or a representative Caucasian sample for a cultural or national group outside of the United States. Ghei (1966) compared the needs of Indian undergraduate women studying in India to white undergraduate women studying in the United States. Ghei found that the Indians differed on ten scales when compared to the undergraduates and on eleven when compared to the EPPS college women. Fuster (1962) compared male and female Indian college students to the EPPS normative populations. He found that men differed on eleven scales while women differed on nine. Chylinski and Wright (1967) compared the scores of Canadian civil service workers to the norms. They found

Table 2 - II

**RANK ORDER CORRELATIONS BETWEEN EPPS NORMS
AND DIFFERENT CULTURE GROUPS**

	Correlations		
Groups	With EPPS Norm Groups		Between Sexes
	Male	Female	
1. EPPS college students	—	—	.56
2. Black college students (Grossack, 1957)	.29	.60	.83
3. Culturally disadvantanged students (Boose & Boose, 1967)	.07	.44	.86
4. Hawaiian Chinese high school students (Fenz & Arkoff, 1962)	.25	.74	.77
5. Filipino high school students (Fenz & Arkoff, 1962)	.20	.61	.61
6. Hawaiian Japanese students (Fenz & Arkoff, 1962)	.42	.63	.81
7. Indian college women (Ghei, 1966)	—	.49	—
8. Indian college students (Fuster, 1962)	.14	.65	.53
9. Second generation Japanese students (Arkoff, 1959)	.37	.63	.66
10. Third generation Japanese students (Arkoff, 1959)	.73	.75	.53
11. Hawaiian college students	.04	.66	.81
12. Western Australian college students (Wheeler, 1962)	.50	.68	.46

Table 2 - II (continued)

Groups	With EPPS Norm Groups		Between Sexes
	Male	Female	
13. Upper South black college students (Brazziel, 1964)	.67	.69	.62
14. Lower South black college students (Brazziel, 1964)	.06	.52	.70

significant differences on thirteen of the scales. Wheeler's (1969) comparison of Western Australian college students to the norms revealed nine scale differences for males and seven for females.

Regardless of ethnic membership, the scales that were lower for all of the minority women than for the norm group was the Heterosexuality Scale; the scale that was consistently higher was the Order Scale. Other scale differences were specific to each culture group and should be examined if one is intending to use the EPPS with minority women. Needs that were lower than the norms for all the male groups (shown in Table 2-III) were heterosexuality, dominance, and autonomy (except for Hawaiians and Australians); higher needs were deference (again excepting Hawaiians and Australians), order, and abasement. Other scale differences existed that varied according to the respondents' cultural background. Needs for which there were few cultural differences were intraception and succorance. Thus, the results to date indicate that the EPPS norms should not be used with minority populations, particularly if they are male.

Marital and/or Relationship Status

There is little evidence that any of the EPPS scales are consistently influenced by a person's marital and/or relationship status. Rogers, Cohen, Dworin, and Lipetz (1972) in their comparison of men who were seeking marital counseling with a relatively comparable sample who had never sought such counseling found that the latter group had higher scores on the Affiliation and Change scales and lower scores on the Succorance Scale than the men whose marriages were in trouble. Sharpe and Peterson (1972) found that "being married and of relatively low [educational] status was associated positively

Table 2 - III

MEANS (AND STANDARD DEVIATIONS) FOR
DIFFERENT CULTURAL GROUPS ON THE EPPS SCALES

Need	Southern Black College Students (Grossack, 1957)		"Culturally Disadvantaged" College Students (Boose & Boose, 1967)		Caucasion High School Students		Chinese High School Students	
						(Fenz & Arkoff, 1962)		
	F (n=108)	M (n=63)	F (n=187)	M (n=119)	F (n=57)	M (n=89)	F (n=95)	M (n=60)
Ach	15.11[1] (6.39)	15.25 (3.57)	14.33[1] (3.67)	15.24[3] (1.66)	11.17	14.93	13.15	13.70[4]
Def	14.09[1] (3.15)	14.32[2] (3.49)	15.01[1,3] (2.86)	14.03[2] (3.66)	11.26	10.63	12.70[5]	12.70[4]
Ord	12.82[1,3] (4.04)	12.71[2] (4.04)	14.02[1] (2.71)	13.58[2] (3.37)	10.61	9.89	12.61[5]	13.47[4]
Exh	10.50[1] (3.42)	11.84[2] (3.58)	10.70[1] (4.51)	12.14[2,3] (3.38)	13.67	16.17	12.93	13.80[4]
Aut	9.73[1] (3.87)	10.90[2] (3.97)	9.06[1] (3.08)	10.76[2,3] (3.67)	12.31	14.73	11.69	11.78[4]
Aff	15.24[1] (7.20)	13.62[2] (3.55)	15.34[1] (3.60)	14.75 (4.24)	17.38	13.69	16.42	14.92
Int	16.13 (7.85)	16.16 (3.83)	17.22[3] (3.11)	15.71 (3.44)	16.84	14.61	17.18	14.22
Suc	10.67[1] (4.62)	10.40 (3.49)	11.90[3] (3.76)	10.98 (3.70)	13.28	10.81	12.28	11.47
Dom	11.97[1] (3.69)	12.86[2] (4.13)	11.29[1] (3.43)	12.92[2,3] (3.83)	11.47	14.92	13.40[5]	13.22[4]
Aba	16.01[1,3] (4.15)	14.38[2] (4.43)	17.50[1,3] (6.14)	16.03[2] (3.90)	16.82	13.73	16.99	15.02[4]
Nur	15.62 (4.04)	14.95 (4.68)	16.68[3] (3.70)	15.19[2] (3.52)	16.82	13.24	17.10	15.20[4]
Chg	16.45[1,3] (3.24)	15.08 (4.54)	16.37[1,3] (3.62)	14.39[2] (3.46)	19.24	17.32	19.42	17.18
End	15.28 (4.65)	15.90[2] (5.04)	17.73[1,3] (3.73)	16.25[2] (4.48)	12.96	13.92	13.92	15.88[4]
Het	10.67[1] (5.18)	13.90[2,3] (6.29)	9.25[1] (5.05)	13.84[2,3] (5.43)	14.40	17.74	9.23[5]	14.03[4]
Agg	11.52[1] (4.11)	13.02[3] (4.06)	11.57[1] (3.73)	13.26[3] (3.81)	12.47	14.49	11.36	11.88[4]
Con			10.37 (1.73)	10.15 (2.15)				

Table 2 - III (continued)

Population

Need	Hawaiian High School Students		Japanese High School Students		Indian Under-grads, (Ghei, 1966)	Indian Undergrads (Fuster, 1962)		Filipino High School Students (Fenz & Arkoff, 1962)	
	F (n=37)	M (n=50)	F (n=319)	M (n=241)	F (n=110)	F (n=141)	M (n=147)	F (n=27)	M (n=40)
Ach	12.32	12.42[4]	12.19	14.15	14.30[1,5] (3.16)	14.20[1] (3.80)	16.20[3] (3.69)	12.55	12.07[4]
Def	12.35	13.72[4]	12.73[5]	12.24[4]	13.33[1,5] (3.59)	12.75 (3.54)	12.92[2] (3.54)	13.10[5]	13.44[4]
Ord	13.49[5]	14.62[4]	12.44[5]	12.09[4]	13.92[1,5] (4.23)	11.33[1] (4.29)	13.31[2,3] (4.63)	13.80[5]	13.67[4]
Exh	13.97	13.82[4]	12.48[5]	12.93[4]	11.61[1,5] (3.42)	12.13[1] (3.76)	12.97 (4.27)	13.44	12.05[4]
Aut	10.62	12.08[4]	11.32	12.35[4]	12.07 (4.29)	12.85 (3.65)	12.57[2] (4.02)	11.32	11.52[4]
Aff	16.73	15.16[4]	17.68	15.68[4]	14.13[1,5] (3.74)	15.56[1,3] (3.77)	12.55[2] (4.16)	16.93	16.20[4]
Int	16.43	14.22	17.16	14.22	16.17[1,5] (3.99)	16.74[3] (4.79)	15.15[2] (4.61)	17.26	15.15
Suc	10.08[5]	9.88	12.44	11.61	12.36 (4.84)	12.89[3] (4.58)	10.88 (4.50)	10.70[5]	12.07
Dom	12.95	13.88	11.76	13.17[4]	13.75[5] (3.95)	12.98[1] (4.83)	15.55[2,3] (4.64)	12.70	13.25[4]
Aba	17.35	15.86[4]	17.84	15.91[4]	16.57[1] (4.64)	17.97[1,3] (4.62)	15.54[2] (5.14)	17.44	15.55[4]
Nur	17.35	14.10[4]	17.86	16.39[4]	18.00[1] (3.51)	18.11[1,3] (4.43)	15.23[2] (4.32)	17.44	15.60[4]
Chg	18.35	16.14	18.99	16.78	16.93 (4.20)	17.54[3] (4.39)	14.81 (4.23)	18.33	16.90
End	15.51	16.46[4]	18.99	16.78	15.85[1,5] (4.75)	13.52 (6.23)	16.23[2,3] (5.32)	15.26	13.90
Het	10.40[5]	13.92[4]	10.08[5]	14.14[4]	7.38[1,5] (6.07)	8.50[1] (6.47)	11.22[2,3] (7.70)	8.70[5]	15.60[4]
Agg	11.84	13.32[4]	11.13	12.27[4]	13.56[1,5] (4.09	12.75[1] (4.86)	14.62[2,3] (4.41)	10.07	13.25
Con									

Table 2 - III (continued)

Need	Japanese American College Students (Arkoff, 1959)				Southern Blacks (Brazziel, 1964)				Western Australian College Students (Wheeler, 1969)	
	Second Generation		Third Generation		Upper South		Lower South			
	F (n=72)	M (n=65)	F (n=113)	M (n=70)	F (n=62)	M (n=60)	F (n=80)	M (n=60)	(n=94)	(n=349)
Ach	12.06	13.17[2]	12.17[1]	13.71[2]	12.0	14.0	16.2[3]	12.8	14.13 (4.05)	15.65[3] (4.04)
Def	13.94[1]	13.28[2]	12.80	12.28[2]	12.8	13.6	12.0	18.0[3]	11.99 (3.79)	11.53 (3.75)
Ord	11.43[1]	11.60[2]	11.75[1]	11.37[2]	11.3	11.0	13.0	13.0	10.38 (4.54)	11.18[2] (5.09)
Exh	11.91[1]	11.55[2]	12.90[1]	13.46	14.0	14.4	13.3	13.5	12.54[1] (3.77)	12.90[2] (3.73)
Aut	12.16	13.35	12.08	13.14[2]	10.0	10.0	9.9	12.2[3]	14.06[1] (4.16)	14.93[2] (4.29)
Aff	17.86	15.46	17.49	15.35	17.0	14.8	16.3	15.6	16.03[1,3] (4.10)	13.76[2] (4.26)
Int	18.64[1]	16.83	17.80	16.54	16.0	16.0	19.9	17.0	17.99[3] (4.06)	15.54 (5.16)
Suc	12.71	11.28	13.32	11.15	13.0	11.0	12.3	10.7	11.95[3] (4.45)	10.24 (4.63)
Dom	11.40[1]	13.28[2]	12.80[1]	14.43[2]	10.3	13.0[3]	11.0	12.0	11.01[1] (4.46)	14.62[2,3] (4.73)
Aba	17.01[1]	15.75[2]	16.05[1]	14.99[2]	12.5	12.6	12.6	12.7	15.78 (4.74)	14.35[2] (4.90)
Nur	17.44	17.31[2]	17.38[1]	15.67[2]	15.0	14.3	18.8	16.4	16.72[3] (4.89)	14.23 (4.84)
Chg	18.69[1]	15.92	19.56[1]	16.36[2]	16.4	15.0	16.0	16.0	18.08[3] (4.56)	15.11 (4.50)
End	13.30	13.91	13.09	13.11	13.1	13.6	18.8[3]	16.2	15.46[1] (4.87)	16.08[2] (5.95)
Het	10.27[1]	14.83[2]	9.81[1]	15.62[2]	11.0	15.5[3]	8.0	12.0[3]	11.15[1] (5.52	14.64[2,3] (6.80)
Agg	10.66	12.38	11.33	13.01	11.0	12.0	11.0	12.0	12.72[1] (4.67)	15.19[2,3] (4.74)
Con					11.0	11.3	11.5	11.5		

[1] differs from female norms [2] differs from male norms

[3] significant male-female difference within the cultural group

[4] differs from a Caucasian sample of males [5] differs from a Caucasian sample of females

deference, order, and endurance while being single and of relatively high [educational] status was positively correlated with heterosexuality and change" (p. 379).

Two other studies support the findings that the Heterosexuality Scale score tends to be elevated for single respondents. McKee and Wildman (1966) categorized their women subjects as frequent or nonfrequent daters. Their with results indicated that frequent daters scored significantly higher on the Heterosexuality and Succorance scales whereas infrequent daters scored higher on the Abasement Scale.

Ladd and Levitt (1967) presented results that suggested that married women score lower on the Heterosexuality Scale than single women even when the items in the scale were adjusted to compensate for implied marital infidelity. However, the married sample was 50 percent black and since other previously cited studies suggest that black women score lower on this scale than white women, Ladd and Levitt's results may have been confounded somewhat by race.

Also, Wilson and Greene's (1971) findings that homosexual and heterosexual women of unspecified relationship status had significantly lower scores on needs for heterosexuality suggest that the scale may not measure a general need for sexuality as much as it does a specific manner of expressing one's sexual needs. Levitt and Brady's (1965) finding that the heterosexual need was not related to male graduate students' reactions to photographs depicting sexual themes also supports this speculation.

Social Class Effects

In studying the effects of social class on EPPS scales, various methods have been used to define social class. Mehlman and Fleming (1963) used an index based on parental occupation and education. They found that Class I (upper class) college students had significantly lower needs for affiliation than all of the five possible classes except the lowest (Class V); they had lower needs for endurance than any of the other classes and higher needs for dominance than the two lowest classes, IV and V. Mehlman and Fleming also found that class V males had significantly lower needs for aggression than Classes III and IV, whereas females in Class V had higher needs for aggression than females in any of the other classes. Autonomy Scale scores were also affected by social class and sex; Class III males had higher autonomy needs than Class II and IV males; women in Class I had higher autonomy needs than women in the middle classes, II, III, and IV; males demonstrated a significantly higher need for autonomy only if they belonged to Classes III or V.

Two studies have investigated social class using correlational approaches. Gunderson (1969) did not specify how she measured socioeconomic status (SES). Nevertheless, among navy personnel, Gunderson found a small but significant negative correlation between SES and order and a small positive correlation between change and SES. Sharpe and Peterson (1972), as previously mentioned, found that educational status was negatively associated with a canonical function, which included negative associations for change and heterosexuality and positive associations for deference, endurance, and order. Their interpretation of these results suggested that people of low educational status were likely to have elevated scores on the Deference, Endurance, and Order scales.

The few other studies in which social class has been a variable of concern have reported different social class effects on the EPPS scales. Among teacher trainees, Garrison and Scott (1962) found that lower class respondents had higher needs for abasement than middle or upper class respondents. George and Marshall (1971) found that college students from the professional-managerial class had a higher need for autonomy than nonprofessional-managerial classes. Using the same classification system, professional/managerial versus not professional, George (1971) found that the respondents from nonprofessionl backgrounds had lower needs for deference and higher needs for autonomy and aggression.

Among southern black college students, Brazziel (1964) found that those from the upper South and from families of middle income had higher needs for achievement, order, and dominance and lower needs for nurturance than the lower middle income students. Those students from the lower South who were middle income had higher needs for order and endurance and lower needs for autonomy and nurturance.

When considering sex differences within classes, Brazziel (1964) found that females in the lowest income group from the lower South exhibited higher needs for nurturance and endurance than males. Women in both social classes from the lower South had higher needs for achievement, but upper South males of middle income revealed higher needs for dominance. His results imply that where black students are concerned region of the country from which they originate may interact with social class variables to influence EPPS scores.

In sum, while it is possible that social class variables do differentially affect the EPPS needs, the existing literature reveals no consistent effects. Perhaps, this lack of consistency is due to the ambiguous and varied manners in which social class variables have been defined.

Summary and Conclusions

Several researchers, e.g. Koons and Birch (1964), Kinnick and Nelson (1970), have recommended the development of local norms to help avoid the problems of interpretation caused by demographically different populations. When norms are as old as are those of the EPPS and/or when one intends to use the inventory with populations differing markedly from the norm populations, such advice is well given and well taken.

It does appear that demographic variables may have significant and differing impact on the EPPS need levels of respondents. To summarize —

    a. For the most part, the male-female scale differences that were originally reported for the norm groups tend to still exist in direction if not in absolute level.

b. Aging possibly contributes to higher deference, order, endurance, and dominance needs and lower needs for heterosexuality and exhibition. This observation means that comparisons involving groups of markedly different ages should not be undertaken without controlling for age effects. In addition, if unusual scale scores appear for older respondents, one must consider the possibility that these scores are merely predictable age-related deviations rather than deviant personality characteristics.

c. The scales that are influenced by religious commitment vary according to the sex of the respondents who have been investigated. Religious female samples have tended to show elevated needs for succorance, order, abasement, and nurturance and depressed needs for achievement, dominance, autonomy, heterosexuality, and change. Only affiliation and autonomy have shown any significant effects due to religion for males. There is currently insufficient data available to determine how the practice of different religions might influence the EPPS scales.

d. Cultural/racial differences on the scales are too diverse and too many, particularly for male subjects, to permit legitimate use of the EPPS norms for minority populations. If one plans to use the EPPS with such groups, then it would be wise to develop appropriate norms.

e. Marital and/or relationship status does not appear to consistently influence scale levels with the possible exception of heterosexuality. Probably, if one is married, then one's heterosexuality need will be lower.

f. Due to the varied and ambiguous ways in which socioeconomic background factors have been defined, it is not possible to make any clear assumptions about how such factors should influence the EPPS scales.

g. Educational persistence and plans to continue formal education beyond two years seem to be positively related to needs for achievement, succorance, and dominance and negatively related to needs for abasement and endurance or deference. Identification with certain academic majors may influence need patterns as well.

REFERENCES

Adams, H.L., Blood, D.F., and Taylor, H.C., Jr.: Student characteristics: A twelve year comparison. *Improving College University Teaching, 22:*16-17, 1974.

Allen, R.M., and Dallek, J.E.: A normative study of the Edwards Personal Preference Schedule. *Journal of Psychology, 43:*151-154, 1957.

Arkoff, A.: Need patterns in two generations of Japanese Americans in Hawaii. *Journal of Social Psychology, 50:*75-79, 1959.

Berrien, F.K., Arkoff, A., and Iwahara, S.: Generation difference in values: Americans, Japanese-Americans, and Japanese. *Journal of Social Psychology, 71:*169-175, 1967.

Boose, B.J., and Boose, S.S.: Some personality characteristics of the culturally disadvantaged. *Journal of Social Psychology, 65:*157-162, 1967.

Brazziel, W.F.: Correlates of Negro personality. *Journal of Social Issues, 20:*45-52, 1964.

Byers, A.P., Forrest, G.G., and Zaccaria, J.S.: Recalled early parent child relations, adult needs, and occupational choice: A test of Roe's theory. *Journal of Counseling Psychology, 15:*324-328, 1968.

Chylinski, J., and Wright, M.W.: Testing in Canada with the Minnesota Multiphasic Personality Inventory (MMPI) and the Edwards Personal Preference Schedule (EPPS). *The Canadian Psychologist, 80:*202-206, 1967.

Eberlein, E.L.: The EPPS need structure of in-service elementary school teachers. *The Journal of Educational Research, 64:*112-114, 1970.

Edwards, A.L.: *Revised Manual of the Edwards Personal Preference Schedule.* New York, Psychological Corporation, 1959.

Fenz, W.D., and Arkoff, A.: Comparative need patterns of five ancestry groups in Hawaii. *Journal of Social Psychology, 58:*67-89, 1962.

Fitzgerald, B.J., and Pasewark, R.A.: Sex differences on the Edwards Personal Preference Schedule. *Psychological Reports, 29:*892, 1971.

Fujita, B.: Applicability of the Edwards Personal Preference Schedule to Nisei. *Psychological Reports, 3:*518-519, 1957.

Fuster, J.M.: A study of the Edwards Personal Preference Schedule on Indian college students. *Journal of Social Psychology, 57:*309-314, 1962.

Garrison, K.C., and Scott, M.H.: The relationship of selected personal characteristics to the needs of college students preparing to teach. *Educational and Psychological Measurement, 22:*753-758, 1962.

Gauron, E.F.: Changes in Edwards Personal Preference Schedule needs with age and psychiatric status. *Journal of Clinical Psychology, 21:*194-196, 1965.

George J.A., and Stephens, M.D.: Personality traits of public health nurses and psychiatric nurses. *Nursing Research, 17:*168-170, 1968.

George, R.L.: Resident or commuter: A study of personality differences. *Journal of College Student Personnel, 12:*216-219, 1971.

George, R.L., and Marshall, J.C.: Personality of young adults: College versus non-college. *Journal of College Student Personnel, 12:*438-444, 1971.

George, R.L., Marshall, J.C., Hoemann, V.H., and Minkevich, G.: Personality differences among community college students. *College Student Journal, 6:*30-36, 1972.

George, R.L., Minkevich, G., and Hoemann, V.H.: Community college transfer students versus career students: A study of personality differences. *Journal of College Student Personnel,* 415-418, 1973.

Ghei, S.N.: Needs of Indian and American college females. *Journal of Social Psychology, 69:*3-11, 1966.

Ghei, S.N.: The reliability and validity of Edwards Personal Preference Schedule: A cross-cultural study. *Journal of Social Psychology, 61:*241-246, 1963.

Grossack, M.M.: Some personality characteristics of southern Negro students. *Journal of Social Psychology, 46:*125-131, 1957.

Gunderson, M.M.: Relationships between expressed personality needs and social background and military status variables. *Journal of Psychology, 71:*217-224, 1969.

Hamachek, D.E., and Mori, T.: Need structure, personal adjustment and academic self-concept of beginning education students. *The Journal of Educational Research, 58:*158-162, 1964.

Izard, C.E.: Personality change during college years. *Journal of Consulting Psychology, 26:*482, 1962.

Kinnick, B.C., and Nelson, T.M.: The EPPS norms: Re-evaluation and necessity. *Journal of Experimental Education, 38:*37-39, 1970.

Klett, C.J.: Performance of high school students on the Edwards Personal Preference Schedule. *Journal of Consulting Psychology, 21:*68-72, 1957.

Koons, P.B., and Birch, R.W.: Re-evalution of the EPPS norms. *Psychological Reports,*

14:905-906, 1964.

Ladd, C.E., and Levitt, E.E.: The EPPS heterosexual scale and marital status. *Journal of Clinical Psychology, 23:*192-194, 1967.

Levitt, E.E., and Brady, J.P.: Sexual preferences in young adult males and some correlates. *Journal of Clinical Psychology, 21:*347-354, 1965.

McClain, E.W.: Personality correlates of church attendance. *The Journal of College Student Personnel, 11:*360-365, 1970.

McKee, N.R., and Wildman, R.W.: EPPS heterosexuality scale and dating frequency. *Journal of Clinical Psychology, 22:*464, 1966.

Mehlman, M.R., and Fleming, J.E.: Social stratification and some personality variables. *Journal of General Psychology, 69:*3-10, 1963.

Meredith, G.M.: Personality correlates to religious belief systems. *Psychological Reports, 23:*1039-1042, 1968.

Minkevich, G., George, R.L., and Marshall, J.C.: Personality differences for two and four year college commuters. *College Student Journal, 6:*87-91, 1972.

Mooman, R.C., and Hayden, C.E.: Personality differences among community college students. *Journal of College Student Personnel, 10:*306-309, 1969.

Murgatroyd, D., and Gavurin, E.I.: Comparison of Edwards Personal Preference Schedule norms with recent college samples. *Journal of Psychology, 91:*71-76, 1975.

Ozehosky, J.R., McCarthy, J.B., and Clark, E.T.: Manifest needs among ROTC and non-ROTC undergraduates. *Psychological Reports, 26:*299-301, 1970.

Reiter, H.H.: Similarities and differences in scores on certain personality scales among engaged couples. *Psychological Reports, 26:*465-466, 1970.

Rogers, L.S., Cohen, I.H., Dworin, J., and Lipetz, M.E.: Edwards personal needs: The choice of comparable groups. *Journal of Personality Assessment, 36:*65-67, 1972.

Satz, P., and Allen, R.M.: A study of the Edwards Personal Preference Schedule: Regional normative approach. *Journal of Social Psychology, 53:*195-198, 1961.

Sharpe, C.K., and Peterson, R.A.: A multi-variate analysis of psychographic variables. *Journal of Personality Assessment, 36:*374-379, 1972.

Simon, W.E., and Primavera, L.H.: EPPS needs of women attending a non-coed Catholic college and those of the normative sample. *Psychological Reports, 30:*966, 1972.

Spangler, D.P., and Thomas, C.W.: The effects of age, sex and physical disability upon manifest needs. *Journal of Counseling Psychology, 9:*313-319, 1962.

Tennison, J.C., and Snyder, W.W.: Some relationships between attitudes toward the church and certain personality characteristics. *Journal of Counseling Psychology, 15:*187-189, 1968.

Thorpe, J.A.: Study of personality variables among successful women students and teachers of physical education. *Research Quarterly of the American Association for Health, Physical Education, and Recreation, 29:*83-92, 1958.

Tisdale, J.R.: Selected correlates of extrinsic religious values. *Review of Religious Research, 7:*78-84, 1966.

Wheeler, D.K.: Edwards Personal Preference Schedule and National Characteristics. *Australian and New Zealand Journal of Sociology, 5:*40-47, 1969.

Wilson, M.L., and Greene, R.L.: Personality characteristics of female homosexuals. *Psychological Reports, 28:*407-412, 1971.

SECTION II

VALIDITY ISSUES

Chapter 3

FAKING ON THE EPPS

Detecting Faked Profiles

MEASUREMENT theorists have speculated that the response set of faking can detract from the validity of personality inventories. Some test constructors have developed special scales to detect faked profiles. For example, the F-scale of the Minnesota Multiphasic Personality Inventory (MMPI) was designed to pinpoint profiles on which the respondent was attempting to appear in an excessively bad light, while the Good Impression (GI) scale of the California Psychological Inventory (CPI) was designed to identify profiles on which the respondent was attempting to make an excessively good impression.

Unlike these two inventories, the Edwards Personal Preference Schedule (EPPS) has no special scale for identifying faked inventories. However, Dunnette, Kirchner, and De Gidio (1958), Stollak (1965a), and Heathers (1959) have speculated about scale variations that should occur were an EPPS profile to be faked.

CPI HYPOTHESIS. Dunnette et al. (1958) found positive correlations between the Good Impression (GI) Scale of the CPI and the Achievement, Deference, Affiliation, Intraception, Dominance, and Endurance scales of the EPPS. The Good Impression Scale was negatively correlated with EPPS needs succorance, heterosexuality, and aggression. Because of these correlations, Dunnette et al. concluded that an inventory on which a respondent was attempting to make a good impression, i.e. "fake good," would possibly result in elevations of the positively correlated scales and depressions of the negatively correlated scales.

STOLLAK HYPOTHESIS. Consistent with his speculation that scale elevations under the fake-good response set were characteristic of female sex-typed responses, Stollak (1965a, 1965b) found that achievement, deference, affiliation, endurance, nurturance, and order were elevated while exhibition, autonomy, change, succorance, heterosexuality, and aggression were depressed.

CONSISTENCY SCORE VARIATIONS. While she does not specifically state how faking should alter EPPS profiles, Heathers (1959) does suggest that faking may partially account for low consistency scores. In this chapter, the CPI hypothesis, the Stollak hypothesis, and Heathers' supposition are tested using data generated by various investigators of faking effects on the EPPS.

Procedure

The CPI and Stollak hypotheses were developed from data provided by presumably male samples (although Stollak subsequently used a female sample as well). Other authors either have not specified their subjects' sexes or have used combined male-female samples. Since adequate tests of the two hypotheses seem to require separate analyses of the two sexes, some arbitrary distinctions were established.

If data were collected in a setting in which one sex typically predominates, the reported sample data were assumed to be of that sex. If a sample consisted of unequal numbers of men and women, reported means were attributed to the dominant sex. Thus, Dicken's (1959) reported means were treated as though they were derived from females. This procedure resulted in the identification of three sets of male subjects (two contributed by French, 1958, and one contributed by Stollak, 1965a) and three sets of female subjects (two from Dicken's study and one from Stollak's 1965b study) who completed the inventory under instructions designed to induce faking of some sort.

SAMPLES. Stollak's (1965a; 1965b) two samples consisted of one group of male and another group of female undergraduates who were instructed to respond to the EPPS in such a way as to make "another person look better to the other person if it were said of him [sic]" (p. 120). French's (1958) groups were tested at entry or seven weeks after entry under instructions to respond as a recruit should or to impress their tactical instructors. Dicken's (1959) subjects who were instructed to answer to make a good impression as well as those who were instructed to elevate their dominance scores formed the remaining two-thirds of the female sample.

For the statistical comparisons, the female groups were compared to Edwards's college female norms; the male samples were compared to male groups in the same setting who had received standard instructions.

Results

Male Respondents

CPI HYPOTHESIS. The Mann-Whitney U-test for differences between independent samples was used to analyze the data in all cases. Means of the male samples under fake-good and standard instruction sets for needs achievement, deference, affiliation, intraception, dominance, and endurance were not significantly elevated ($U' = 115$; n_1, n_2 = 18, 18; $p > .05$) contrary to the CPI hypothesis. As shown in Figure 3-1, achievement, deference, affiliation, and endurance were elevated for three groups of respondents, dominance was elevated for two groups, while intraception was elevated for only one.

Regarding the succorance, heterosexuality, and aggression needs, which should have been depressed under fake-good conditions, there was no significant difference ($U = 27$; n_1, n_2 = 9, 9; $p > .05$) between standard and faked profiles. For two of the male groups (college students and new Air Force

Elevated Scales[1]

	CPI Hypothesis		Stollak Hypothesis

CPI Hypothesis   Stollak Hypothesis

Ach (3)   Ach (3)
Def (3)   Def (3)
Aff (3)   Aff (3)
End (3)   End (3)

Dom (2)   Nur (2)

Int (1)   Ord (3)

Suc (2)   Suc (2)
Het (2)   Het (2)
Agg (2)   Agg (2)
                                              Exh (3)
                                              Aut (3)
                                              Chg (3)

Depressed Scales

[1]Number in parentheses equals number of samples affected.

Figure 3-1. ELEVATED AND DEPRESSED SCALES FOR MALE SAMPLES. Scales influenced by "fake" instructions.

recruits), these three means were lower than those for the standard condition. However, for the seven-week recruits, they were not. The discrepancy suggests that needs succorance, heterosexuality, and aggression may be biased by environmental factors.

STOLLAK HYPOTHESIS. The needs subsumed under the Stollak hypothesis were significantly elevated under the good impression set (U' = 86; n_1, n_2 = 18, 18; p < .01; one-tailed test). Four of these needs, achievement, deference, affiliation, and endurance, were in common with the CPI hypothesis. Thus, as shown in Figure 3-1, these four needs were elevated for each of the three groups as tested under the separate hypotheses. However, the Stollak hypothesis also predicts elevations of the Nurturance and Order scales. Nurturance was elevated for two of the three groups and, thus, appears to be comparable to the

Dominance Scale. Order was elevated for all three.

The expected composite of six needs was significantly depressed under the fake good set (U = 102; n_1, n_2 = 18, 18; p < .05; one-tailed test). Of course, succorance, heterosexuality, and aggression were depressed for the same two out of three groups under the Stollak hypothesis as under the CPI hypothesis. However, exhibition, autonomy, and change were depressed for all three groups, suggesting that they may be less susceptible to environmental influences.

Female Samples

The six scales designated by the CPI hypothesis were significantly elevated (U = 78, n_1, n_2 = 18, 18; p < .01; one-tailed test) under the fake good set as were the six scales designated by the Stollak hypothesis (U = 90; n_1, n_2 = 18, 18; p < .25; one-tailed test). Only one of the scales suggested by the CPI hypothesis (Achievement) was elevated for all three groups. Only two of the scales (Achievement and Order) were elevated for all three groups as predicted by the Stollak hypothesis. Nurturance was the least likely of the designated scales to be elevated. However, the one group for which it was elevated was the only indisputably female sample.

The three scales designated by the CPI hypothesis were significantly lower than Edwards's norm group when respondents were faking good (U = 6, n_1, n_2 = 9, 9; p < .01; one-tailed test). Stollak's six scales were also significantly lower than the norm group under the fake-good set (U = 75, n_1, n_2 = 18, 18; p < .01; one-tailed test).

Scales that were depressed for all female groups in support of both hypotheses were the Succorance and Heterosexuality scales. Additionally, the Autonomy and Change scales were depressed, according to the Stollak hypothesis.

CONCLUSIONS. For female test takers, responding under instructions to fake good, 67 percent of the designated scales were depressed for all three samples in support of both the CPI and Stollak hypotheses. When men were the fakers, 0 percent of the scales designated by the CPI hypothesis and 50 percent of those designated by the Stollak hypothesis were appropriately depressed for all three samples. However, only 17 percent and 33 percent for women as compared to 67 percent and 83 percent for men under the CPI and Stollak hypotheses, respectively, were *elevated* for all three samples as suggested. Possibly, faked inventories produced by women can be more reliably identified by the depressed scales, while those produced by men can be more reliably identified by Stollak's elevated scales.

Consistency Scores

Although authors have used consistency scores of different levels for

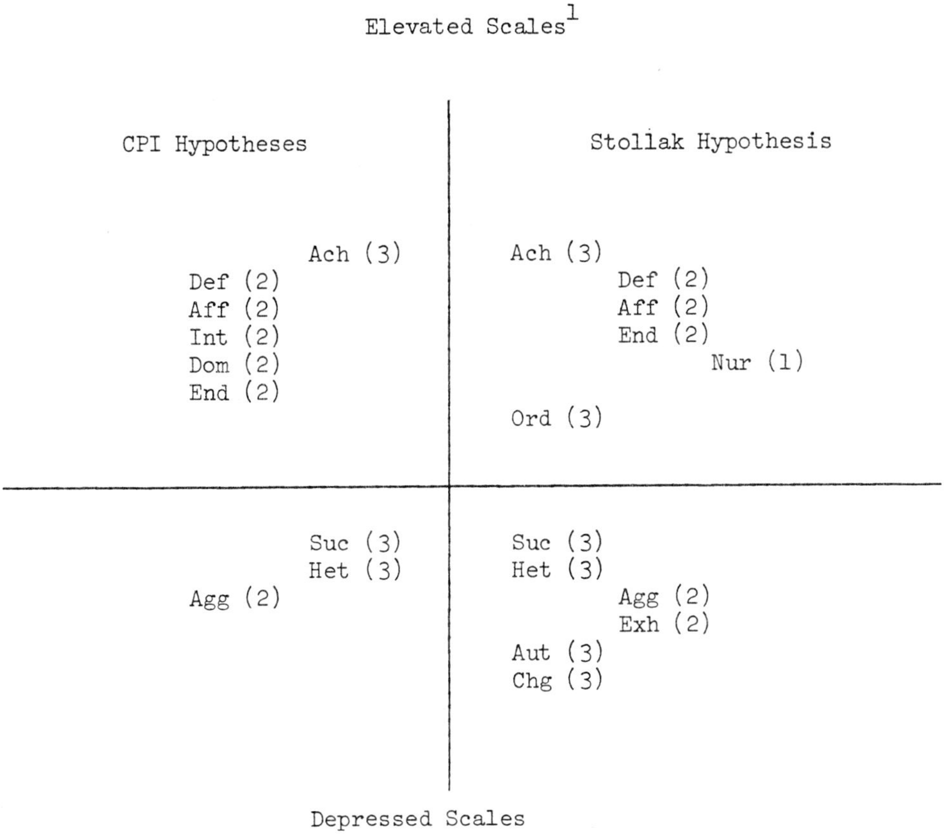

Elevated Scales[1]

CPI Hypotheses	Stollak Hypothesis
Ach (3) Def (2) Aff (2) Int (2) Dom (2) End (2)	Ach (3) Def (2) Aff (2) End (2) Nur (1) Ord (3)
Suc (3) Het (3) Agg (2)	Suc (3) Het (3) Agg (2) Exh (2) Aut (3) Chg (3)

Depressed Scales

[1]Number in parentheses equals number of samples affected.

Figure 3-2. ELEVATED AND DEPRESSED SCALES FOR FEMALE SAMPLES. Scales influenced by fake instructions.

distinguishing faked profiles from those produced under standard instructions, it appears that instructions to fake scores result in a greater proportion failing to meet the various consistency score criteria. Table 3-I shows that combining the standards used by various authors results in the elimination of a significantly greater proportion of faked than standard profiles ($z = 2.20$; $p < .05$).

Perhaps the only practical significance of this finding is that the higher the consistency score, the more confidence the test user can place in the validity of the results. It appears that consistency scores of 10 or less will detect invalid inventories when a person is attempting to create a generally good impression. However, when a person is responding according to an "ideal self" or personal desirability (PDI), then the consistency score level might not differ from that produced under standard instructions (Borislow, 1958). Therefore, if possible,

Table 3 - I

NUMBER OF FAKED AND STANDARD PROFILES
WITH LESS THAN CRITERION CONSISTENCY SCORE

Author	Author's Criterion Consistency Score	Type of Instructions			
		Standard[1]	Social Desirability	Dominance	Personally Desirable Impression
Stollak (1965a)	8	14 (206)	25 (178)*		
Stollak (1965b)	8	-	4 (59)[2]		
Dicken (1959)	10	6 (36)	5 (17)	6 (19)	
Borislow (1958)	9	4 (25)	1 (6)		0 (7)
Total		24 (267)	31 (201)*	6 (19)**	0 (7)

*p < .05

**p < .01

[1] Number in parentheses equals total n.

[2] Not included in total

the test user should discuss with the test taker whether the obtained profile reflects the test takers' perceptions of their real or of their ideal selves.

Basically, the evidence concerning consistency scores as well as scale variations supporting the argument that a person *can* fake a profile does not necessarily mean that he or she will. Orpen (1971), using a self-developed consistency score, found that clerical job applicants responding first as part of a selection procedure and later as part of a research project were more consistent than college students who responded first under standard instructions and later under a simulated employment situation.

Kirchner (1962) suggests that differential personality characteristics may intercede to determine whether a person will fake a personality inventory when he or she knows it is to be used for selection purposes. He found, for instance, that retail sales applicants as compared to retail sales employees were likely to show scale elevations characteristic of faking, but industrial sales applicants were not. His description of retail applicants as having stronger sales interests and tendencies to plan and to be persistent, as compared to the industrial person who shows less interests in sales and has greater reasoning ability, suggests the explanation that people who fake personality inventories may be those who exhibit other personality characteristics reflecting a desire to sell themselves.

In addition, Korman and Coltharp's (1962) investigation of the transparency of the EPPS scales, i.e. respondents' ability to match scale items to the appropriate scale, indicates that certain scales may be more easily faked than others. For the ninety-eight medical students whom they used, the five most transparent scales, in descending order, were Order, Dominance, Heterosexuality, Succorance, and Abasement; the five least transparent scales were Deference, Achievement, Nurturance, Autonomy, and Aggression.

Discussion and Summary

In spite of the diversity of methodology used by investigators of faking effects on the EPPS, it appears that under a fake-good set, certain scales are likely to be elevated while other scales are likely to be depressed. For women, the most reliably elevated scales as evidenced by the data at hand were Achievement, Deference, Affiliation, Intraception, Dominance, and Endurance. For men, the significantly elevated scales were Achievement, Deference, Affiliation, Endurance, Nurturance, and Order. Significantly depressed scales for women were Aggression, Succorance, Heterosexuality, Autonomy, Exhibitionism, and Change. The same scales were depressed for men, but with less consistency.

The above conclusions must be tempered somewhat by the knowledge that the male and female samples may not have been strictly comparable. Researchers have been less inclined to use female samples than male samples. Thus, a good proportion of the data that has been treated in the present review as though it were female is really a mixture of the two sexes. Also, studies of female respondents have not typically included a separate standard instruction group as have the studies of males. Therefore, it was necessary to substitute the means reported in the EPPS manual for the missing data. A limitation of this procedure was, of course, that the female data were less variable than were the male data. It remains for future researchers to retest these hypotheses using samples that are more comparable.

Scales that are elevated and depressed under a general good impression or fake-good set may differ from scale variations produced under a specific fake set. That is, when a person is attempting to look good with respect to a particular characteristic(s) (Blumenfeld, 1972; Dicken, 1959) or to conform to an ideal self (Borislow, 1958), the designated scales may not pertain. Therefore, the person using the EPPS for selection purposes would do well to explore with the test taker her or his biases concerning the target situation.

Regarding the consistency score, it appears that Heathers was at least partially correct in asserting that consistency scores would be lower under a fake set. However, there is no way of ascertaining whether an obtained low consistency score was the result of faking or other extra test factors. Nevertheless, the test user is justified in considering a profile with consistency scores of 10 or more as probably valid.

Furthermore, investigators have not addressed the question of scale variations relevant to a fake-bad set. Yet, where there is the capacity to create an image in one direction, is there not the same capacity for creating an image in an opposite direction? The question remains to be answered by future researchers.

In conclusion, it appears that consistency score level in combination with certain scale variations can be used to detect faked inventories, particularily when the respondents are male. Stollak has proposed that if faking is suspected the user readminister the EPPS with instructions to the testee to "attempt to make a good impression." Changes in scales can be assessed. However, it must be noted that the person (other than a research participant) who willingly completes the inventory twice may already be providing sufficient behavioral information about his or her deference and endurance.

References

Blumenfeld, W.S.: Effects of various instructions on personality inventory scores. *Personal Administration and Public Personnel Review, 1:*67-71, 1972.

Borislow, B.: The Edwards Personal Preference Schedule (EPPS) and fakability. *Journal of Applied Psychology, 42:*22-27, 1958.

Dicken, C.F.: Simulated patterns on the Edwards Personal Preference Schedule. *Journal of Applied Psychology, 43:*372-378, 1959.

Dunnette, M.D., Kirchner, W.K., and De Gidio, J.: Relations among scores on Edwards Personal Preference Schedule, California Psychological Inventory, and Strong Vocational Interest Blank for an industrial sample. *Journal of Applied Psychology, 42:*178-181, 1958.

French, E.G.: A note on the Edwards Personal Preference Schedule for use with basic airmen. *Educational and Psychological Measurement, 18:*109-115, 1958.

Heathers, L.: In Edwards, A.L.: *Edwards Personal Preference Schedule Manual.* California, Psychological Consulting Press, 1959.

Kirchner, W.K.: "Real-life" faking on the Edwards Personal Preference Schedule by sales applicants. *Journal of Applied Psychology, 46:*128-130, 1962.

Korman, M., and Coltharp, F.: Transparency in the Edwards Personal Preference Schedule. *Journal of Consulting Psychology, 26:*379-382, 1962.

Orpen, C.: The fakability of the Edwards Personal Preference Schedule in personnel selection. *Personnel Psychology, 24:*1-4, 1971.

Stollak, G.E.: EPPS performance under social desirability instructions. *Journal of Personality and Social Psychology, 2:*430-432 (a), 1965.

Stollak, G.E.: EPPS performance under social desirability instructions: College females. *Psychological Reports, 16:*119-122 (b), 1965.

Chapter 4

ARE THE EPPS SCALES MEASURES OF SOCIAL DESIRABILITY?

S INCE Cronbach (1946, 1950) presented his argument that various test taker response sets or respondent attitudes could invalidate test results, test constructors have devised various means of identifying or controlling for response sets. By far, the most popular technique had been to construct ancillary scales whose purpose is to measure specific styles of response. Examples of such scales are the K Scale of the MMPI (Hathaway and McKinley, 1951) or the Ac (Acquiescence) Scale of the California Psychological Inventory. Edwards used a rather unique approach for his time, which was to form forced-choice items by combining pairs of statements, which had been equated as much as possible for their social desirability. Thus, test respondents' selection of one or the other item as descriptive of themselves should indicate that the item is an actual descriptor rather than an endorsement inspired by a desire to appear in a desirable light. Naturally Edwards's claim that he had minimized the effects of social desirability within the EPPS was enough to launch more than a decade of research aimed primarily at disproving his contention.

Aspects of Social Desirability

Edwards used college students' judgments of single items to equate pairs of statements for social desirability. Because they believed that differences in social desirability might exist between the EPPS, couplets that did not exist when the items were rated singly by judges, Corah, Feldman, Cohen, Gruen, Meadow, and Ringwall (1958) had fifty male and thirty-one female introductory psychology students rate thirty pairs of items comprising the Achievement, Order, Succorance, Abasement, Heterosexuality, and Aggression scales. Of the ten pairs of items in which it was a member, achievement was judged the more socially desirable of the two items in seven of those pairs; order was judged the more desirable for four out of ten pairs; succorance and abasement were judged more desirable in three of ten pairs; heterosexuality was judged the more socially desirable item for only two pairs; aggression was the more socially desirable for only one pair. Whenever achievement items were matched with succorance or heterosexuality items, the achievement items were judged the more socially desirable. Likewise, when order and aggression items were paired, order was the more socially desirable and when abasement and heterosexuality items were paired, abasement was the more socially desirable.

59

The correlation between social desirability indices and subjects' endorsement of items was .88 suggesting that differential perceptions of the social desirability of combinations of items influenced respondents' response selection.

MULTIDIMENSIONAL SOCIAL DESIRABILITY. Messick (1960) speculated that social desirability was not a unidimensional characteristic of the EPPS traits, which could be successfully controlled by judges' ratings along a single continuum. Instead, he suggested that different viewpoints might exist concerning the nature of social desirability and that these viewpoints could be discovered by factor analyzing the social desirability ratings of a sample of items selected from the various EPPS scales.

To explore his hypothesis, Messick (1960) used the social desirability judgments generated by Klett's (1957) sample of mental hospital patients in response to forty-two EPPS items, three from each of fourteen scales. His analysis revealed that there was no single social desirability factor, but that nine types of desirability seem to exist. He named these factors: interpersonal concern or interpersonal sensitivity, aggressive arrogance or criticalness, emotional dependence or succorance, sexual interests, intellectual aggressiveness or active intellectual independence, interpersonal involvement, interest in travel, compulsive conformity, and achievement-oriented, middle-class stereotype [or desirable behavior]. This last factor accounted for the greatest percentage of variance. Items constituting the factors are summarized in Table 4-I.

To the extent that single items are similar to their scale mates, which were not included in the study, and to the extent that mental health patients share viewpoints that are similar to nonpatients, then it is likely that the Deference, Order, Endurance, Achievement, Change, Affiliation, Succorance, Aggression, and Nurturance scales might be elevated for the person who is attempting to conform to some aspect of social desirability according to Messick's (1960) data. By comparing the single item responses with those used by Messick, the test user can possibly get a clue as to the kind of social desirability set that might be operating.

PERSONAL DESIRABILITY. The multidimensional social desirability hypothesis essentially assumes that groups of people share perceptions of needs that influence the manner in which they respond to the need inventory. An alternate hypothesis, personal desirability, postulates that each person has a unique perception of what is desirable and it is this individual perception rather than a shared group norm that influences the person's test responses.

Saltz, Reece, and Ager (1962) demonstrated that individuals did consistently identify certain statements as being more desirable than their alternates. To explore the impact of personal desirability on actual response tendencies, Bernhardson and Fisher (1971) used various analyses of the personal desirability ratings and the EPPS scores of approximately sixty-nine psychology students of unspecified sex. The first measure, a categorization based on the social desirability differences between the pairs of statements that composed an item,

Table 4 - I

SUMMARY OF MESSICK'S SOCIAL DESIRABILITY FACTORS

ITEM	EPPS ITEM NO.	SCALE	FACTOR[1] NUMBER
1.	17A	Deference	VIII
2.	178A	Endurance	II
3.	114A	Dominance	I
4.	2A	Deference	IX
5.	68A	Order	IX, VI
6.	152A	Change	VII
7.	41A	Achievement	I
8.	45A	Autonomy	III
9.	14A	Exhibition	III, V
10.	78A	Succorance	IX
11.	221A	Nurturance	I, III
12.	5A	Autonomy	IX
13.	214A	Heterosexuality	--
14.	11A	Achievement	IX
15.	222A	Change	III
16.	98A	Succorance	III
17.	39A	Exhibition	III
18.	82A	Intraception	I
19.	94A	Dominance	--
20.	224A	Heterosexuality	IV
21.	168A	Endurance	VI
22.	42A	Deference	VIII
23.	91A	Affiliation	VI, IX

Table 4 - I (continued)

ITEM	EPPS ITEM NO.	SCALE	FACTOR[1] NUMBER
24.	169A	Heterosexuality	IV
25.	146A	Affiliation	VI
26.	33A	Order	VIII
27.	51A	Achievement	IX
28.	190A	Aggression	II
29.	102A	Intraception	IX
30.	180A	Aggression	V
31.	70A	Autonomy	V
32.	65B	Endurance	IX
33.	93A	Succorance	III
34.	76A	Affiliation	IX
35.	49A	Exhibition	II, III
36.	206A	Nurturance	IX
37.	185A	Aggression	II
38.	18A	Order	VIII
39.	166A	Nurturance	VI
40.	104A	Dominance	V
41.	197A	Change	VII
42.	112A	Intraception	V

[1]Factor I = Interpersonal Concern; Factor II = Aggressive Arrogance; Factor III = Emotional Dependence; Factor IV = Sexual Interests; Factor V = Intellectual Aggressiveness; Factor VI = Interpersonal Involvement; Factor VII = Interest in Traveling; Factor VIII = Compulsive Conformity; Factor IX = Achievement-Oriented - Middle-class stereotype [of desirable behavior].

indicated that the AB item pairs were not viewed as being equally desirable, only an average of 51.6 items (out of a possible 210) were rated as equally desirable; on the other hand, most items were not considered to differ extremely from one another either as evidenced by the finding that only an average of 9.8 items were rated as differing by as much as five of the eight possible Social Desirability Scale points. Excluding two questionable subjects, reliabilities for this particular social desirability measure ranged from + .46 to + .86.

A second measure used by Bernhardson and Fisher (1971) was designed to examine the degree or level to which a response keyed for a particular scale differed in social desirability from its nonkeyed partner. Their results indicated that small, variable differences of low to moderate reliability (range: .58 to .81) existed for the fifteen needs. The keyed response tended to be evaluated more personally desirable for the Achievement, Order, Affiliation, Intraception, Nurturance, Change, Endurance, and Heterosexuality scales. Their third measure, a simple count of the number of items in which the keyed response was considered to be more personally desirable, indicated that only the need for change was evaluated more desirable for as many as half of the twenty-eight times that it appeared. Test-retest reliabilities for the count of personal desirability ranged from .39 (Succorance Scale) to .80 (Order Scale).

In general, Bernhardson and Fisher's (1971) three measures of personal desirability converge to suggest that subjects endorse the items that they perceive to be more desirable. The average correlation between subjects' responses and desirability ratings was – .40 for the first measure. The correlations between their ratings of desirability and their responses to each of the fifteen scales ranged from .41 (Deference Scale) to .70 (Abasement Scale). Correlations between the count of desirable keyed responses and EPPS scale scores ranged from .45 (Deference and Aggression Scales) to .70 (Dominance Scale).

The question of whether perceptions of the desirability of the EPPS needs were correlated with respondents' scores was also addressed by Navran and Stauffacher (1954), who found a correlation of – .01 between the composite EPPS raw score of nursing students and their composite ideal self-ranking. Using EPPS T scores, Korman and Coltharp (1962) found a significant correlation, .46, between need scores and self-rankings for their sample of medical students. Heilbrun (1958) also found moderate correlations of .56 and .63 between personal desirability rankings of the fifteen needs and actual scores for a standard instruction group and for a group who had received instructions designed to make the members attempt to appear normal. Mann (1958) correlated each need with the respondents' ratings of "themselves as they wished they were" (p. 267) with respect to each of the needs. He found only one chance correlation between the two measures. Therefore, of the four studies in which ideal self-ratings were used as measures of social desirability, two have indicated that social desirability effects were eliminated and two have not.

Heilbrun and Goodstein (1959a) speculated that the pairs of statements that make up the EPPS items might differ in level of personal as well as social desirability and that these two types of desirability might independently influence test responses. They compared the likelihoods that 166 male and eighty-two female undergraduate students would endorse items (a) when the two statements in a pair differed maximally in their level of personal and social desirability and the higher personal or social desirability value was associated with different statements; (b) when the higher social and personal desirability items were associated with the same statement and the social desirability values were the same as for the first group; and (c) when the social and personal desirability values differed maximally and the higher values for both types were associated with the same statement in the pair. Their results indicated that respondents were significantly more likely to endorse items when the social and personal values were associated with the same statement and less likely to select a socially desirable item when it opposed a personally desirable statement.

Although Heilbrun and Goodstein (1959a) concluded that "it would appear that utilization of only social values for matching purposes does not represent a crucial flaw in Edwards' attempt to minimize desirability of verbal statements as an important source of performance variance" (p.304), they do suggest that certain scales may be differentially influenced by desirability factors. They reported that for the twenty items having the higher combined desirability values, items tended to be distributed rather evenly across ten scales: Endurance, Intraception, Succorance, Dominance, Order, Affiliation, Heterosexuality, Exhibition, Change, and Nurturance. Therefore, scores on these scales might tend to be slightly inflated, with the Endurance and Intraception scales being most susceptible to social and personal desirability inflation. Less desirable statements were associated with the scales Aggression, Exhibition, Dominance, Abasement, and Autonomy, suggesting that these scales might tend to be somewhat deflated. The authors recommend particular caution in interpreting the Aggression Scale since in most of the pairs in which an aggression statement was a member, the aggression statement had lower personal as well as social desirability values.

In a study of the relationship between personal and social desirability ratings of the statements that make up the needs, Goodstein and Heilbrun (1959b) reported a correlation of .90 indicating that the two types of ratings were very similar. However, when the need *scales* were divided into categories of high and low personal desirability on the basis of a different set of ratings, the authors found that for the high personal desirability needs, social and personal desirability ratings at a *statement* level did not differ. However, for the low personally desirable needs, social desirability ratings were higher than personal desirability ratings at a statement level. The latter finding would suggest that people may present lower scores for needs that they personally perceive as undesirable even though they may perceive that these needs are positive as far as other people are concerned.

In later studies, Heilbrun and Goodstein (1961) and Heilbrun (1962) noted that the tendency of people to respond to items in a socially desirable direction did not necessarily destroy the validity of the measure. In the first study, Heilbrun and Goodstein developed Special Achievement and Abasement scales in which item statements were equated for individuals' personal desirability ratings. The individualized and regular EPPS Achievement and Abasement Scales scores of thirty-four females and nineteen males were correlated with their grade point average for the semester and with their self-reported expectancy for future academic performance.

Use of the individualized scales did not result in a better prediction of grade point average than did the standard scale. The correlation between achievement and grade point with intelligence partialed out was .07 for the former and .28 for the latter. Both the original and the modified Abasement scales differentiated high and low abasing males to the same extent. However, for both scales subjects predicting semester GPAs, i.e. high abasing, lower than the group average had lower Abasement Scale scores than subjects predicting higher GPAs, i.e. low abasing, — a reversal of expected direction. The regular scale was the best discriminator and in an appropriate direction for female high versus low abasing subjects, but neither version of the scales significantly differentiated the two groups of women.

In the second study, Heilbrun (1962) compared the validities of the original EPPS Achievement Scale and an achievement scale that he constructed in which social desirability was uncontrolled. Using academic performance as the criterion, he found that the EPPS scale did not discriminate between achievers and nonachievers. The social desirability contaminated scale discriminated the two groups of male achievers, but it did not discriminate for females. His results suggested that in some situations a scale in which social desirability has not been eliminated might be a more useful predictor.

Social Desirability Stereotypes

It is possible that one's view of socially desirable characteristics may be influenced by the fact of belonging to certain cultural and subcultural groups. If group membership were a significant contributor to social desirability perceptions, then different groups of people should respond differently to the inventory simply by virtue of their group membership characteristics.

A question that concerned Klett (1957a, 1957b) was whether other groups would use the same social desirability standards as did Edwards's college student samples. In one investigation of this question, he compared the judgments of high school students to those of the college sample. Although the correlation of .94 between the scaled values for the two groups indicated a shared perception of socially desirable characteristics, Klett noted that the pairs of items were not as well equated for social desirability as they had been for the college students. Thus, the relationship between social desirability and probability of endorsement was slightly higher for the high school students.

In the second study, Klett (1957b) compared the social desirability judgments of a combined sample of eighty-nine psychotic and twenty-nine nonpsychotic hospitalized veterans to the judgments of his sample of high school students and Edwards's (1953) sample of college students. He found correlations of .88 and .87 between the patient responses and the college students and between the college students and high school students, respectively. These correlations suggest a high degree of similarity between the student and hospital groups.

However, Klett (1957b) did find systematic scale differences that might be expected to influence respondents' scores. The hospitalized group perceived deference, order, and aggression items to be more socially desirable than did the college students and order to be more desirable than did the high school students and, consequently, could be expected to endorse these items more frequently. Affiliation was judged to be more undesirable relative to the college and high school students' judgments and intraception was less desirable for the patients as compared to the college students; change was less desirable for the patients as compared to high school students' judgments of change items.

Two studies have been designed to examine and compare stereotypes of other cultural groups to those of Americans. Klett and Yaukey (1959) compared the social desirability evaluations of six cultural groups: 165 male and thirty-three female Lebanese students, Fujita's (1957) sample of Nisei college students, Lovaas's sample of Norwegians, Edwards's college sample, and Klett's high school and hospital groups. They found that the groups differed significantly in their ratings of social desirability on only seven of the needs. The greatest agreement occurred among the various American student groups (predominantly white college students, Nisei college students, and high school students), and the Norwegians exhibited the greatest divergence.

Patterns that Klett and Yaukey (1959) reported were the Lebanese students judged achievement, autonomy, dominance, and aggression to be more socially desirable than the other groups. Deference, exhibition, succorance, and nurturance were judged by them to be less desirable relative to the judgments of most of the other five groups. Nisei students evaluated endurance, heterosexuality, deference, and order as socially desirable and change as socially undesirable. Norwegians valued exhibition, change, and succorance and reacted more negatively to achievement, intraception, order, and endurance. The authors suggest that the pattern of needs that were revealed may be used cautiously to gain an impression of the character types of the populations who were studied.

In the other cross-cultural study, Diers (1965) intercorrelated the social desirability judgments of 123 male and 103 female Canadian university students, seventy male Hungarian student exiles, and forty institutionalized delinquent girls. She compared responses of these groups to those reported by Klett and Yaukey (1959). Correlations reported for the Hungarians and the juvenile delinquents were the most deviant. Her results also suggested that the tendency to respond in a socially desirable manner had not been controlled for these two groups. In terms of the mean level of their social desirability ratings, Diers found that American, Canadian, and Hungarian students shared similar perceptions of the needs for achievement, exhibition, intraception, change, endurance, and heterosexuality, but there were differences among the groups in their perceptions of affiliation, dominance, and order.

In interpreting her results, Diers states that "it may be that what has been called the social desirability stereotype persists across widely different groups provided these groups are comparable in intelligence, education, and social class within the Western European cultural continuum" (p. 103). Nevertheless, she warns against concluding that subgroups within a nationality will necessarily share the same stereotype.

Interscale Comparisons

Another way of assessing the residual social desirability of the EPPS items is to compare them in some manner to other instruments that have been designed to measure social desirability. Of course, high positive (in most cases) correlations would indicate a relationship between social desirability-response set and tendency toward item endorsement.

Silverman (1957) theorized that the presence of a social desirability-response set would be revealed by correlations between the EPPS scales and two other scales, the K Scale and a Taylor Manifest Anxiety (Taylor, 1953) difference score, designed for the specific purpose of measuring social desirability-response sets. Two scales, Deference and Order, correlated positively with the K Scale, and two, Autonomy and Aggression, correlated negatively. In an earlier validity study, Edwards had also found negative correlations between the K Scale and Autonomy and Aggression and a third scale, Succorance. Silverman's difference score measure correlated negatively with the Achievement, Autonomy, and Aggression scales and positively with the Abasement and Endurance scales. Edwards had also found a positive correlation between need endurance and a specially constructed measure of social desirability. Thus, needs that consistently appeared in both the Silverman and Edwards studies to involve some component of social desirability were autonomy, aggression, and endurance, but the relationships in both cases were of small magnitude ($rs = -.32$)

Two studies in which different measures of social desirability were correlated with the EPPS scales yielded consistent findings. In his study of the correlation between Edwards' Social Desirability Scale and subjects' tendencies to endorse the items having the higher social desirability ratings, Kelleher (1958) found insignificant correlations in most instances for both sexes. For a sample of seventy-two male students, Stollak (1965) found that the Marlowe-Crowne Social Desirability Scale correlated significantly with respondents' scores if their scores were similar to those of males who had been instructed to respond in a socially desirable direction, but that their typical performance did not correlate with Social Desirability Scale scores.

In a series of studies ending with Heilizer and Gerdine (1965), Heilizer and Gerdine (1964) concluded that social desirability effects had not been completely eliminated from the EPPS but that the simple linear relationship between social desirability and item endorsement had been reduced. They also suggested that the end effect of reducing the social desirability component was that the instrument that resulted was more sensitive to the effects of respondents' sex, age, and education.

Shifting to a patient population, Klett and Tamkin (1957) found a high correlation (r = .90) between psychotic and nonpsychotic patients' social desirability ratings of the items that comprise the EPPS scales. They also reported that patients who had high scores on the Pathology Scale and/or low scores on the Social Desirability Scale of the MMPI judged Endurance Scale items to be less socially desirable and Heterosexuality Scale items more desirable than did people who were characterized by a reverse pattern of MMPI scores. Patients with high Ego Strength Scale scores as compared to those with low scores considered achievement and endurance to be more desirable and heterosexuality and autonomy to be less desirable. The authors suggested that the MMPI scales had separated people into groups according to their degree of conformity to group judgments about social desirability.

Instructional Sets

A final means of discovering the effect of the social desirability-response set of subjects' responses has been to compare profiles taken under standard instructions to profiles generated under instructions to make a good impression. Edwards, Wright, and Lunneborg (1959) found correlations of .69 and .61 between the scores of a group of subjects responding under social desirability instructions and a group who responded under standard instructions and a portion of the original normative group, respectively. These correlations were less than the correlation of .93 that they found between standard and normative scores. Yet, the correlations still seemed to confirm Corah, Feldman, Cohen, Gruen, Meadow, and Ringwall's (1958) conclusion that social desirability had not been totally eliminated.

In two later studies, the effects of social desirability instructions were examined for male (Stollak, 1965a) and female (Stollak, 1965b) college students. For male subjects, social desirability instructions resulted in the elimination of a greater proportion of invalid profiles. Scales that were elevated under social desirability instructions were Achievement, Deference, Order, Affiliation, Nurturance, Endurance, and Dominance. Scales that were elevated under regular instructions were Exhibition, Autonomy, Succorance, Change, Heterosexuality, and Aggression. For female students, Stollak's comparison of female scale scores obtained under social desirability instructions to the female college norms was .77. Elevated scales were Achievement, Deference, Order, Affiliation, Nurturance, and Endurance. Depressed scales were Exhibition, Autonomy, Change, Heterosexuality, Aggression, and Succorance. Stollak recommends that one identify test takers with social desirability needs from those with a low need by comparing their standard instruction profile to one (such as his) obtained under social desirability instructions.

Summary and Discussion

The one assertion that can be made with any certainty about the EPPS scales with regard to social desirability is that it is possible for respondents to answer the items in a socially desirable direction should they so desire. Nevertheless, the presence of a social desirability component in the need scales has been reduced to a moderate level at worst depending on the kind of criteria one is using to define social desirability. Enough interstudy differences occurred to make it probable that certain aspects of social desirability are group specific and that one's personal standards of desirability or other personality characteristics may override more general social desirability influences.

Despite the diversity of methods and populations used to investigate the social desirability of the EPPS, a few scales have been identified rather consistently as being *socially desirable*, and a few have been identified rather consistently as being less desirable. Included in the desirable group are achievement, endurance, deference, change, order, and affiliation; less desirable needs include aggression, exhibition, and autonomy.

While it would not be surprising to see elevated need profiles with respect to the desirable needs and depressed profiles with respect to the undesirable ones, it is not clear what either would mean. Virtually none of the literature presented in this chapter, for instance, demonstrates that the presence of a social desirability-response set in any way destroys the validity of the EPPS. Unfortunately, the test user is left in the position of knowing that a person *can* respond to the EPPS in a desirable direction if he or she wants to or is instructed to so respond, but how such knowledge is useful is not readily apparent.

References

Bernhardson, C.S., and Fisher, R.J: The relationship between personal desirability and endorsement with a forced-choice technique. *Multivariate Behavioral Research, 6:*63-73, 1971.

Corah, N.L., Feldman, M.J., Cohen, I.S., Gruen, W., Meadow, A., and Ringwall, E.A.: Social desirability as a variable in the Edwards Personal Preference Schedule. *Journal of Consulting Psychology, 22:*70-72, 1958.

Cronbach, L.J.: Response sets and test validity. *Educational and Psychological Measurement,* 6:475-494, 1946.

Cronbach, L.J.: Further evidence on response sets and test design. *Educational and Psychological Measurement, 10:*3-31, 1959.

Diers, C.J.: Social desirability ratings of personality items by three subcultural groups. *Journal of Social Psychology, 67:*97-104, 1965.

Edwards, A.L., Wright, C.E., and Lunneborg, C.E.: A note on "social desirability as a variable in the Edwards Personal Preference Schedule." *Journal of Consulting Psychology, 23:*558, 1959.

Fujita, B.: Applicability of the Edwards Personal Preference Schedule to Nisei. *Psychological Reports, 3:*518-519, 1957.

Goodstein, L.D., and Heilbrun, A.B., Jr.: The relationship between personal and social desirability scale values of the Edwards Personal Preference Schedule. *Journal of Consulting Psychology. 23:*183, 1959.

Hathaway, S.R., and McKinley, J.C.: *The Minnesota Multiphasic Personality Inventory Manual.* New York, Psychological Corporation, 1951.

Heilbrun, A.B., Jr: Relationships between the Adjective Check List, Personal Preference Schedule and desirability factors under varying defensive conditions. *Journal of Clinical Psychology, 14:*283-287, 1958.

Heilbrun, A.B. Jr.: Social desirability and the relative validities of achievement scales. *Journal of Consulting Psychology, 26:*383-386, 1962.

Heilbrun, A.B., Jr., and Goodstein, L.D.: Relationship between personal and social desirability sets and performance on the Edwards Personal Preference Schedule. *Journal of Applied Psychology, 43:*302-305, 1959a.

Heilbrun, A.B., and Goodstein, L.D.: Social desirability response set: Error or predictor variable? *Journal of Psychology, 51:*321-329, 1961.

Heilizer, F., and Gerdine, P.V.: Social desirability effects in the EPPS. *Psychological Reports, 15:*243-258, 1964.

Heilizer, F., and Gerdine, P.V.: Comparison of how two content variables are changed by the special format of the EPPS. *Psychological Reports, 16:*3-15, 1965.

Kelleher, D.: The social desirability factor in Edwards' EPPS. *Journal of Consulting Psychology, 22:*100, 1958.

Klett, C.J.: Stability of the social desirability scale values in the EPPS. *Journal of Consulting Psychology, 21:*183-185, 1957a.

Klett, C.J.: Social desirability stereotype in a hospital population. *Journal of Consulting Psychology, 21:*419-421, 1957b.

Klett, C.J., and Tamkin, A.S.: Social desirability stereotype and some measures of psychopathology. *Journal of Consulting Psychology, 21:*450, 1957.

Klett, C.J., and Yaukey, D.W.: A cross-cultural comparison of judgements of social desirability. *Journal of Social Psychology, 49:*19-26, 1959.

Korman, M., and Coltharp, F.: Transparency in the Edwards Personal Preferences Schedule. *Journal of Consulting Psychology, 26:*379-382, 1962.

Lovaas, O.I.: Social desirability ratings of personality variables by Norwegian and American college students. *Journal of Abnormal Social Psychology, 57:*124-125, 1958.

Mann, J.H.: Self-ratings and the EPPS. *Journal of Applied Psychology, 42:*267-268, 1958.

Messick, S.: Dimensions of social desirability. *Journal of Consulting Psychology, 24:*279-287, 1960.

Navran, L., and Stauffacher, J.D.: Social desirability as a factor in Edwards' Personal Preference Schedule performance. *Journal of Consulting Psychology, 18:*442, 1954.

Saltz, E., Reece, M., and Ager, J: Studies of forced choice methodology: individual differences in social desirability. *Educational and Psychological Measurement, 22:*365-370, 1962.

Silverman, R.E.: Edwards Personal Preference Schedule and social desirability. *Journal of Consulting Psychology, 21:*402-404, 1957.

Stollak, G.E.: EPPS performance under social desirability instructions: College females. *Psychological Reports, 16:*119-122, 1965.

Stollak, G.E.: Relationship between EPPS and Marlowe-Crowne SD Scale. *Psychological Reports, 16:*731-732, 1965.

Stollak, G.E.: EPPS performance under social desirability instructions. *Journal of Personality and Social Psychology, 2:*430-432, 1965a.

Taylor, J.A.: A personality scale of manifest anxiety. *Journal of Abnormal and Social Psychology, 48:* 285-290, 1953.

Chapter 5

NONRESPONSIVE AND RANDOM RESPONDING ON THE EDWARDS PERSONAL PREFERENCE SCHEDULE

T HE Edwards Personal Preference Schedule (EPPS) is one of few personality inventories that has been developed for the purpose of assessing normal personality characteristics. Perhaps for this reason it has been used extensively by researchers and practitioners alike since its debut in 1954. Neither the original manual nor the sequel published in 1959 provides much information relevant to the validity of the instrument. Noticeably absent are data concerning how the test user can identify a profile produced under potentially biasing test taker response sets.

One response set that has received little consideration in the literature is random or nonresponsive answering. Yet, information about nonresponsive answering on the EPPS is important because the manual suggests that low consistency scores may be the result of test taker's "irritation with the difficult forced choices the EPPS demands" (p. 18). Wittenborn (1956) has also suggested that the answer sheet, while convenient for the test scorer, may be rather tedious from the test taker's viewpoint.

As the EPPS manual and Wittenborn's (1956) comments suggest, partially random responding is a potential response set on the EPPS. Partially random answering would occur in situations in which the test taker began by attempting to respond to the items seriously, but shifted to a random pattern of responding at some point during the test. In the present paper, profiles produced in such a way will be called nonresponsive.

Totally random responding is a second type of random response set that might occur on EPPS profiles. Totally random profiles result when an individual answers all of the items with little or no regard for item content. In the present paper, this type of response set will be referred to as random responding. A random profile might be produced by an individual with a reading deficiency or a language difficulty that hindered her/his ability to respond accurately to the items.

The purpose of the present paper was to investigate the question of whether random and nonresponsive profiles could be distinguished from authentically produced profiles. The sole means for determining the validity of an EPPS profile is the consistency score. Thus, the primary question in the investigation was whether the profiles produced under three different response conditions, two random and one genuine, would yield markedly different consistency scores. However, a secondary question was whether there were other profile characteristics that could be used to identify invalid profiles.

Profile Generation

AUTHENTIC. Puig-Casaranc[1] asked 185 female junior and senior undergraduates at a Northwestern university to take the EPPS for research purposes. The only inducement for their participation was that they could receive a test interpretation if they wished. Presumably, then, the participants completed the inventories because they chose to complete them. Puig-Casaranc's subjects were distributed across female-dominated (e.g. nursing), male-dominated (e.g. accounting), and neutral (e.g. pharmacy) college majors. The authentic comparison group consisted of a random sample of fifty of these answer sheets; an additional fifty were used to create the nonresponsive profiles.

NONRESPONSIVE. Prior to completing each of the nonresponsive answer sheets, a different number was selected from a table of random numbers, the only stipulation for the selected numbers being that they exceed one and not exceed 210. Each answer sheet was marked as one of the authentic respondents had marked her answer sheet until the item numbered the same as the preselected random number was reached. At this point, the answer sheet was completed in the same manner as the random answer sheets.

RANDOM. The random answer sheets were hand-produced using a table of random numbers. Whenever an odd number appeared in the table, the A response was marked; whenever an even number appeared, the B response was marked. A total of fifty answer sheets were produced in this manner.

Thus, the analysis consisted of 150 profiles: fifty authentically produced, fifty random, and fifty nonresponsive. All of the profiles were scored for consistency scores. A lenient standard for determining the validity of a profile according to the manual is that the consistency score should reach a minimum of 10. A more rigid standard requires a consistency score of 11 or more. In the present study, those profiles having a consistency score less than 10 were discarded.

Results

Whether one uses the lenient standard of a consistency score of 10 or the more rigid standard of 11 or more makes little difference in distinguishing valid from invalidly produced profiles. As shown in Table 5-I, when 10 was used as a minimum standard, all except four of the authentic profiles were considered valid. However, only nine of the nonresponsive and six of the random profiles were retained. A chi-square computed for the difference between amount of

[1]The author wishes to thank Mela Puig-Casaranc for donating the data used in the present study.

profiles retained under the random and nonresponsive set with 10 as the standard was not significant (chi-square = .71, df = 1). However, the chi-square computed for the three response conditions was significant (chi-square = 82.08, df = 2, $P < .001$) — indicating that more authentic than nonauthentic profiles were retained.

Table 5 - I

NUMBER OF VALID PROFILES
WITH CONSISTENCY SCORE AS A CRITERION

Type of Profile [1]	Minimum Consistency Score		Total
	10	11-15	
Nonresponsive	7	2	9
Random	3	3	6
Authentic	5	41	46

[1] N for each of the three profile types equals 50.

Using a minimum consistency score of 11 resulted in the rejection of forty-eight, forty-seven, and nine profiles for the nonresponsive, random, and authentic profiles, respectively. Thus, a consistency score of 10 is about as effective as a minimum score of 11 in eliminating invalid profiles under the circumstances of the present study.

Although the majority of invalid profiles would be eliminated if a minimum consistency score of 10 were used as the discriminating criterion, some would still be considered valid. To determine whether these profiles had distinguishing characteristics, the individual scale values for each profile were compared. As shown in Table 5-I, authentic profiles are likely to have a greater percentage of scales with extreme values. For example 77 percent of the authentic profiles had one or more scales within the range of from 0 to 6. By contrast, none of the nonresponsive or random profiles had one or more scales within the raw score range from 0 to 6. For the upper extreme, 16 to 28, 66 percent of the nonresponsive and 17 percent of the random profiles had five or more within that range, while 98 percent of the authentic scales had from five to nine scales that were very high.

The middle range of scores seems to be most descriptive of the random and nonresponsive profiles. From 84 to 99 percent of these profiles had nine or more scales within the range of from 7 to 15. Among authentic profiles only 30 percent had eight or more scales within the midrange.

Group means for the three response conditions were computed for each

Table 5 - II

DISTRIBUTION OF SCALE VALUES
FOR THREE RESPONSE CONDITIONS

Number of Scales on Profile	Raw Score Intervals								
	0-6			7-15			16 - 28		
	A[1]%	NR%	R%	A%	NR%	R%	A%	NR%	R%
12					22	17			
11				2	11	67			
10				15	33			11	
9				13	33		2		
8				26		17	4		
7				11			26		17
6				15			33	33	
5				13			33	22	
4	4			2			2	11	67
3	17			2				22	17
2	17								
1	39								

A[1] Authentic (n=46), NR= Nonresponsive (n=9), R= Random (n=6)

need scale and rounded to the nearest whole number. These means were converted to percentiles using the college female norms presented in the EPPS manual (p. 12). Figure 5-1 shows the individual groups profiles. Interestingly, the random data *appear* more real than do the authentic data. That is, the random and nonresponsive profiles exhibit more exaggerated peaks and valleys than does the authentic profile. Of the fifteen needs measured by the Edwards, six of the random and nonresponsive and five of the authentic scales exceeded the 60th percentile; three of the authentic and nonresponsive scales and five of the random scales were below the 40th percentile. Thus, it appears that the more random the responses, the more extreme the percentiles. About half of the authentic scales were in the percentile range from 40 to 60 as compared to two for the random and five for the nonresponsive. Therefore, if the interpreter of an EPPS inventory relies on the percentile norms alone, he or she runs a risk of being duped by the ostensible scale variation which occurs with random data. In addition, although the specific scales for which evaluations oc-

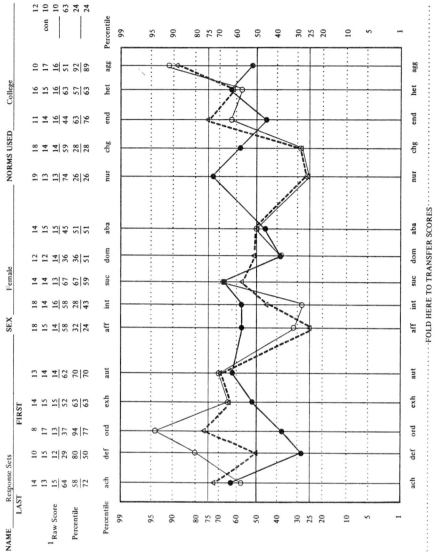

Figure 5-1. EDWARDS PERSONAL PREFERENCE SCHEDULE. Group Profiles of EPPS Need Percentiles. Reproduced from *Edwards Personal Preference Schedule Manual* by permission.

cur may differ from study to study, extreme evaluations, e.g. aggression, or depression, e.g. affiliation, on sex inappropriate scales may suggest the presence of some random responding.

Discussion

The results of the present study suggest that there is no absolute method of distinguishing randomly produced profiles from those produced under more serious responding conditions. However, one can have greater confidence in the validity of a profile if it has a consistency score of 10 or higher in combination with one or more other profile characteristics. These characteristics in order of descending effectiveness are (a) one or more scales within the range from 0 to 6, (b) five or more scales within the range from 16 to 28, and (c) seven or fewer scales within the range of 7 to 15.

Because the investigation of random response sets on the Edwards Personal Preference Schedule is a neglected area in the measurement research, additional cross-validating studies are a necessity. Such studies might focus on determining whether profiles produced under other authentic conditions, e.g. solicited counseling, conform to the guidelines presented in the present study.

It should also be noted that the profiles used in the present study were contributed by women respondents. Therefore, caution should be used in generalizing these conclusions to profiles produced by men.

References

Edwards, A.L.: *Edwards Personal Preference Schedule Manual.* New York, The Psychological Corporation, 1959.

Puig-Casaranc, M.C.: Personality and interest characteristics of females in traditional and non-traditional fields of academic study and their relationship to psychological androgyny. Unpublished doctoral dissertation, Washington State University, Pullman, Washington, 1976.

Wittenborn, J.R.: A review of Edwards Personal Preference Schedule. *Journal of Consulting Psychology, 20:*321-323, 1956.

Chapter 6

A NOTE ON THE CONVERGENT AND DISCRIMINANT VALIDITY OF THE EPPS

To be useful to a practitioner, it is desirable that measures bearing the same trait names (assuming that they refer to conceptually similar content) correlate highly with one another and that measures bearing dissimilar names do not correlate highly with one another. These two observations refer to the convergent and the discriminant validity, respectively, of measures and are particularly true when the measures derive from theoretically similar ancestry. Most of the multiscale studies of the EPPS have involved another measure descended from Murray's need theory, the Adjective Check List (Gough and Heilbrun, 1965), although other "first cousins," including self-ratings and the Personality Research Form (Jackson, 1967), have been used occasionally.

Convergent Validity

Table 6-I summarizes the convergent validity studies in which the Adjective Check List was the criterion variable, and Table 6-II summarizes those studies in which self-ratings were the criteria. By testing the hypothesis that the total number of significant findings that occurred across studies exceeded chance, it is possible to determine for which scales the weight of evidence balances in favor for convergent validity. In both tables, the original authors' significance levels are maintained since different authors tended to use different standards, e.g. one-tailed versus two-tailed tests.

When both test and self-rating intercorrelations were considered, scales that yielded significant findings across studies more often than chance were Order, Exhibition, Autonomy, Succorance, Dominance, Abasement, Nurturance, and Aggression (a one-tailed test of significance was used). In their validity study, Bessmer and Ramanaiah (1979) included the Personality Research Form, which limited the number of scales that they could consider. Nevertheless, they also reported convergent validity for the Aggression, Autonomy, Dominance, Exhibition, and Order scales in the male sample and for the Aggression, Autonomy, Dominance, Exhibition, and Nurturance scales for the female sample. Although their study did not include the Succorance or Abasement scales, it can be concluded safely that all of the EPPS scales except Achievement, Deference, Intraception, Change, Endurance, Affiliation, and Heterosexuality share content with the investigated similarly named measures.

Table 6 - I

SUMMARY OF CONVERGENT VALIDITY STUDIES INVOLVING THE ADJECTIVE CHECK LIST

Samples

EPPS Need	College[a] Students (Heilbrun, 1958) N = 77	Peace Corps Women (McGargee & Parker, 1968) N = 86	Peace Corps Men (McGargee & Parker, 1968) N = 77	College Women & Men (Bouchard, 1968) N = 78	University Students (Poe, 1969) N = 131	University Honor Students (Wohl & Palmer, 1970) N = 46	University Non-honors Students (Wohl & Palmer, 1970) N = 76	University Males (Bessmer & Ramanaiah, 1979) N = 85	University Females (Bessmer & Ramanaiah, 1979) N = 103
Ach	.01	-.15	-.07	.11	.18*	.46**	.11	.26**	.09
Def	.39**	.33**	.02	.28**	.22**	.40**	.21	—	—
Ord	.31**	.44**	.34**	.49**	.34**	.33*	.40**	.26**	.14
Exh	.36**	.25*	.22*	.52**	.40**	.21	.38**	.25**	.28**
Aut	.31**	.15	.42**	.23	.41**	.41**	.45**	.32**	.38**
Aff	.28**	.22	.18	.32**	.23**	.47**	.22**	.21	.19
Int	.04	.22*	.14	.19	.22**	.46**	.12	—	—
Suc	.33**	.26*	.23*	.14	.39**	.30**	.06	—	—
Dom	.41**	.22*	.20	.44**	.49**	.62**	.41**	.29**	.37**
Aba	.39**	.23*	.20	.57**	.46**	.50**	.28*	—	—
Nur	.32**	.23*	.16	.30**	.30**	.26	.41**	.20	.29*
Chg	.19	.18	.05	.25*	.36**	.49**	.21	—	—
End	.14	.48*	.17	.45**	.43**	.38**	.53**	.19	.16
Het	.18	.22*	-.02	.00	.19*	.12	.22	—	—
Agg	.48**	.42**	.21	.32**	.49**	.23	.48**	.42***	.37***

[a] Heilbrun's correlations were reported in the Adjective Check List Manual.

*p < .05
**p < .01
***p < .001

Table 6 - II

SUMMARY OF CONVERGENT VALIDITY STUDIES
INVOLVING SELF-RATINGS

Samples

EPPS Needs	Medical Students (Korman & Coltharp, 1962) N = 98	University Men & Women (Bouchard, 1968) N = 78	University Men & Women (Poe, 1969) N = 131	(Mann, 1958) N =
Ach	.16	.26*	.58**	.12
Def	.20	.19	.46**	.28*
Ord	.52**	.56**	.65**	.27*
Exh	.26*	.27*	.60**	.06
Aut	.43**	.49**	.67**	.13
Aff	.35**	.32**	.74**	.00
Int	.26*	.25*	.71**	.07
Suc	.37**	.47**	.70**	.22*
Dom	.04	.59**	.74**	.26*
Aba	.24*	.15	.75**	.39*
Nur	.37**	.20*	.69**	.34*
Chg	.44**	.43**	.60**	.42*
End	.26*	.50**	.57**	.41*
Het	.36**	.34**	.71**	.40*
Agg	.23*	.31**	.56**	.24*

Discriminant Validity

Investigators of the discriminant validity of the EPPS scales usually have not analyzed all of the scales, some for theoretical reasons (Bessmer and Ramanaiah, 1979) and others for inexplicable reasons (Bouchard, 1968). Therefore, it is not possible to make definitive statements about the scales.

Bouchard (1968), who used only the Dominance, Endurance, and Order scales, found strong evidence for the discriminant validity of the Dominance and Order scales and partial support for the validity of the Endurance scale. McGargee and Parker (1968) reported partial confirmation of the discriminant validity of the Aggression, Endurance, Order, and Succorance scales when women were the respondents and for Autonomy, Exhibition, and Order when men were the respondents. Poe's (1969) summary of his data suggests the presence of discriminant validity for all of the scales when self-ratings were the other measure. Though it is not easy to tell with any certainty because of the manner in which his data are presented, it appears that the Dominance, Aggression, Succorance, Abasement, Change, and Endurance scales demonstrated at least partial evidence of discriminant validity.

Finally, in their study in which they used nine of the EPPS scales, Bessmer and Ramanaiah (1979) reported strong discriminant validity for Aggression, Autonomy, Dominance, Exhibition, and Nurturance scales for their female sample and for the Aggression, Autonomy, Dominance, Exhibition, and Order scales for the male sample. Partial support for both sexes were found for all nine scales.

Taken together the discriminant validity studies provide strong evidence for the discriminant validity of the Dominance, Order, Aggression, Autonomy, and Exhibition scales and probable evidence for the discriminant validity of the Endurance scale.

Summary

Scales that reoccur consistently enough across studies to support the presence of both discriminant and convergent validity are Order, Exhibition, Autonomy, Dominance, and Aggression. Of course, it is never possible to state that a measure does or does not have validity since validity depends to a large extent on the criterion that one is considering. The critieria on which the studies in this chapter were based were tests and self-ratings that were derived from Murray's need theory.

References

Bessmer, M.A., and Ramanaiah, N.V.: Convergent and discriminant validity of selected need scales from the ACL, the EPPS, and the PRF. *In Technical Reports in Applied Experimental Psychology,* Vol. 1. Carbondale, Southern Illinois University, Department of Psychology, 1979.

Bouchard, T.J., Jr.: Convergent and discriminant validity of the Adjective Check List and Edwards Personal Preference Schedule. *Educational and Psychological Measurement, 28:*1165-1171, 1968.

Gough, H.G., and Heilbrun, A.B.: *The Adjective Check List Manual.* Palo Alto, California, Consulting Psychologists Press, 1965.

Jackson, D.N.: *Personality Research Form Manual.* Goshen, New York, Research Psychologists Press, 1967.

Korman, M., and Coltharp, F.: Transparency in the Edwards Personal Preference Schedule. *Journal of Consulting Psychology, 26:*379-382, 1962.

Mann, J.H.: Self-ratings and the EPPS. *Journal of Applied Psychology, 42:*267-268, 1958.

McGargee, E.I., and Parker, G.V.C.: An exploration of the equivalence of Murrayan needs as assessed by the adjective check list, the TAT and Edwards Personal Preference Schedule. *Journal of Clinical Psychology, 24:*47-51, 1968.

Poe, C.A.: Convergent and discriminant validation of measures of personal needs. *Journal of Ed-*

*ucational Measurement, 6:*103-107, 1969.

Wohl, J., and Palmer, A.B.: Correlations between Adjective Check List and Edwards Personal Preference Schedule measures of Murray's needs. *Psychological Reports, 27:*525-526, 1970.

SECTION III

PERSONALITY CHARACTERISTICS

Chapter 7

DIMENSIONS OF THE EPPS SCALES:
NORMAL POPULATIONS

A NUMBER of studies have sought to investigate whether correlational or factor analytic procedures could be used to reduce the fifteen scales to fewer scales or dimensions. Both approaches have involved some studies that used only the EPPS and some that combined it with other instruments designed to measure normal personality characteristics. Because some of these studies have involved normal populations as well, they are useful in forming hypotheses about the characteristics measured by the scales.

EPPS Studies

CORRELATIONAL STUDIES. While some authors, e.g. Stolz (1958), have questioned the appropriateness of using correlational procedures with the EPPS scales because of their inevitable interdependence, others (Allen, 1958; Tisdale, 1965; Dixon and Ahern, 1973; Manners and Steger, 1975) have continued to use correlational procedures simply because there are few viable statistical alternatives readily available for use with small samples.

In the second edition of the manual for the EPPS, Edwards presented a correlation matrix of the fifteen needs as evidence that the need scales were relatively independent of one another.

To determine the level of similarity between the correlational matrix reported by Edwards and the nine matrices reported by subsequent investigators, the individual correlations within the matrices were treated as scores, which were then correlated with the EPPS matrix of scores, i.e. correlations. Obtained between-matrix correlations ranged from .20 ($p \leq .02$) to .87 ($p \leq .0001$) with an average correlation of .70, suggesting a high degree of similarity between the pattern of scale relationships reported by Edwards and those obtained in subsequent validational studies.

In Tables 7-I and 7-II, the results of attempted replications of Edwards's original correlational study are summarized. Only correlations that were statistically significant in a minimum of three studies and whose signs were in the same direction are presented. If one considers the average correlation across the five studies, then it appears that the only pair of scales that show a positive correlation of any consequence are affiliation and nurturance. This correlation should indicate that when one member of this pair is elevated or depressed for a respondent so should be the other member to some extent. The average correlations for the negatively correlated pairs of scales were all negligible.

The previously discussed studies were based on combined samples of women and men, entirely male samples or samples of unspecified sex. Allen's (1958) study suggests that scales may be correlated differently for the two sexes, but his findings are in need of further replication.

FACTOR ANALYTIC STUDIES. Table 7-III summarizes the factor analysis studies for normal populations, primarily male and female undergraduates. For details about factor characteristics the reader is referred to these original sources. In the eight studies in which the EPPS has been factor analyzed exclusively (Wright, 1961; Bendig and Martin, 1962; Milton and Lipetz, 1968; Dixon and Ahern, 1973; Sherman and Poe, 1970; Sherman and Poe, 1972; Manners and Steger, 1975), the number of factors identified has ranged from 4 to 8, with 5 being the most common number extracted. For the most part, the investigations of the factor composition of the EPPS alone have involved statistical alterations of the original scales designed either to eliminate or to measure the statistical bias assumed to be inherent in the original version.

The concern about the possible interdependence between the EPPS scales, which held for the correlational studies of the inventory also, applies to those studies in which investigators have attempted to identify the underlying dimensions of the EPPS via factor analysis. In addition, several of the factor analysis studies have been characterized by sample sizes that only barely exceeded the number of variables under investigation. Of course, the result of small sample sizes is that one may discover factors in one study that will not appear in future investigations of the scale. Therefore, in order to have confidence in the factors discovered in a particular study it is necessary to have evidence that the factors occur across studies as well.

One factor that was identified by various authors has been variously named altruism vs. narcissism (Caron and Wallach, 1959), n [need for] ego self-direction (Dixon and Ahern, 1973), assertive aggressiveness (Sherman and Poe, 1970; 1972), and need for status-dominance (Milton and Lipetz, 1968). This factor consists of some combination of unidirectional factor loadings for the Achievement, Exhibition, Autonomy, Dominance, Aggression, and Heterosexuality scales and opposite direction loadings on some combination of the Deference, Order, Affiliation, Abasement, Nurturance, and Succorance scales. Thus, this dimension represents an attention-seeking and impulse-satisfaction orientation as opposed to a self-effacing, impulse-inhibiting orientation.

In a comparison of their reanalysis of Wright's (1961) correlation matrix with their own data, Bendig and Martin (1962) identified virtually identical factors for both samples that appeared to represent the two poles of the impulse-satisfaction factor. However, each pole was represented by two different factors. The impulse-satisfaction sets of scales were named *achievement*

Table 7 - I

SUMMARY OF NEGATIVELY CORRELATED NEED SCALES

	Negatively Correlated Pairs	Original EPPS Correlations	Subsequent[1] Correlations	Mean Correlation
1.	achievement-nurturance	-.30	-.31, -.31, -.20, -.19	-.26
2.	affiliation-aggression	-.33	-.36, -.27, -.23, -.30	-.30
3.	dominance-abasement	-.34	-.30, -.18, -.17, -.32	-.26
4.	endurance-heterosexuality	-.27	-.31, -.41, -.18, -.21	-.28
5.	achievement-abasement	-.28	-.22, -.10, -.15, -.29	-.20
6.	deference-autonomy	-.30	-.40, -.26, -.04, -.26	-.25
7.	deference-dominance	-.22	-.18, -.22, -.01, -.05	-.14
8.	deference-heterosexuality	-.28	-.32, -.32, -.09, -.29	-.26
9.	order-exhibition	-.21	-.17, -.20, -.06, -.16	-.16
10.	order-autonomy	-.15	-.28, -.13, -.02, -.15	-.14
11.	order-heterosexuality	-.16	-.31, -.21, -.09, -.31	-.22
12.	exhibition-abasement	-.18	-.15, -.21, -.03, -.17	-.14
13.	exhibition-endurance	-.27	-.27, -.22, -.00, -.13	-.18
14.	autonomy-abasement	-.26	-.21, -.25, -.02, -.15	-.18
15.	autonomy-nurturance	-.36	-.37, -.29, -.09, -.31	-.28

Table 7 - I (continued)

Negatively Correlated Pairs	Original EPPS Correlations	Subsequent[1] Correlations	Mean Correlation
16. autonomy-endurance	-.13	-.17, -.11, -.05, -.22	-.14
17. intraception-heterosexuality	-.19	-.27, -.23, -.04, -.21	-.18
18. succorance-endurance	-.31	-.34, -.33, -.13, -.09	-.24
19. abasement-heterosexuality	-.29	-.23, -.16, -.02, -.26	-.19
20. nurturance-change	-.12	-.19, -.18, -.14, -.12	-.15
21. nurturance-aggression	-.33	-.39, -.31, -.05, -.24	-.26
22. nurturance-heterosexuality	-.21	-.21, -.02, -.00, -.14	-.12

[1]First figure: Allen's (1958) n = 130

Second figure: Tisdale's (1965), n = 292

Third figure: Dixon & Ahern's (1973) Study I, n = 167

Fourth figure: Manners & Steger (1975), n = 325

via independence or *general ambition* and *need for attention* or *emotional immaturity.* The first was composed of positive loadings for needs Achievement, Autonomy, Dominance, Endurance, Intraception, and Change and a negative loading for Succorance. The second was composed of positive loadings for Exhibition, Aggression, Succorance, and Heterosexuality.

The self-effacing pole was represented by an obsessive-compulsive syndrome factor and a social dependency factor. The former was composed of positive loadings for Deference, Order, Endurance, and Abasement needs; the latter was composed of positive loadings for Affiliation, Nurturance, Change, and Succorance and negative loadings for Aggression.

Some version of the obsessive factor occurred with some regularity in several other studies. In about 50 percent of the studies, the Deference, Order, and Endurance scales were opposed by the Heterosexuality Scale, suggesting a conventionality versus unconventionality dimension.

Dixon and Ahern (1973) called the factor having highest loadings on the first three of the mentioned scales *n* [need for] social control; Sherman and Poe

Table 7 - II

SUMMARY OF POSITIVELY CORRELATED NEED SCALES

	Positively Correlated Pairs	Original EPPS Correlations	Subsequent[1] Correlations	Mean Correlation
1.	abasement-endurance	.07	.09, .09, .26, .19	.14
2.	abasement-nurturance	.23	.27, .11, .41, .19	.24
3.	achievement-autonomy	.14	.16, .16, .26, .12	.16
4.	affiliation-nurturance	.46	.34, .44, .60, .46	.46
5.	affiliation-succorance	.09	.25, .21, .13, .12	.16
6.	autonomy-aggression	.29	.26, .14, .33, .32	.26
7.	autonomy-change	.15	.27, .14, .26, .23	.21
8.	deference-endurance	.22	.29, .21, .31, .13	.23
9.	deference-intraception	.10	.11, .17, .25, .20	.16
10.	deference-order	.26	.41, .23, .41, .42	.34
11.	dominance-aggression	.21	.13, .02, .35, .18	.18
12.	exhibition-aggression	.11	.13, .06, .29, .12	.14
13.	exhibition-autonomy	.09	.06, .06, .26, .26	.14
14.	exhibition-dominance	.11	.06, .19, .42, .13	.18
15.	exhibition-heterosexuality	.12	.22, .10, .07, .22	.14

Table 7 - II (continued)

Positively Correlated Pairs	Original EPPS Correlations	Subsequent[1] Correlations	Mean Correlation
16. heterosexuality-aggression	.15	.26, .12, .15, .13	.16
17. order-endurance	.33	.48, .36, .40, .33	.38
18. succorance-nurturance	.16	.22, .17, .24, .24	.20

[1]First figure: Allen's (1958), n = 130

Second figure: Tisdale's (1965), n = 292

Third figure: Dixon & Ahern's (1973) Study I, n = 167

Fourth figure: Manners & Steger (1975), n = 325

(1970) called the factor having highest loadings on Order and Endurance persistence-dependence; Manners and Steger (1975) who found notable loadings for all four of the scales when they reanalyzed Edwards's original data as well as a new sample of their own called it the *drone* pattern. These scales seem to reflect a need for a structured and conventional environment.

The EPPS and Other Personality Measures

The primary reason for intercorrelating and/or factor analyzing some combination of the EPPS need scales plus other personality tests has been to determine whether the EPPS scales measure something distinct from these other inventories or can be used interchangeably. This issue is of particular concern when the EPPS scales are compared to scales from other tests of similar names and/or underlying rationales.

CORRELATIONAL STUDIES. Three studies represented efforts to discover relationships between the EPPS scales and personality characteristics measured by other multiscale personality inventories designed to measure some aspect of normal behavior. Dunnette, Kirchener, and DeGidio (1958) intercorrelated the EPPS and the California Psychological Inventory (CPI), a measure of interpersonal behaviors; Edwards and Abbott (1973) intercorrelated the EPPS and the Edwards Personality Inventory (EPI); Cunningham, Wakefield, and Ward (1975) used canonical correlation to study the relationship between the EPPS and the Work Motivation Inventory, a measure of Maslow's needs. Significant scale correlations from the first two studies are shown in Table 7-IV.

Table 7 - III

SUMMARY OF FACTOR ANALYSES USING NORMAL POPULATIONS

Study	Sample	N	Measures	EPPS Response Format	Factoring Method	Type of Rotation	Number of Factors Extracted
1. Lorr, O'Connor Seifert (1977)	a. College men and women	216	1. EPPS 2. PRF 3. Two Additional Instruments	True-False (Abasement Items	Prinicipal Components	Promax	12
	b. High school boys	327					
2. Wright (1961)	a. Undergraduate women	48	EPPS	Forced Choice and Rating Scale	Principal Components	None	8
	b. Men	44					
3. Milton & Lipetz (1968)	a. Undergraduate males	150	EPPS	Corrected Forced Choice	Centroid	Varimax	5
	b. Undergraduate females	150					
4. Edwards & Abbott (1973)	a. Male students	109	1. EPPS 2. EPI 3. PRF 4. Two Social Desirability Scales 5. One Additional Measure	Forced Choice	Principal Components	Varimax	18
	b. Female students	109					
5. Edwards & Abbott (1973)	a. Female students	171	1. EPI 2. CPI 3. EPPS 4. Three Additional Measures	Forced Choice	Principal Components	Varimax	22
	b. Male students	115					
6. Dixon & Ahern (1973)	a. Senior high school students	167	EPPS	Forced Choice	Image Analysis	Varimax	5
	b. Introductory psychology students						
	c. "Innovative" college students						
7. Edwards, Abbott,& Klockars (1972)	a. Males b. Females	109 109	1. PRF 2. Two Social Desirability Scales 3. One Additional Measure	Forced Choice	Principal Components	Varimax	11

Table 7 - III (continued)

Study	Sample	N	Measures	EPPS Response Format	Factoring Method	Type of Rotation	Number of Factors Extracted
8. Borgatta (1962)	a. Female under-graduates b. Male under-graduates	32 82	1. Thurstone Temperament Schedule 2. EPPS 3. 16 PF	Forced Choice			8
9. Krug & Moyer (1961)	a. Female freshmen under-graduates b. Male freshmen under-graduates	194 490	1. EPPS 2. F Scale	Forced Choice	Centroid	Quartimax	10
10. Sherman & Poe (1972)	Under-graduates	314	EPPS	Likert Format	Principal Axes		4
11. Hartley & Allen (1962)	Under-graduates	130	EPPS MMPI	Forced Choice	Centroid		10
12. Cook, Linden, & McKay (1961)	Under-graduates	196	EPPS	Forced Choice	Multiple Group Centroid	Varimax	6
13. Sherman & Poe (1970)	a. College men b. College women	169 146	EPPS	Likert Format	Principal Axes	None	4
14. Manners & Steger (1975)	Male industrial employees	325	EPPS	Standard	Alpha	Varimax	5
15. Bendig & Martin (1962)	a. Under-graduate males b. Under-graduate women	133 195	EPPS Short Form	True-False	Complete Centroid	Analytic	10

[1] Forced choice is the regular response format.

Samples involved were entirely male, 60 percent female, or of unspecified sex. Most of the EPI correlations exceeded .40; only two of the CPI correlations, succorance-good impression ($r = -.42$) and dominance-sociability ($r = .41$) exceeded .40.

    Cunningham et al. identified three significant canonical dimensions involv-

Table 7 - IV

SUMMARY OF MULTISCALE CORRELATIONAL STUDIES

	Related CPI Scales	Correlation	Related EPI Scales	Correlation
1. Achievement	dominance	.20	desires recognition	.49
	responsibility	.26		
	socialization	.25		
	good impression	.25		
2. Deference	responsibility	.22	conforms	.39
	self-control	.26		
	good impression	.25		
3. Order	dominance	-.24	plans and organizes things	.60
	capacity for status	-.37		
	sociability	-.28		
	social presence	-.26		
	tolerance	-.32		
	communality	-.24		
	achievement via independence	-.24		
	intellectual efficiency	-.30		
	psychological-mindedness	-.24		
	flexibility	-.23		
	femininity	.23		
4. Exhibition	dominance	.34	enjoys being the center of attention	.38
	capacity for status	.23		
	sociability	.35		
	social presence	.31		
	self-acceptance	.29		
	intellectual efficiency	.21		
5. Autonomy			conforms	-.57
6. Affiliation	tolerance	.26	feels superior	-.34
	good impression	.21		
7. Intraception	capacity for status	.21	interested in the behavior of others	.42
	sociability	.21		
	well-being	.24		
	responsibility	.23		
	self-control	.20		
	tolerance	.21		
	good impression	.27		
	achievement via conformance	.34		

Table 7 - **IV** (continued)

		Related CPI Scales	Correlation	Related EPI Scales	Correlation
8.	Succorance	dominance	-.26	wants sympathy	.47
		capacity for status	-.25		
		well-being	-.32		
		responsibility	-.36		
		tolerance	-.24		
		good impression	-.42		
		achievement via conformance	-.30		
9.	Dominance	dominance	.34	assumes responsibility	.72
		capacity for status	.26		
		sociability	.41		
		self-acceptance	.29		
		responsibility	.37		
		tolerance	.31		
		good impression	.20		
		achievement via conformance	.29		
		intellectual efficiency	.24		
10.	Abasement	dominance	-.31	self-critical	.47
		capacity for status	-.21		
		sociability	-.21		
		socialization	-.21		
		tolerance	-.20		
		achievement via conformance	-.36		
11.	Nurturance	self-acceptance	-.24	helps others	.44
		well-being	.21		
		self-control	.20		
12.	Change	social pressure	.28	seeks new experience	.44
13.	Endurance	well-being	.23	is a hard worker	.51
		self-acceptance	-.22		
		responsibility	.23		
		self-control	.29		
		good impression	.26		
		communality	-.23		
		achievement via conformance	.28		
14.	Heterosexuality	well-being	-.29	is a hard worker	-.29
		responsibility	-.26		
		socialization	-.20		
		good impression	-.38		
		achievement via conformance	-.20		

Table 7 - IV (continued)

	Related CPI Scales	Correlation	Related EPI Scales	Correlation
15. Aggression	responsibility	-.29	critical of	.52
	well-being	-.29	others	
	self-control	-.31		
	tolerance	-.25		
	good impression	-.36		

ing EPPS scales: (a) the first consisted of negative weightings for Maslow's safety and belonging needs and the EPPS need for order and positive weightings for his status need and the EPPS achievement need; (b) the second dimension had positive weights for basic, status needs, and need for succorance and negative weights for belonging, self-actualization, intraception, and nurturance; and (c) the third dimension consisted of basic self-actualization and change needs that were negatively weighted and safety, belonging, status, and achievement needs that were positively weighted.

Although the CPI correlations tended to be small, the correlations taken from the three studies lend additional meaning to the scales particularly when a person has extremely high or low scores on a given scale. By combining test authors' descriptions of their scales plus Lorr's (1975) review of studies involving the Personality Research Form, the Comrey Personality Scale, the Interpersonal Style Inventory, and the EPPS, the following summaries were developed. The descriptions were developed using high scorers as referents; one would expect opposite tendencies among low scorers.

ACHIEVEMENT. People with high scores are motivated by a desire for recognition and status. They tend to be ambitious, capable people who are perceived as being organized and reasonable by others. Although they may appear to be adaptable, flexible, risk takers, they also may appear to be rather conventional because they tend to evaluate their performance according to prescribed external standards of excellence.

DEFERENCE. Tendencies toward conformity or conventionality are indicated by this scale. Control of one's self and of one's impulses receive some emphasis.

ORDER. High scores probably indicate a need to be planful, systematic, and organized in one's personal and interpersonal environment. Development of intellectual abilities and insight may be deficient in such individuals. Other personality characteristics may include coldness, discomfort in social situations and intolerance of others.

EXHIBITION. People who score high on this scale enjoy being the center of attention and are freely responsive to their environments. Lorr (1975) suggests that they attract attention to themselves by means of speech, behavior, and appearance because of a generalized expectation that other people will respond positively to such behaviors. They tend to be outgoing and to look for and enjoy social interactions. Personality characteristics that may apply to them are spontaneous, adventurous, witty, and unconventional.

AUTONOMY. No CPI scales correlated significantly with the Autonomy Scale. The high negative correlation with the EPI "conforms" scale suggests that it may indicate a certain amount of rebelliousness, lack of willingness to conform, or resistance to social influence.

AFFILIATION. High scorers tend to be considerate, kind, self-denying, and thoughtful. They can be expected to possess progressive, humanitarian feelings.

INTRACEPTION. Intellectual understanding of other people's behavior may be characteristic of the person with high scores. They perform well in situations where the criteria for excellence are specified. Adjectives that may apply are considerate, thoughtful, socially poised, imaginative, reasonable, and dependable.

SUCCORANCE. High scorers need attention from other people, possibly because of a lack of self-confidence. Such people would likely desire emotional support and reassurance from others. They may appear to be apathetic or inhibited, irritable or temperamental, pessimistic, lazy, careless, and shallow.

DOMINANCE. The person with high dominance scores is one who seeks out and enjoys interpersonal situations in which he or she can take the initiative and be the leader. Traits that may be characteristic of this person are ambitious, reasonable, good-natured, outgoing, and sociable. Lorr (1975) warns that low scores should not be confused with submissiveness or compliance.

ABASEMENT. Self-criticalness is characteristic of people who score high on this scale. This person may be an underachiever who lacks self-confidence as well as an effective means for achieving status in her or his social environment. She or he may appear to be gloomy, meek, mild, retiring, tense, and submissive or he or she may be defensive, headstrong, unconventional, and rebellious.

NURTURANCE. The nurturant person is involved in helping others, in offering them emotional support and sympathy. This person tends to be dependable and good natured, peaceable, and self-denying. Belonging to a social group of some sort may be a strong part of the person's identity.

CHANGE. The desire for new and novel experiences (as opposed to the conventional and familiar) may be characteristic of people who show a high need for change. They may be unconventional, witty, adventurous, and spontaneous.

ENDURANCE. Persistence at tasks characterizes the person who scores high on this scale. He or she is dependable and enjoys situations where performance standards are structured and the criteria for excellence are specified. This person tends to be reliable, self-denying, and self-controlled.

HETEROSEXUALITY. This scale seems to be a measure of impulsivity or rebelliousness. Persons who score high on this scale tend to reject the conventional. They may be complainers or cynics who are at odds with themselves and others. Traits that may characterize this person are headstrong, irresponsible, mischievous, and outspoken.

AGGRESSION. The Aggression Scale seems to measure aggressive impulses directed toward one's interpersonal environment. The person who scores high on this scale tends to be self-centered and opportunistic and may exploit or manipulate others in order to achieve her or his aims. He or she is more concerned with changing others to fit her or his needs than in changing her or himself to meet other's needs. Descriptive adjectives include headstrong, complaining, fault-finding, rebellious, anxious, impulsive, and defensive.

FACTOR ANALYSIS STUDIES. The factors identified when various combinations of tests were factor analyzed are presented in Table 7-V. For the sake of brevity, only those factors accounting for at least 3 percent of the test variance and having at least one EPPS scale with an absolute factor loading of .30 are presented.

Three of the studies (Hartley and Allen, 1962; Krug and Moyer, 1961; Cook et al., 1961) identified some factors that were composed entirely of EPPS scales. However, only a factor that had deference, order, and endurance as its core was repeated across studies. This factor seems to evidence a need for structured relationships, a predictable environment, and personal compulsivity. Negative loadings for exhibition, heterosexuality, autonomy, or change were sometimes characteristic of the structure factors as well.

The combination of achievement and dominance opposed by affiliation and nurturance occurred frequently enough to suggest that these scales may represent the core of a second factor: need for a social community. People who have high need scores on the positive pole of this factor tend to prefer close social groups in which much nurturing can occur and to eschew leadership roles.

Murray's personality theory was the basis for the twenty personality scales of Jackson's (1967) Personality Research Form (PRF) as it was for the EPPS scales. All but seven of the PRF scale names are the same as those of the EPPS scales. Therefore, comparable factor loadings on similarly named scales would provide one type of evidence of the validity of the scales, but would also suggest which scales could be used interchangeably.

The data in Table 7-V regarding the PRF scales are incomplete since some of the authors, e.g. Lorr et al. (1977); Edwards and Abbott, 1973, did not report the complete array of factor loadings. However, the most complete of the reported results (Edwards et al., 1972) suggests that the factors extracted are fairly equally balanced, including comparable numbers of scales from both inventories. Although some like-named scales appear on all of the factors except VI, VII, IX, and XI, all of the scales sharing a trait name do not consistently occur together. The Edwards et al. (1972) and the Lorr et al. (1977) studies suggest that the following PRF scales could be substituted for like-named EPPS scales: Autonomy, Order, Affiliation, Nurturance, Succorance, Aggression, Dominance, Endurance, Exhibition, and Change.

Table 7 - V

COMPOSITION OF FACTORS FORMED BY
ANALYZING EPPS AND OTHER PERSONALITY TESTS

Hartley and Allen's (1962) MMPI Study

Original Factor Name	No. EPPS[1] Variables	EPPS[2] Scales	No. other test scales	Name of[3] other test scales	Total No. Scales
1. K	4	+Suc, -Int, -Aut, +Aff	0		4
2. A	5	+Def, +Ord, -Aut, -Chg, +End	0		5
3. H	5	-Ach, -Exh, +Nur, -Agg, +Aba, +Con	1	-Pd	6
4. G	1	+Con	4	-L, -F, +MF +Pt	5
5. F	4	+Ach, -Dom, +Chg, -Agg	1	+Mf	5
6. C	2	-Def, -End	1	+ ?	3
7. D	4	-Aff, -Dom, +Aba, +End	4	-K, -Hs, -Hy +Si	8
8. J	1	-Int	6	+L, +Hy, +Pa, +Pt	7

Edwards et al.'s (1972) PRF Study

Original Factor Name	No. EPPS Variables	EPPS Scales	No. other test scales	Name of other test scales	Total No. Scales
1. I	4	-Def, -Ord, +Aut, -End	6	+Au, +Chg, -Or, -Cs, -Ha, +Im	10
2. II	6	-Aut, +Aff, +Suc, +Aba, +Nur, -End	5	+Af, -Au, +Nu, +Sr, +Su	11
3. III	3	+Aff, +Nur, -Agg	3	-Agg, -De, +Nur	.6
4. IV	3	+Dom, -Aba, +Agg	4	+Do, +Ex, +Dy +Sd	7
5. V	2	-Suc, +End	3	+Ac, +En, -Ha, +Se	5
6. VI	2	-Int, +Het	2	+Se, -Un	4

Table 7 - V (continued)

Original Factor Name	No. EPPS Variables	EPPS Scales	No. other test scales	Name of other test scales	Total No. Scales
7. VII	2	+Ach, -Het	4	-Aff, +Ha, -Pl, +R	6
8. VIII	3	-Exh, +Suc, +Nur	3	-Ex, -Pl, -Sr	6
9. IX	3	+Def, -Aut, -Het	2	+Ab, -De	5
10. X	3	+Aff, +Chg, -Agg	2	+Ch, +Se	5
11. XI	1	-Ach	2	+In, +Mc	3

Edwards & Abbott's (1973) EPI and PRF Study[4]

Original Factor Name	No. EPPS Variables	EPPS Scales	No. other test scales	Name of other test scales	Total No. Scales
1. I	2	+Dom, -Aba	4	+Do, +Ex, +Leader +Responsibility	6
2. II	1	+Aba	6	-Dy, +De, +Anxious +Sensitive -Sd, -Mc	7
3. III	1	-Ord	4	-Cog, -Or, -Routine, -Plans	5
4. IV	2	+End, -Suc	4	+Ach, +End, +Worker, +Persistent	4
5. V	2	+Nur, +Aff	5	+Nu, -Ag, +Kind, +Helps, +Mc	7
6. VI	1	-Aut	4	+Sr, -Aut, -Independent +Conforms	5
7. VII	1	-Suc	4	-Su, +Au, -De, -Sympathy	5
8. VIII	1	+Int	4	+Un, +Se, +Interested +Understands	5

Lorr et al.'s (1977) PRF, CPS, & ISI Study

(high school sample)

Original Factor Name	No. EPPS Variables	EPPS Scales	No. other test scales	Name of other test scales	Total No. Scales
1. Directive	1	+Dom	2	+Do, +Di	3
2. Succorant	1	+Suc	3	+Help, +Su	4

Table 7 - V (continued)

Original Factor Name	No. EPPS Variables	EPPS Scales	No. other test scales	Name of other test scales	Total No. Scales
3. Novelty Seeking	1	+Chg	2	+Novelty seeking, +Change	3
4. Orderly	1	+Ord	3	Orderly (ISI, CPS, PRF)	4
5. Endurance	1	+End	3	+Achieving +Activity +En	4

(college sample)

1. Directive	2	+Dom, +Ach	2	+Di, +Do	4
2. Succorant	1	+Suc	2	+Help, +Su	3
3. Novelty Seeking	1	+Chg	2	+Novelty seeking +Change	3
4. Orderly	1	+Ord	3	+Orderly, +Order (CPS & PRF)	4
5. Endurance	1	+End	1	+Endurance	2

Krug and Moyer's (1961) Guilford Zimmerman
Temperament Survey and F Scale

(male sample)

1. I	5	+Ord, +Def, +End, -Het, -Exh	2	+R, +CO	7
2. II	1	+Dom	4	+A, +S, +G, +E	5
3. IV	1	+Int	2	+T, +R	3
4. V	4	+Nur, +Aff, -Ach, -Dom	0		4
5. VI	1	+Aba	1	+P	2
6. VII	2	-Suc, +Chg	0		2
7. VIII	4	+Aff, +Nur, -Agg, -Aut	3	+F, +P, -M	7

Table 7 - V (continued)

Original Factor Name	No. EPPS Variables	EPPS Scales	No. other test scales	Name of other test scales	Total No. Scales
		(female sample)			
1. I	5	+Def, +Ord, +Aba, +End, -Aut	2	-M, +CO	7
2. II	1	+Dom	3	+G, +A, +S	4
3. III	3	-Suc, +End, -Agg	5	+E, +O, +F +P, -Pro	8
4. IV	2	+Ach, +Int	2	+R, +T	4
5. V	7	-Ach, -Exh, +Aff, +Suc, -Dom, +Aba, +Nur	0		7
6. VI	3	-Exh, +Aba, -Het	0		3
7. VIII	2	-Int, +Suc	0		2
		Cook et al. (1961) Guilford-Zimmerman Temperament Survey Study			
1. I	1	-Agg	5	+R, +E, +O, +P	6
2. II	4	-Ach, -Aut, +Aff, +Nur	0		4
3. III	3	-Suc, +Dom, -Aff	4	+A, +S, +E, +O	7
4. IV	6	+Def, +Ord, -Exh, -Suc, -End, -Het	0		6
5. V	1	+Int	2	+R, +T	3
6. VI	1	-Het	3	+G, +A, +S	4

[1]Variables listed for which authors reported an absolute factor loading of at least .30

[2]Positive and negative signs represent the direction of the factor loading.

[3]See Appendix I for test legends.

The Guilford-Zimmerman Temperament Survey shares neither scale names nor theoretical foundations with the EPPS. Therefore, overlap between the scales of the two inventories should help to further define the components measured by the various scales. Few consistent relationships between the scales were identified. Examination of the separate sex samples of Krug and Moyer (1961) and the combined sex sample of Cook et al. (1961) suggests that the following are perhaps related: need for dominance and ascendance and sociability; need for intraception and thoughtfulness and restraint. The GZST ascendance scale purportedly measures leadership characteristics; sociability measures the desire for many friends and social activity. Borgatta (1962) found a similar clustering of EPPS dominance need and GZST ascendance and sociability characteristics. He suggested that the scales might form a part of an extroversion cluster of personality scales. The second triplet of scales suggests a shared introversion dimension.

Only one study (Hartley and Allen, 1962) has involved the analysis of normal subjects' responses to an inventory designed to diagnose abnormal conditions, the MMPI. As shown in Table 7-V, it appears that the EPPS and MMPI scales are relatively independent for normal populations.

Discussion and Summary

When correlational and factor analytic studies involving normal populations were examined, patterns of similar relationships occurred often enough to suggest that (a) the patterns of scale relationships reported by Edwards have been characteristic of later studies and (b) specific scales from different inventories measure similar personality characteristics. Although descriptive summaries of the various EPPS scales were developed, sometimes these descriptions were based on statistically significant correlations of debatable practical significance and sometimes they were based on correlations of respectable size.

From his review of the correlational/factor analysis literature (which did not include the Deference, Aggression, Heterosexuality, Abasement, Affiliation, and Intraception scales), Lorr (1975) concluded that there was evidence of good convergent validity for the following scales: Dominance, Succorance, Nurturance, Autonomy, Order, Change, and Endurance. Probably most confidence can be placed in the personality summaries involving these seven scales.

References

Allen, R.M.,: An analysis of Edwards Personal Preference Schedule intercorrelations for a local college population. *Journal of Educational Research, 57:*591-597, 1958.

Bendig, A.W., and Martin, A.M.: The factor structure and stability of fifteen human needs. *Journal of General Psychology, 67:*229-235, 1962.

Borgatta, E.F.: The coincidence of subtests in four personality inventories. *Journal of Social Psychology, 56:*227-244, 1962.

Cook, D.L., Linden, J.D., and McKay, H.E.: A factor analysis of teacher trainee responses to selected personality inventories. *Educational and Psychological Measurement, 21:*865-872, 1961.

Cunningham, C.H., Wakefield, J.A., Jr., and Ward, G.R.: An empirical comparison of Maslow's and Murray's Needs Systems. *Journal of Personality Assessment, 39:*594-596, 1975.

Dixon, P.W., and Ahern, E.H.: Factor pattern comparisons of EPPS scales of high school, college, and innovative college program students. *Journal of Experimental Education, 42:*23-35, 1973.

Dunnette, M.D., Kirchener, W.K., and DeGidio, J.: Relations among scores on Edwards Personal Preference Schedule, California Psychological Inventory, and Strong Vocational Interest Blank for an industrial sample. *Journal of Applied Psychology, 42:*178-181, 1958.

Edwards, A.L., and Abbott, R.D.: Relationships between the EPI scales and the 16 PF, CPI, and EPPS scales. *Educational and Psychological Measurement, 33:*231-238,. 1973.

Edwards, A.L., and Abbott, R.D.: Relationships among the Edwards Personality Inventory scales, the EPPS, and the Personality Research Form Scales. *Journal of Consulting and Clinical Psychology, 40:*27-32, 1973.

Edwards, A.L., Abbott, R.D., and Klockars, A.J.: A factor analysis of the EPPS and PRF personality inventories. *Educational and Psychological Measurement, 32:*23-29, 1972.

Hartley, R.E., and Allen, R.M.: The Minnesota Multiphasic Personality Inventory (MMPI) and the Edwards Personal Preference Schedule (EPPS): A factor analytic study. *Journal of Social Psychology, 58:*153-162, 1962.

Krug, R.E., and Moyer, K.E.: An analysis of the F scale: II. Relationship to standardized personality inventories. *Journal of Social Psychology 53:*293-301, 1961.

Lorr, M.: Convergences in personality constructs measured by four inventories. *Journal of Clinical Psychology, 31:*182-189, 1975.

Lorr, M., O'Connor, J.P., and Seifert, R.F.: A comparison of four personality inventories. *Journal of Personality Assessment, 41:*520-526, 1977.

Manners, G.E., and Steger, J.A.: The stability of the Edwards Personal Preference Schedule and the Guilford-Zimmerman Temperament Survey. *Personnel Psychology, 28:*501-509, 1975.

Milton, G.A., and Lipetz, M.E.: The factor structure of needs as measured by the EPPS. *Multivariate Behavior Research, 3:*37-46, 1968.

Sherman, R.C., and Poe, C.A.: Factor analytic scales of a normative form of the EPPS. *Measurement and Evaluation in Guidance, 2:*243-248, 1969.

Sherman, R.C., and Poe, C.A.: Factor-analytic scales of a normative form of the EPPS replicated across samples and methodologies. *Psychological Reports, 30:*479-484, 1972.

Stolz, R.E.: Note on the intercorrelation of Edwards' Personal Preference Schedule variables. *Psychological Reports, 4:*239-241, 1958.

Tisdale, J.R.: Comparison of Edwards Personal Preference Schedule data for three groups. *Psychological Reports, 15:*203-210, 1965.

Wright, C.E.: A factor dimension comparison of normative and ipsative measurement. *Educational and Psychological Measurement, 21:*433-444, 1961.

Chapter 8

SCALE INTERCORRELATIONS

T HE studies summarized in this chapter have in common only that they are attempts to establish the construct validity of measures by intercorrelating them with other measures that bear some conceptual similarities. The non-EPPS measures have included personality measures of individual traits and personality styles as well as measures of interpersonal characteristics, including family dynamics and various social behaviors.

Personality Traits

ANXIETY. Fortunately, three of the studies (Williams, Tallarico, and Tedeschi, 1960; Weitzner, Stallone, and Smith, 1967; Saper, 1965) that have involved investigations of the relationship between the EPPS scales and level of anxiety have used the Taylor Manifest Anxiety Scale (Taylor, 1953) as the primary measure of anxiety. Williams et al. compared EPPS scores of samples of twenty-three male and fifteen female college students who were high anxious to those obtained by samples of nineteen males and twenty low anxious female students. All were volunteers from a previously identified larger sample of people who scored in extreme directions on the Anxiety Scale. Low anxious males had significantly lower needs for Succorance and Abasement and significantly higher needs for Dominance than high anxious males; low anxious females had greater needs for Deference, Intraception, and Endurance and significantly lower needs for Abasement and Aggression than did high anxious females.

Dividing ninety-six undergraduate males into groups of high, middle, and low anxiety, Weitzner et al. (1967) found that high anxious respondents as compared to those who formed a middle anxious group had a greater need for succorance and a higher need for abasement than those in the low anxious group. Correlations between anxiety and succorance, abasement, and intraception were .44, .25, and -.21, respectively. Finally, Saper (1965), comparing a sample of twenty-eight high anxious subjects of unspecified sex to a low anxious sample similar in age, sex, educational, vocational and marital status, found that low anxious subjects had a higher need for deference and affiliation and a lower need for abasement, aggression, and autonomy, but Ford and Sempert (1962) who used only the Aggression Scale and the Taylor Anxiety Scale with a sample of tenth, eleventh, and twelfth graders found no significant correlation for either sex.

In a fourth study involving the correlation between an anxiety measure and the EPPS scales, Walsh (1969) used the Alpert-Haber Achievement Anxiety Test, a measure of test anxiety. Facilitating and debilitating anxiety scores and the difference between the two were analyzed separately for male and female subjects. For males, achievement (r = .25), intraception (r = .21), exhibition (r = .21), and nurturance (r = .17) were positively correlated with facilitative anxiety and succorance (r = -.17) and affiliation (r = -.25) were negatively correlated; achievement (r = -.19), deference (r = -.17), exhibition (r = -.28) and dominance (r = -.19) were negatively correlated with debilitating anxiety and abasement (r = .28) was positively correlated. The difference scores indicated that greater facilitating anxiety was positively related to needs for achievement (r = .26), deference (r = .18), exhibition (r = .31), dominance (r = .21) and negatively related to needs for abasement (r = -.25), nurturance (r = -.20), and heterosexuality (r = -.17).

Regardless of the differences in sample characteristics, the need that appeared across studies to be characteristic of high anxious subjects was an elevated need for abasement. Low anxiety or facilitative anxiety seems to be related to the absence of a high need for succorance for male subjects.

LOCUS OF CONTROL. People who believe that the things that happen to them are controlled by forces outside of themselves, e.g. fate, luck, chance, are said to have an external locus of control whereas those who believe that they control their own fate are said to have an internal locus of control. Three studies have explored the relationship between the EPPS scales and Rotter's (1966) locus of control measure.

DiGiuseppe (1971) speculated that people whose locus of control tended toward internality would have high scores on dominance, achievement, endurance, and autonomy. Using a sample of thirty male undergraduates, he only found support for a relationship between dominance and internality (r = .50), but Tseng (1970) found that vocational trainees with an internal locus of control had a higher need for achievement than those with an external locus of control. Becker's (1974) study of thirty-two male college students and fifty-seven female college students revealed a relationship between heterosexuality and externality for males (r = .35) as well as for females (r = .43) indicating that as externality scores increased so did heterosexuality scores. The three locus of control studies suggest that none of the EPPS scales reliably relate to locus of control, but that the characteristics of the sample may determine which needs are pertinent.

Becker's (1975) study of two groups of persisters and nonpersisters in a boring psychology experiment indicated that while locus of control was not related to persistence, needs order, endurance, and autonomy were related. Persisters had higher needs for order and endurance and lower needs for autonomy as predicted. Abasement was negatively correlated with self-esteem for both groups.

INTROVERSION-EXTROVERSION. A variety of labels are used to refer to personality characteristics that attempt to distinguish people who are attuned to, responsive to, or sensitive to internal processes from those who are attuned to or sensitive to environmental forces. One such label is field dependence, where the field independent person tends to be an internally oriented person and the field dependent person tends to be socially oriented. Marlowe (1958) found a positive correlation between field independence and intraception ($r = .34$) and a negative correlation between field independence and succorance ($r = -.30$) for a combined sample of fifty-seven college women and twelve college men. There were no significant correlations between field independence and other EPPS needs, achievement, autonomy, and dominance, which he hypothesized should be related. Testing their hypothesis that people who desired to influence others might have a high need for achievement, Carver and Glass (1976) found no significant correlation between achievement and a public self-conscious scale using a sample of male undergraduates.

Farley (1968) investigated the relationship of extroversion, a descriptor for environmental sensitivity, to need for endurance using two different samples of British trade apprentices. In both studies, he found negative correlations between the two variables. His results suggest that extroverted males do not tend to self-report high endurance needs. Caron and Wallach (1959) found some evidence that exhibition was correlated with extroversion for college freshmen of unspecified sex.

Two other variables relating to a person's responsivity to environmental stimulation are sensation seeking and conventionality. In a cross-validation study of the former variable, Waters and Waters (1969) used two male and female samples of college students separated by a two-year period. For male subjects only needs for change and order were significantly correlated in the original as well as the validational study. Correlations between change and sensation seeking were positive ($rs = .35, .39$); correlations with order were negative ($rs = -.26, -.36$). For female subjects, positive correlations occurred in both studies between sensation seeking and dominance ($rs = .23, .34$), change ($rs = .32, .38$), and aggression ($rs = .23, .33$) and negative correlations occurred between sensation seeking and deference ($rs = -.20, -.23$), order ($rs = -.49, -.39$), and succorance ($rs = -.29, -.34$). Thus, for both sexes, the tendency actively to seek stimulation in the environment seems to be associated with a liking for change and an aversion to order.

In an investigation of the latter environmental variable, conventionality, Graine (1957) found a significant positive correlation between a group conformity rating and the need for autonomy ($r = .26$), suggesting that one of the scales was not measuring what it was supposed to be measuring. Separate sex correlations were not significant.

DEFENSIVE STYLES. The construct of defensive styles has also been used to describe a person's responsivity to environmental cues. Gayton and Bernstein (1969) compared maladjustment as indicated by incompatible EPPS need scores of sensitizers (people who approach environmental stress via intellectualization, worrying, and/or obsessive behavior) and repressors (people who avoid environmental stress by using avoidance defenses such as denial, repression, and rationalization). Overall incompatible need scores, i.e. Trehub's Ego Disjunction Scale scores, were higher for sensitizers than for repressors. As compared to repressors, sensitizers had higher scores on the incompatible need pairs of autonomy-abasement and succorance-nurturance. There were no significant sex differences. Gayton and Bernstein's results seem to suggest that maladjustment is more characteristic of the sensitizing defensive style.

Caron and Wallach (1959) attempted to identify personality, intellectual, and achievement variables related to repressive and obsessive reactions to stress caused by failure. The authors identified one EPPS factor that they called other-orientation versus self-orientation (nurturance, affiliation, abasement versus achievement) which, however, did not significantly relate to whether one remembered success or failure experiences.

In two studies (Jordan and Kempler, 1970; O'Neill and Kempler, 1969), a combination of the EPPS Aggression, Change, and Abasement scales and the Guilford-Zimmerman Temperament Survey scales, General Activity, Personal Relations, and Masculinity, were used to distinguish hysterical personalities from nonhysterics. Hysteric personality was a label that they used to describe people whom the authors described as confused about their sexuality and who, consequently, approach sexual situations with ambivalence. O'Neill and Kempler demonstrated that hysterics, identified by the combination of scales, were overly sensitive to sexual stimuli in neutral situations and avoided such stimuli in sexual situations. Jordan and Kempler found that hysterics were more responsive to sexual stimuli in situations in which their femininity was threatened.

Two studies suggest that EPPS variables as indicants of perceptual styles may not be related to behaviors that are other than objective self-report measures. Van de Castle (1960) found that college students, who were classified as high or low aggressive on the basis of their EPPS aggression scores did not perceive different amounts of aggressive words during a binocular rivalry perception task.

Tanck and Robbins's (1970) effort to correlate pupil dilation responses with three measures of reactions to situations designed to evoke Murrayan needs indicated that EPPS needs didn't correlate with pupil dilation. However, needs for heterosexuality ($r = .39$), dominance ($r = .36$), and order ($r = .36$) correlated with subjects' self-reports of their level of arousal.

On the other hand, Greenspan and Pollock (1969) showed that certain needs were correlated with Bekesy audiogram tracing width. Achievement, succorance, and dominance were negatively correlated and abasement and aggression were positively correlated.

INSIGHT. Three studies have investigated the usefulness of the Intraception Scale for identifying people who should be differentially insightful or knowledgeable about other people. Williams and Bruel (1968) found that psychology majors as compared to nonmajors had a higher mean need for intraception. Tolor (1961), investigating the relationship between scores on an insight test and intraception, found an overall positive correlation ($r = .31$) for a mixed sex sample of psychiatric aides. Female aides who had high insight scores as compared to those who had low scores showed greater need for intraception. No differences were found for high and low insightful male aides. Brien, Eisenman, and Thomas (1972) found that middle and top level management applicants who had low needs for intraception also tended to have inanimate movement responses on the Rorschach. More than two such responses have been assumed to be characteristic of people who engage in "habitual psychological self-observation." The three studies of the intraception scales offer some support for its usefulness as a measure of insight or insight-related personality characteristics.

Dogmatism and Rigidity

A few studies have searched for needs that might account for open-mindedness or flexibility as opposed to close-mindedness or rigidity. Various labels have been used for this dimension including dogmatism in the case of attitudes, rigidity in the case of nonverbal perceptions, and flexibility-inflexibility in the case of conceptual processes.

Studies of dogmatism have not consistently identified relevant EPPS needs. Using a sample of education students of unspecified sex distribution, Borgers and Ward (1974) found that high dogmatic respondents who were identified by their scores on Rokeach's Dogmatism Scale had significantly higher needs for order, abasement, and aggression and a lower need for autonomy than low dogmatic respondents. Vacchiano, Strauss, and Schiffman (1968) used a predominantly male sample of college students and found that dogmatism correlated positively with succorance ($r = +.25$) and negatively with intraception ($r = -.21$) and change ($r = -.25$). Bernhardson and Fisher's (1970) search for dogmatism and EPPS needs that correlated consistently across studies revealed no more significant correlations than would have been expected by chance.

Swindell and Lieberman (1968) suggested that the failure of investigators to find consistent dogmatism correlates may have been because they did not analyze the sexes separately. They found that intraception correlated negatively with dogmatism for the sexes individually and combined; for women, deference and dogmatism correlated negatively ($r = -.21$) and aggression correlated positively ($r = .27$); for men, consistency and dogmatism correlated negatively ($r = -.22$).

Only one study involved the investigation of perceptual rigidity. Simon, Primavera, Klein, and Cristal (1972) found that needs for deference ($r = .44$), order ($r = .29$), abasement ($r = .20$), and endurance ($r .19$) correlated positively with perceptual rigidity; the needs for autonomy (r = -.23), change (r = -.26), heterosexuality (r = -.16), and aggression (r = -.26) correlated negatively. The authors contend that perceptual rigidity may be indicative of an obsessive-compulsive personality type.

In any case, only aggression, order, abasement, autonomy, change, and intraception appeared to be related in the same direction in as many as two studies.

CONCEPTUAL BEHAVIOR. The way that a person organizes or makes sense of her or his environment is potentially related to psychological needs. Tutko and Sechrest (1962) found that for college males who used concepts that were easily communicated, nurturance (r = .28), affiliation (r = .19), and intraception (r = -.21) were significantly correlated.

Hardison and Purcell (1959) divided male college students into groups of independent or dependent and flexible or constricted cognitive styles. The first dimension was defined according to subjects' scores on the Deference and Autonomy scales, with those whose scores exceeded the 15th percentile classified as dependent or independent, respectively. Hardison and Purcell regarded the dependence-independence dimension as the person's ability to ignore internal stimuli that could interfere with their ability to make appropriate environmental responses. The flexible-constricted dimension, measured by Stroop's color word interference measure, they viewed as a general ability to ignore external stimuli that might interfere with appropriate responding. Results of their study of the effects of socially induced stress on performance of a block design test indicated that independent flexibles improved their performance under stress while that of dependent constricteds deteriorated. They use their results to argue for the use of more efficient classification of cognitive types in investigations of the relationship between stress and task performance.

How male and female subjects use language to organize their world was the topic of Nunnally and Flaugher's (1963) study. Three semantic patterns that they identified, the tendency to evaluate concepts negatively, the tendency to evaluate concepts positively, and the tendency to categorize concepts, were related to a number of EPPS needs for males, but not for females. The tendency to make negative evaluations was positively correlated with affiliation (r = .15), succorance (r = .18), abasement (r = .15), and nurturance (r = .10) and negatively correlated with intraception (r = -.09), dominance (r = -.12), and endurance (r = -.12). The tendency to make positive evaluations was positively correlated with affiliation (r = .20), succorance (r = .09), and nurturance (r = .10) and negatively correlated with achievement (r = -.09), deference (r = -.09), and order (r = -.12). Categorization responses considered to be a higher level of abstraction than the other two types of responses were positively correlated with dominance (r = .12), order (r = .11), and endurance (r = .10) and negatively correlated with succorance (r = -.13). For female subjects, only order (r = -.17), achievement (r = -.18), and achievement (r = -.18) were correlated with categorization, positive evaluation, and negative evaluative responses, respectively.

Studies of conceptual behavior have been so varied in focus and methodology that it is impossible to determine with any certainty which, if any, of the EPPS needs are consistently related to any aspects of conceptual behavior. It does appear that nurturance and affiliation may be positively related and intraception may be negatively related to male subjects' ability to organize their environment in socially desirable ways. Evidence, to date, does not suggest the EPPS needs are related to women's conceptual behavior.

Personality Styles

Some personality theorists imply that people have general personality styles or basic personality orientations that they use in their interactions with the world. Various traits have been proposed to explain these orientations.

SUPEREGO FUNCTIONS. Mosher (1966) postulated a guilt orientation in which a person's social behaviors would be influenced by her or his generalized expectancy that violation or contemplated violation of internalized standards of socially acceptable behavior should result in self-monitored punishment.

In an attempt to discover which of the EPPS needs were related to three components of guilt measured by the Mosher Guilt Scale, Abramson, Mosher, Abramson, and Woychowski (1977) found that different needs were relevant for males and female undergraduates. Sex guilt or guilt over sex and responses to sexual stimuli were correlated with affiliation (r = .25), endurance (r = -.22), and heterosexuality (r = -.29) for males and autonomy (r = - .39), endurance (r = .31), and heterosexuality (r = -.44) for females.

Morality conscience guilt, one's judgment and feelings of guilt over misdeeds, was correlated with autonomy (r = -.25), abasement (r = .44), nurturance (r = .27), change (r = .20), and heterosexuality (r = .22) for males; affiliation (r = .31), abasement (r = .52), nurturance (r = .44, and heterosexuality (r = -.40), and autonomy (r = -.34) were significantly correlated with mortality conscience guilt for females.

Hostility guilt, feelings of guilt caused by aggressive behavior or the anticipation of aggressive behavior, was only correlated with three needs for females: abasement (r = .41), nurturance (r = .34), and aggression (r = -.32). For males, the six significantly correlated needs were affiliation (r = .27), intraception (r = .24), abasement (r = .32), nurturance (r = .35), heterosexuality (r = -.20), and aggression (r = -.43).

One might conceptualize cheating as being the opposite of a guilt personality disposition. Hetherington and Feldman (1964) proposed that there were four types of cheaters for whom different EPPS needs might be relevant and used a sample balanced for sex who responded to a variety of personality and demographic measures including the EPPS to explore their hypothesis.

They set up various types of classroom situations that would make cheating possible and found that "independent-opportunistic cheating which is unplanned and impulsive" (p. 212) was positively correlated with affiliation (r = .29). "Independent-planned cheating which involves an element of foresight and activity preliminary to the actual test situation" (p. 212) was significantly correlated with none of the EPPS scales. "Social cheating [active] which involves two or more people and in which the subject actively instigates the cheating" (p.213) was positively correlated with succorance (r = .36). "Social cheating [passive] which involves two or more people but in which the individual plays a passive role" (p. 213) was significantly correlated with nurturance (r = .29), intraception (r = .27), and deference (r = .24).

MASCULINITY-FEMININITY. Although it is customary to think about masculinity and femininity as traits that reside within the person, it is also possible to consider that there may be attitudes or social roles that characterize men or women. Studies in the area of sex role characteristics can be categorized as focusing on one of three issues: general interests, body perceptions, and male-female differences.

In the former category, Mussen (1961) conducted a longitudinal study of men as adolescents, and sixteen years later he found that men whose interests had been highly masculine during high school had higher need for abasement as adults than those whose needs were more feminine. Posited explanations include the possibility that highly masculine adolescent males may develop into men who are less self-accepting or they may just be more willing than their counterparts to admit shortcomings during adulthood.

In the category of body perception, Fisher (1964) used a male sample to address the question of how power aspiration was related to needs for achievement, aggression, and dominance. He found that power aspiration as inferred from degree of subjects' height overestimation was positively related to achievement and dominance. However, in a similar study, Berkowitz found no correlation between height estimates of subjects of unspecified sex and their needs; nor were their needs correlated with their perceptions of their friends' heights.

Blazer (1966) attempted to correlate a potentially sex-typed behavior, leg position, and the EPPS scales using a diverse sample of female respondents. For the ten leg positions that he investigated, Blazer found that high levels of different needs tended to characterize each position.

Hartnett, Bailey, and Gibson (1970) used male and female subjects to determine whether the Heterosexuality Scale was associated with body positioning, i.e. the degree of physical closeness subjects were willing to allow for same and opposite sex experimenters. They found that male subjects with high heterosexuality need were willing to allow a female experimenter to walk closer to them than were males with a low heterosexuality need. For females, none of the social distance measures were related to the need for heterosexuality.

Phares and Adams's (1961) findings that males with high Heterosexuality

Scale scores as compared to those with low needs liked sexual photographs more (though they did not remember sexual material better) support the possibility that the Heterosexuality Scale may measure initial heterosexual approach behavior when used with male respondents.

Tolor and LeBlanc (1974), who used the Autonomy, Affiliation, and Nurturance scales to investigate various aspects of interpersonal spacing, found that different scales were related for males and females. For females, autonomy and nurturance were positively correlated with sitting closer to someone else of the same sex, but need for autonomy was positively correlated with a desire for distance when a schematic representation of figures was used to measure body positioning. For males, the need for affiliation was inversely related to the amount of distance they allowed between human replicas.

Two studies examined the effects of specific needs on visual behavior. Speculating that female subjects with a high need for affiliation would spend more time looking at pictures with high rather than low affiliation themes, Leckart, Waters, and Tarpinian (1967) found that high affiliation women looked longer at all stimuli regardless of content than did women with low need for affiliation.

Libby and Yaklevich (1973) also found some evidence for a relationship between visual contact and needs. They found that males and females with a high nurturance need looked at an interviewer more than those with low nurturance need. In addition, people high on abasement need were less likely than low abasing interviewees to break eye contact by looking to the right.

In the category of sex differences, Walberg, Welch, and Rothman (1969) studied the hypothesis that teachers' heterosexuality needs were differentially related to high school boys' and girls' attitudes toward a traditionally masculine subject, physics. They found several significant relationships for male students, but not for females. Teacher's heterosexuality was positively correlated (r = .34) with boys' understanding of science, but was negatively correlated with affective dimensions such as whether the boys perceived that the subject was important (r = -.31) or fun (r = -.45). The results can be interpreted as meaning that males had to earn attention from male teachers by achieving whereas such attention could have been noncontingent on performance for females.

As mentioned in earlier chapters, it is a fairly common finding that men and women differ in their levels of most of the EPPS needs. Harshbarger (1974) suggested that the reason for these observed differences might be because the needs measured are not equally socially desirable characteristics for women and men. He selected eighteen of the EPPS items he believed were more desirable for men or women. His findings indicate that men tend to endorse items that are desirable *in others* whereas women endorse items that are desirable *in women*. Although based on a limited number of items, his study suggests an alternative approach by which social desirability of instruments can be measured.

Familial and Biographical Correlates

Most of the detailed studies of family characteristics as they relate to psychological needs have used birth order of respondents as a crucial characteristic. For the most part, such studies have presented inconclusive results. Query and Query (1973) found that for their sample of fifty-six high school males, mean affiliation scores were higher for firstborns than for later-borns and that firstborns participated in more extracurricular activities. Payne (1971) found no significant differences in mean scores for either need affiliation or achievement when firstborn freshmen Air Force cadets were compared to other birth-order positions.

On the other hand, Nowicki (1967) found that middle-born, adult male schizophrenics had a greater need for achievement than firstborns, last-borns, and only children. Other needs that differed according to birth-order position of respondents were nurturance, abasement, dominance, and endurance.

Family patterning may influence the manner in which needs are related to birth order. Sampson and Hancock (1967) found that although need for achievement was higher for their second-born male and female subjects, having an older brother or a younger sister was more likely to contribute to high need achievement than having a younger brother or an older sister. Though they found no relationship between birth order and need affiliation, Sampson and Hancock did find that only male children had a lower need for autonomy than firstborn males; only female children had lower need for autonomy than any of the females who had sisters.

In an attempt to make sense of the hodgepodge of birth-order studies, Cornoldi and Fattori (1976) proposed that the number of years separating siblings was a more crucial variable in determining psychological needs than ordinal position per se. They administered an adaptation of the EPPS to a mixed sex sample of Italian students. Students who had siblings less than three years younger than themselves had higher needs for affiliation and succorance than those whose siblings were more widely spaced (as predicted).

Obviously, it is difficult to state anything conclusive about the birth-order studies because of the number of variables that have been confounded across studies. These include age, sex, number of scales used, culture, and spacing of children. Another approach that has been used to identify family factors that influence psychological needs has been to correlate biographical data with EPPS needs.

Sundberg et al. (1969) compared family cohesiveness and need for autonomy using a sample of American and Indian ninth grade students of both sexes. Family cohesiveness was defined as the number of family activities in which the person participated combined with a positive attitude toward family interactions. Autonomy was partially measured by scores on an adaptation of the EPPS Autonomy Scale. Results indicated that Americans perceived themselves as more autonomous and their families as less cohesive than did Indian students.

In a more extensive study of biographical factors, Hearn, Charles, and Wolins (1965) correlated a variety of self-biographical items with EPPS scale scores. Their results, also obtained from a male college student sample, can be summarized as follows:

(a) Need for achievement was most strongly related to a perceived lack of father's success (r = .25). Only influential factors included achievement as a high school student and academic achievement (as evidenced by some college) on the mothers' part;

(b) High Deference was most strongly associated with not dating in high school (r = .30) and having read twelve or more books the previous year (r = .25). Other significant contributing variables suggested a lack of paternal leadership role modeling;

(c) High order scores tended to be characteristic of married students who came from rather impoverished environments and in which personal expression was not encouraged;

(d) Need for exhibition was characterized by early personal as well as parental achievement. Both parents led active social lives and neither praised nor punished their sons very much;

(e) High need for autonomy was characteristic of men who had considerable freedom within the family. Their parents imposed few restrictions and they were accepted by their siblings and peers. In addition, their parents probably modeled autonomous behavior;

(f) Men who showed a high need for affiliation tended to be young (under twenty-one years of age) and single. Most indicants suggested that they came from protected family and early academic environments. They were, for instance, likely to be a teacher's pet (r = .25) and to have had parents who were interested in their class work (r = .26);

(g) Intraception, most characteristic of younger students, seemed to have developed in response to autonomous behavior on the part of parents coupled with low socioeconomic status and a lack of paternal education and success;

(h) Succorance seemed to occur as a result of growing up in an environment that encouraged dependence. These men came from families of high financial status (r = .26) but did not choose their own clothes until they were in high school (r = .20). As college students, they still reported uncertainty about their vocation (r = .24);

(i) Early leadership qualities and social poise were characteristic of men for whom dominance was a high need. They dated frequently (r = .25), planned their future early in life (r = .21), and were noticed by others in elementary school. Perhaps, they were encouraged in their social pursuits by mothers who were fearless themselves (r = .23);

(j)   Men with high abasement needs tended to be under twenty-one years of age (r = .20) and to have come from a settled, but socially isolated family. Lack of paternal occupational achievement was present as was a lack of personal high school achievement;

(k)   Nurturance was characteristic of those who maintained early peer relationships and whose parents were prone to entertaining;

(l)   A high need for change was characteristic of men who came from an atmosphere in which their family was occupationally secure (r = .25) and in which they were seldom punished (r = .21);

(m)   High endurance need seemed to result from having been raised in a lower class environment with few luxuries, but in which the child fantasized about making great scientific achievements;

(n)   People whose religious affiliation was Protestant tended to have high scores on the Heterosexuality Scale. Whereas those who were Catholic did not. The need characterized people who had been somewhat rebellious toward their parents during their youth and who had been socially oriented in fantasy as well as activities;

(o)   High need for aggression developed in home environments that were reported to be somewhat combative although the fights were perceived as being caused by someone else (r = .30). In the home, the father was regarded as the leader (r = .23) and social activities occurred somewhere other than the home (r = .22).

Measures of Interpersonal Characteristics

MATERNAL CHARACTERISTICS. An issue in two studies has been the question of whether a woman's needs find expression in her maternal attitudes or behaviors. The Parental Attitude Research Inventory allegedly measures several parental attitude factors, including authoritarian control or suppressive and punitive attitudes, hostility-rejection or rejection of the maternal role, and democratic attitudes or a social desirability response set pertaining to child-rearing attitudes (Zuckerman and Oltean, 1959). Zuckerman and Oltean used a sample of twenty-four mothers of college students and a second sample of student nurses who had never been parents to test the accuracy of the authors' predictions that certain of the EPPS scales should be related to the first two parental attitude factors.

For the mothers, they found a negative correlation between affiliation and the authoritarian factor (r = -.43), positive correlations between the hostility factor and achievement (r = .48) and aggression (r = .41) and negative correlations between hostility and nurturance (r = -.59) and affiliation (r = -.67). For the student nurses, there was a positive correlation between the authoritarian factor and deference (r = .36), a positive correlation between the social desirability factor and nurturance (r = .25), and a negative correlation between deference (r = -.38) and the same factor. Zuckerman and Oltean suggest that the difference in correlational patterns for the two samples may be because the *hypothetical* attitudes of the nonparents are less influenced by their personality needs than are the *actual* attitudes of parents.

Crandall and Preston (1961) used behavioral observations in their homes of the child-rearing behaviors of thirty eight middle-class mothers. They found that nurturance was positively related to mothers' tendencies to be protective toward their children; need for aggression tended to be negatively related to the amount of positive affection expressed toward the children; need for autonomy was negatively correlated with tendencies toward child-centeredness; need for dominance did not relate to any of the maternal behaviors.

In a study of female and male college students' attitudes toward breast-feeding, Magnussen and Kemler (1969) found that female advocates of breast-feeding (as opposed to bottle feeding) had greater needs for dominance, nurturance, and endurance and lesser needs for achievement and heterosexuality. Only a higher need for achievement differentiated male breast-feeding advocates from those who preferred bottle-feeding. Magnussen and Kemler interpret the higher characteristic of the women preferring breast-feeding as being indicative of overprotectiveness while those that are higher for women who prefer bottle-feeding are said to characterize rejectiveness.

The Zuckerman and Oltean (1959), the Crandall and Preston (1961), and Magnussen and Kemler (1959) studies taken together offer some support for the use of the Nurturance Scale to predict affectionate maternal behaviors and attitudes of women and the use of the Aggression and Achievement scales to predict rejecting or nonaffectionate mother-child interactions and attitudes.

INTERPERSONAL BEHAVIOR. Other than the maternal behavior studies, three studies have dealt with interpersonal behavior as a personality variable, qua personality variable. Gynther, Miller, and Davis (1962) derived four dimensions, dominance, love, competitiveness, and responsibility, from Leary's Interpersonal Check List. Their sample consisted of ninety-five male undergraduates. Dominant interpersonal behaviors were positively related to needs for dominance (r = .32) and exhibition (r = .22) and negatively related to need for succorance (r = -.28); self-reports of loving behaviors were positively related to affiliation (r = .22) and nurturance (r = .27) and negatively related to autonomy (r = -.40) and aggression (r = -.47); competitive self-reported behaviors were positively related to autonomy (r = .35), dominance (r = .28), and aggression (r = .34) and negatively related to affiliation (r = -.20), succorance (r = -.26), abasement (r = -.23), and nurturance (r = -.23); responsible behavior was positively correlated with exhibition (r = .20) and negatively correlated with autonomy (r = -.24) and aggression (r = -.34).

Cairns and Lewis (1962) used Leary's docile-dependent items (Octant VI) in their study of the relationship between various indices of dependency. Defining high dependent subjects as those college males who scored high on deference (> 70th percentile) and low on autonomy (< 50th percentile), they found that high dependent subjects as compared to low dependent subjects selected more Octant VI responses to describe themselves.

Nichols et al. (1972) developed a self-report scale of previous behaviors to be used in differentiating A- and B-type personalities. A-types were described as active, impulsive, aggressive, and present-oriented; B-types were described as inactive, compulsive, deferent, cautious, and future-oriented. They used a sample of male Army members and found that dominance and aggression loaded positively on an A-type factor and deference and order loaded negatively; a B-type factor was characterized by a negative dominance loading and positive succorance and abasement loadings.

Certain values have been assumed to be important in the quest for self-actualization. LeMay and Damm (1969) investigated the relationship between EPPS needs and Shostrom's Personal Orientation Inventory, a measure of self-actualization values. They found that need for aggression and acceptance of aggression were positively correlated for men and women. The need for order in women seemed to be roughly equivalent to the need for abasement in men as evidenced by negative correlations with POI scales, inner directness, existentiality, spontaneity, and acceptance of aggression. However, for men lack of self-regard, lack of capacity for intimate contact, and absence of feeling reactivity were also correlated with need abasement, suggesting the presence of values that are not consistent with self-actualization when need abasement is elevated. Among women, need for change was positively related to time competence, inner directness, existentiality, and capacity for intimate contact; among men, autonomy was positively related to inner directness, feeling reactivity, spontaneity, self-acceptance, and capacity for intimate contact.

NURTURANCE. Although the Nurturance Scale has emerged as being related to a variety of personality variables, only two studies have been designed to test the validity of the Nurturance Scale in a hospital setting. Unfortunately, they have yielded contradictory results. Smith (1972) found that of the thirty-five female adolescent hospital volunteers whom he studied, those with high self-esteem showed a positive relationship between their level of satisfaction with their volunteer work and their need for nurturance ($r = .52$). The relationship was present for testing that occurred during the fifth and seventh months of service, although it decreased somewhat at the later testing. Volunteers with low self-esteem revealed no relationship between the nurturance need and satisfaction with their presumably nurturing volunteer activities.

Woodmansee (1978) found an inverse relationship between nurturing behaviors as measured by supervisors' ratings of state mental hospital nurses and the nurses' needs for nurturance for the female nurses ($r = -.32$) and no relationship for male nurses. Given the variety of other studies that support the validity of the Nurturance Scale as an adequate measure for a variety of nurturant behaviors, it is tempting to attribute Woodmansee's results to interrater error. However, another possible explanation may be that the scale may measure a level of protectiveness that is less appropriate for hospitalized patients.

Summary and Discussion

Some evidence summarized in the foregoing presentation suggests that certain EPPS scales do offer some level of construct validity. Although one set of authors cautions against using the scale as a global measure of adjustment (Rosenkrantz and Halloran, 1965), high scores on the abasement scale tend to be associated with high anxiety (at least as indicted by the Taylor Manifest Anxiety Scale). For male subjects, high need for succorance tends to be associated with high anxiety, a lack of dominating and competitive behaviors, and possibly a tendency to be field dependent.

For both sexes, need for affiliation and nurturance tend to correspond to loving and affectionate behaviors and attitudes and to be contrary to competitive and hostile attitudes and behaviors. On the other hand, high need for aggression seems to be characteristic of people who do not display loving and nurturing relationships, who are competitive, and possibly hostile and primarily self-centered.

References

Abramson, P.R., Mosher, K.L., Abramson, L.M., and Woychowski, B.: Personality correlates of the Mosher Guilt Scales. *Journal of Personality Assessment, 41:*375-382, 1977.

Becker, W.M.: Internal-external scale correlated with Edwards Personal Preference Schedule. *Psychological Reports, 35:*1182, 1974.

Becker, W.M.: I-E locus of control, selected Edwards Personal Preference scales and task persistence. *Psychological Reports, 36:*97-98, 1975.

Berkowitz, W.R.: Perceived height, personality, and friendship choice. *Psychological Reports, 24:* 373-374, 1969.

Bernhardson, C.S., and Fisher, R.J.: Personality correlates of dogmatism (abstract). *Journal of Consulting and Clinical Psychology, 34:*449, 1970.

Blazer, J.A.: Leg position and psychological characteristics. *Psychology, 3:*5-12, 1966.

Borgers, S.B., and Ward, G.R.: Differences in the needs of low dogmatic and high dogmatic prospective teachers. *Educational Leadership, 31:*697-699, 1974.

Brien, R.L., Eisenman, R., and Thomas, D.: Edwards intraception score and inanimate movement responses on the Rorschach. *Journal of Clinical Psychology, 28:*203, 1972.

Cairns, R.B., and Lewis, M.: Dependency and the reinforcement value of a verbal stimulus. *Journal of Consulting Psychology, 26:*1-8, 1962.

Caron, A.J., and Wallach, M.A.: Personality determinants of repressive and obsessive reactions to failure-stress. *Journal of Abnormal and Social Psychology, 59:*236-245, 1959.

Carver, C.S., and Glass, D.C.: The self-consciousness scale: A discriminant validity study. *Journal of Personality Assessment, 40:*169-172, 1976.

Cornoldi, C., and Fattori, L.C.: Age spacing in firstborns and symbiotic dependence. *Journal of Personality and Social Psychology, 33:*431-434, 1976.

Crandall, V.J., and Preston, A.: Verbally expressed needs and overt maternal behaviors. *Child Development, 32:*261-270, 1961.

DiGiuseppe, R.A.: Correlation of locus of control with four EPPS items. *Psychological Reports, 28:* 290, 1971.

Farley, F.H.: Extraversion and the self-description of endurance. *British Journal of Social and Clinical Psychology, 7:*1-2, 1968.

Fisher, S.: Power orientation and concept of self height in men: Preliminary note. *Perceptual and Motor Skills, 18:*732, 1964.

Ford, L.H., Jr., and Sempert, E.L.: Relations among same objective measures of hostility, need aggression, and anxiety. *Journal of Consulting Psychology, 26:*486, 1962.

Gayton, W., and Bernstein, S.: Incompatible need strength and the repression-sensitization dimension. *Journal of Clinical Psychology, 25:*192-194, 1969.

Graine, G.N.: Measures of conformity as found in the Rosenzweig P-F study and the Edwards Personal Preference Schedule. *Journal of Consulting Psychology, 21:*300, 1957.

Greenspan, C.F., and Pollock, K.C.: Response variability and personality factors in automated audiometry. *Journal of Auditory Research, 9:*386-390, 1969.

Gynther, M.D., Miller, F.T., and Davis, H.T.: Relations between needs and behavior as measured by the Edwards PPS and interpersonal check list. *Journal of Social Psychology, 57:*445-451, 1962.

Hardison, J., and Purcell, K.: The effects of psychological stress as a function of need and cognitive control. *Journal of Personality, 27:*250-258, 1959.

Harshbarger, T.R.: Differential desirability. *Journal of Clinical Psychology, 30:*535-540, 1974.

Hartnett, J.J., Bailey, K.G., and Gibson, F.W., Jr.: Personal space as influenced by sex and type of movement. *Journal of Psychology, 76:*139-144, 1970.

Hearn, J.L., Charles, D.C., and Wolins, L.: Life history antecedents of measured personality variables. *Journal of Genetic Psychology, 107:*99-110, 1965.

Hetherington, E.M., and Feldman, S.E.: College cheating as a function of subject and situational variables. *Journal of Educational Psychology, 55:*212-218, 1964.

Jordan, B.T., and Kempler, B.: Hysterical personality: An experimental investigation of sex-role conflict. *Journal of Abnormal Psychology, 75:*172-176, 1970.

Leckart, B.T., Waters, L.K., and Tarpinian, J.: Duration of attention and need for affiliation. *Perceptual and Motor Skills, 25:* 817-824, 1967.

LeMay, M.L., and Damm, V.J.: Relationship of the Personal Orientation Inventory to the Edwards Personal Preference Schedule. *Psychological Report, 24:*834, 1969.

Libby, W.L., and Yaklevich, D.: Personality determinants of eye contact and direction of gaze aversion. *Journal of Personality and Social Psychology, 27:*197-206, 1973.

Magnussen, M.G., and Kemler, W.M.: Infant feeding preference as related to personality test scores. *Journal of Clinical Psychology, 25:*258-260, 1969.

Marlowe, D.: Some psychological correlates of field independence. *Journal of Consulting Psychology, 22:*334, 1958.

Mosher, D.L.: The development and multitrait — multimethod matrix analysis of three measures of three aspects of guilt. *Journal of Consulting Psychology, 30:*25-29, 1966.

Mussen, P.: Some antecedents and consequents of masculine sex-typing in adolescent boys. *Psychological Monographs, 75:*1-24, 1961.

Nichols, M.P., Gordon, T.P., and Levine, M.D.: Development and validation of the Life Style Questionnaires. *Journal of Social Psychology, 86:*121-125, 1972.

Nowicki, S., Jr.: Birth order and personality: Some unexpected findings. *Psychological Reports, 21:* 265-267, 1967.

Nunnally, J.C., and Flaugher, R.L.: Correlates of semantic habits. *Journal of Personality, 31:*191-202, 1963.

O'Neill, M., and Kempfler, B.: Approach and avoidance responses of the hysterical personality to sexual stimuli. *Journal of Abnormal Psychology, 74:*300-305, 1969.

Payne, D.L.: Birth-order, personality and performance at the Air Force academy. *Journal of Individual Psychology, 27:*185-187, 1971.

Phares, E.J.: and Adams, C.K.: The construct validity of the Edwards PPS Heterosexuality. *Journal of Consulting Psychology, 25:*341-344, 1961.

Query, W.T., and Query, J.M.: Birth order: Urban-rural effects on need affiliation and school activity participation among high school male students. *Journal of Social Psychology, 90:*317-320, 1973.

Rosenkrantz, P.S., and Halloran, W.J.: Are abasement scores predictive of adjustment? *Journal of Psychology, 61:*33-37, 1965.

Rotter, J.: Generalized expectancies for internal versus external control of reinforcement. *Psychological Monographs, 80* (1, Whole No. 609), 1966.

Sampson, E.E., and Hancock, F.T.: An examination of the relationship between ordinal position personality, and conformity: An extension, replication, and partial verification. *Journal of Personality and Social Psychology, 5:*398-307, 1967.

Saper, B.: Motivational components in the interpersonal transactions of married couples. *Psychiatric Quarterly, 39:*303-314, 1965.

Simon, W.E., Primavera, L.H., Klein, B., and Cristal, R.M.: Personality and nonverbal rigidity: Some preliminary findings. *Journal of Psychology, 82:*127-132, 1972.

Smith, R.C.: Self-esteem as moderator variable in the relationship between manifest need of nurturance and satisfaction. *Journal of Clinical Psychology, 28:*347-348, 1972.

Sundberg, N., Sharma, V., Wodtli, T., and Rohila, P.: Family cohesiveness and autonomy of adolescents in India and the United States. *Journal Marriage and the Family, 31:*403-407, 1969.

Swindell, D.H., and Lieberman, L.R.: Effect of sex on the correlation between the dogmatism scale and the Edwards Personal Preference Schedule. *Psychological Reports, 23:*893-894, 1968.

Tanck, R.H., and Robbins, P.R.: Pupillary reactions to sexual, aggressive, and other stimuli as a function of personality. *Journal of Projective Techniques and Personality Assessment, 34:*227-282, 1970.

Taylor, J.A.: A personality scale of manifest anxiety. *Journal of Abnormal and Social Psychology, 48:*285-290, 1953.

Tolor, J.A.: Relationship between insight and intraception. *Journal of Clinical Psychology, 17:*188-189, 1961.

Tolor, A., and LeBlanc, R.F.: An attempted clarification of the psychological distance construct. *Journal of Social Psychology, 92:*259-267, 1974.

Tseng, M.S.: Locus of control as a determinant of job proficiency, employability, and training, satisfaction of vocational rehabilitation clients. *Journal of Counseling Psychology, 17:*487-491, 1970.

Tutko, T.A., and Sechrest, L.: Conceptual performance and personality variables. *Journal of Consulting Psychology, 26:*481, 1962.

Vacchiano, R.B., Strauss, P.S., and Schiffman, D.C.: Personality correlates of dogmatism. *Journal of Consulting and Clinical Psychology, 32:*83-85, 1968.

Van de Castle, R.L.: Perceptual defense in a binocular rivalry situation. *Journal of Personality, 28:*448-462, 1960.

Walberg, H.J., Welch, W.W., and Rothman, A.I.: Teacher heterosexuality and student learning. *Psychology in the Schools, 6:*258-261, 1969.

Walsh, R.P.: Test-taking anxiety and psychological needs. *Psychological Reports, 25:*83-86, 1969.

Waters, C.W., and Waters, L.K.: Relationships between a measure of "sensation-seeking" and personal preference schedule need scales. *Educational and Psychological Measurement, 29:*983-985, 1969.

Weitzner, M., Stallone, F., and Smith, G.M.: Personality profiles of high, middle, and low MAS subjects. *Journal of Psychology, 65:*163-168, 1967.

Williams, C.D., and Bruel, I.: Evidence for the validity of the construct of intraception. *Journal of Clinical Psychology, 24:*188-189, 1968.

Williams, C.D., Tallarico, R.B., and Tedeschi, J.T.: Manifest needs and manifest anxiety. *Journal of Consulting Psychology, 24:*371, 1960.

Woodmansee, J.J.: Validation of the nurturance scale of the Edwards Personal Preference Schedule. *Psychological Reports, 42:*495-498, 1978.

Zuckerman, M., and Oltean, M.: Some relationships between maternal attitude factors and authoritarianism personality needs, psychopathology, and self-acceptance. *Child Development, 30:*27-36, 1959.

Chapter 9

USE OF THE EPPS FOR ASSESSING NONNORMAL
POPULATIONS

T HE most recent version of the EPPS manual makes no mention of how
the inventory is to be used for assessment and/or diagnosis of psychiatric
populations. Nevertheless, since the EPPS was introduced, researchers have
attempted to discover which of the scales could be used to diagnose psychiatric
conditions. The typical procedure in such studies has been to administer the
EPPS to respondents who have been diagnosed by some other means as
evidencing psychopathology. Scales that deviate significantly from the norms
or from other diagnostic classification groups are then assumed to be
characteristic of the particular clinical syndrome. While the other means used
for the clinical diagnoses have been rather vague, in general they appear to
have included some combination of the following: (a) the standard clinical
evaluation procedures followed by a particular agency and (b) responses to inventories designed to detect nonnormal conditions.

Five kinds of studies have evolved from investigators' curiosity about the
EPPS's usefulness for assessing other than normal populations. The first might
be called nosological studies. In these studies, investigators divide clinical
populations into various diagnostic categories, e.g. neurotic versus psychotic,
and then attempt to discover the scales which differentiate one from the other.
In the second kind of study, the investigator attempts to discover the scales that
are characteristic of people who indulge in unhealthy behavior practices. Most
of these studies have involved the examination of addictive behaviors, such as
drug addiction or cigarette smoking. A subclassification of the unhealthy
behavior studies are those studies that have been searches for relationships between personality characteristics and physiological symptoms or responses. A
small group of studies has involved an examination of the relationship between
the EPPS scales and other personality inventories. A major purpose of these
studies has been to determine the uniqueness of the various measures. A final
small collection of the studies has been examinations of therapy process and
outcome. In these studies, investigators attempt to determine which scales can
be used to predict therapy-related behaviors of patients or therapists.

Nosological Studies

Goss (1968) surveyed the literature in which psychiatric populations had
been compared to an EPPS norm group and concluded that differences between the groups had been misrepresented because the authors had used the

wrong norm group. Tables 9-I and 9-II represent an adaptation and updating of his reanalysis of these data. Trends that are evident in the table are that male patient groups exhibit a lower need for dominance than noninstitutionalized samples and that female patient samples excepting adolescents exhibit higher needs for autonomy and lower needs for affiliation. Hospitalized nonpsychotic males also appear to have higher need for abasement.

The limited data available for female populations suggest that hospitalized adult females have a higher need for exhibition and heterosexuality than non-hospitalized samples. For the general adult sample of women, autonomy, ex-hibition, and heterosexuality are among their five lowest ranking needs while affiliation is the second highest in terms of ranking. Thus, women psychiatric clients may be people who exhibit a sex role reversal of some consequence.

Evidence for such a reversal among male clients is not so apparent although Goss hypothesized that such might be the case. Yet, Heilizer and Trehub (1962) did find higher correlations between the profiles for adult and college women and male schizophrenics than existed between these hospitalized groups and the adult and college men.

Adolescent hospitalized samples tended to differ from adult samples in the kinds of needs that differed when compared to an appropriate age norm group. As compared to a nonhospitalized group of girls, Pasewark et al. (1968) found that the hospitalized girls did not differ on any of the needs. Of eight needs reported by Gauron (1965) for hospitalized girls aged fifteen to nineteen years, order was higher and change and heterosexuality were lower than the same needs reported for Klett's (1957) high school sample. Delinquent girls in Wat-son et al.'s (1970) study had lower needs for deference and endurance and higher needs for heterosexuality.

Hospitalized boys in Pasewark et al.'s (1968) study had lower needs for deference, dominance, and heterosexuality and higher need for order than their respective comparison group. Comparison of Gauron's (1965) data for fifteen- to nineteen-year-old male psychiatric patients to Klett's high school norms supported the finding that the former had lower need heterosexuality. Delinquent boys as compared to nondelinquents had lower needs for achieve-ment, deference, affiliation, and dominance (Watson et al., 1970). Thus, the needs that stand out as having some importance for adolescent patient samples are an elevated need for order or depressed needs for deference or endurance and a deviant need (either higher or lower than a comparable comparison group) for heterosexuality.

Another way to examine similarities between clinical groups is Q-typing, which is the factor analysis of intercorrelated profiles. Heilizer (1963) used such a procedure and found evidence for a factor peopled by male personality disorder, neurotics, and schizophrenics. These groups were characterized by high needs for endurance, abasement, nurturance, and order and low needs for heterosexuality, aggression, and autonomy. Heilizer theorized that this factor

Table 9 - I

COMPARISON OF MALE PSYCHIATRIC SAMPLES AND EPPS ADULT NORMS

EPPS Scale	Diagnostic Groups[1]						
	Newman & Fisher Neurotics (n = 50)	Kissinger Schizophrenics (n = 45)	Gauron mixed (n = 159)	Rosenberg obsessional (n = 10)	Personality Disorders (n = 200)	Nowick Neurotics (n = 200)	Psychotics (n = 200)
Ach	0	0	0	H	0	0	0
Def	0	0	0	0	0	H	0
Ord	0	0	L	0	0	0	0
Exh	0	0	H	0	0	0	0
Aut	0	0	0	0	L	0	0
Aff	0	0	0	L	L	0	0
Int	0	0	H	0	L	0	0
Suc	0	H	H	0	0	H	0
Dom	L	L	L	L	L	L	L
Aba	H	0	H	0	H	H	L
Nur	H	L	H	0	0	H	0
Chg	0	0	0	0	0	0	0
Erd	0	0	L	0	0	L	0
Het	0	0	0	0	H	H	H
Agg	L	L	L	0	L	L	L

[1]
0 = no difference; L = lower than norm group; H = higher than norm group

Table 9 - II

COMPARISON OF FEMALE PSYCHIATRIC SAMPLES AND EPPS ADULT NORMS

EPPS Scale	Diagnostic Groups[1]				
	Kissinger	Gauron	Rosenberg	Paseward et al.	Watson et al.
	Schizophrenics (n = 62)	mixed (n = 162)	obsessional (n = 19)	Hospitalized Girls (n = 39)	Delinquent Girls (n = 46)
Ach	0	0	0	0	0
Def	H	L	0	0	L
Ord	0	L	0	0	0
Exh	H	H	0	0	0
Aut	H	H	H	0	0
Aff	L	L	L	0	0
Int	0	0	0	0	0
Suc	0	0	0	0	0
Dom	H	0	0	0	0
Aba	L	0	0	0	0
Nur	0	0	0	0	0
Chg	L	0	L	0	0
Erd	0	L	L	0	L
Het	H	H	0	0	0
Agg	0	0	H	0	H

[1] See note at Table 9-I.

described personality trait disturbances.

Gordon and Sait (1969) applied Q-typing to forty-five samples that they had located in the literature, seven of which were psychiatric populations and four of which were prison populations. Three of the psychiatric populations, i.e. female psychiatric patients, male schizophrenics, male psychiatric patients, had their highest loading on a factor that Gordon and Sait call *docility*. Groups with high loadings on this factor were characterized by high needs for deference, order, succorance, abasement, and nurturance and low needs for dominance and heterosexuality. Nonpsychiatric groups that also had high loadings on this factor included male and female adults, female prisoners, male psychiatric aides, Air Force enlistees, and black male and female college students. Male neurotics had their highest loadings on a predominantly female factor called *friendly interest*. Groups with high loadings on this factor had high needs for affiliation, intraception, and change and low needs for aggression, endurance, and achievement.

Van Evra and Rosenberg (1963) explored the possibility that different need scores might occur within diagnoses. They divided ninety-eight white male diagnosed sociopaths into two groups: neurotic sociopaths, those reporting high anxiety, and primary sociopaths, those reporting little anxiety. A comparison of the Ego-Disjunction Scale scores (conflicting EPPS need variables) of the two groups indicated that the neurotic group had a higher level of incompatible needs. The Ego-Disjunction Scale score is composed of unindirectional scores on the following pairs: deference-aggression, autonomy-abasement, succorance-nurturance, order-change. Thus, the neurotic sociopaths had need patterns similar to Heilizer's (1963) personality trait disturbance factor as well as Gordon and Sait's (1969) docility factor.

Together the nosology studies suggest that high needs for abasement, nurturance, order, heterosexuality, and low needs for dominance characterize adult male clinical samples and samples composed of both sexes. Males and females seemed to deviate in opposite directions on three of the scales: heterosexuality, affiliation, and autonomy; adult women tended to have higher needs for autonomy and heterosexuality and lower needs for affiliation. Low need for aggression seems to be uniquely characteristic of male patients.

Addictive Behavior

Identification of needs characteristic of alcoholics has been a primary area of concern in the literature concerning addictive behavior. Some of these studies have involved comparisons of alcoholic samples and the EPPS norm groups (Manaugh and Scott, 1976; Goss, Morosko, and Sheldon, 1968; Fitzgerald, Pasewark, and Tanner, 1967; Hoffman and Nelson, 1971). With the exceptions of Fitzgerald et al. (1967) and Scott and Manaugh (1976), all of these studies have involved exclusively male samples. Most have involved populations exhibiting markedly differing or unknown individual characteristics, including marital status and age. Nevertheless, an examination of these studies indicates that although some of the studies have reported within study differences among groups, virtually none of the scale differences have occurred across studies. Likewise, none of the needs have consistently appeared to be characteristic of the alcoholic samples in the various studies.

Focusing on the drinking behavior of a nondiagnosed population, Reiter (1970) used a mixed sex sample of college students to compare heavy drinkers to light drinkers. A heavy drinker was defined as one who drank more than three drinks more than two times a week and felt she or he drank too much.

Reiter reported that heavy drinkers had higher needs for achievement, order, exhibition, dominance, endurance, and aggression and lower needs for intraception, nurturance, and change. Also, when using a standard college population, Primavera, Simon, and Camisa (1975) found no need differences between female undergraduate users of caffeine as compared to nonusers.

Efforts to distinguish completers of treatment programs have been equally unsuccessful. Neither Goss et al. (1968) nor Pryer and Distefano (1970) found any evidence that the EPPS scales could distinguish premature terminators from people who completed treatment.

Hoffmann and Miner (1973) found that former male alcoholics who participated in a training program for alcoholic counselor trainees had higher needs for affiliation, heterosexuality, and aggression and lower needs for change and endurance after training than before. Following training their needs for affiliation, intraception, endurance, and heterosexuality were higher and their needs for order and autonomy were lower than those of a normative group.

Narcotics abuse and smoking have been the other two areas that have generated some investigator interest. Sheppard, Ricca, Fracchia, and Merlis (1974) tested male and female applicants to a methadone maintenance program. They found that a significant number of addicts scored below the 40th percentile on the Affiliation and Endurance scales. In a comparison of female marijuana users and nonusers, Simon et al. (1974) found that users had significantly higher needs for autonomy, change, and aggression; nonusers had significantly higher needs for deference, order, and endurance.

Field and Madigan's (1974) study of drug usage on a college campus revealed that nonusers had greater need for order than those students who used marijuana only or those who used hallucinogens. Marijuana and hallucinogen users as compared to nonusers had higher autonomy and aggression needs. Users of hallucinogens also had higher needs for exhibition than the other two groups and lower needs for affiliation than nonusers.

Weatherley (1965) compared four categories of smokers: people who had never smoked, smokers who had never attempted to quit, relapsed smokers, and former smokers. He found that former smokers had lower needs for deference, affiliation, and change and higher needs for achievement and aggression than the nonsmokers and the current smokers. Former smokers also had a higher need for achievement and a lower need for change than the relapsers. Rieter (1970) compared a mixed sex sample of college students who were designated as smokers or nonsmokers on the basis of whether or not they smoked each day. He found that smokers had higher needs for exhibition and change and that nonsmokers had higher needs for deference and nurturance.

Although some data raise the possibility that autonomy, aggression, order, and affiliation are related to drug abuse behavior, the data at hand indicate that the EPPS scales cannot be reliably used to differentiate alcoholics, narcotic addicts, or cigarette smokers from groups that are presumably not drug abusers. Nevertheless, they beg the question of whether there is an addictive personality that could be evidenced by *patterns* of the EPPS scales rather than single scale scores. Unfortunately, only two of the available studies (Reiter, 1970; Manaugh and Scott, 1976) provided enough information to permit a reanalysis of the data. Rank correlations computed between the smoker and alcoholic groups (rho = .50), between the smokers and the total college students norms (rho = .70), and between the alcoholics and the adult male norms (rho = .00) suggest that the students, smokers or nonsmokers, were more like each other than they were like the alcoholics, but that the alcoholics were more similar to the students who were smokers as well as the college student norms (rho = .60) than they were to the adult men norms. It is possible that in terms of the ordering of their psychological needs that alcoholics have not reached the level of maturity that would be expected of men of their age.

Scott and Manaugh's (1976) analysis of patterns of similarity among profiles of men and women alcoholics and the EPPS men and women adult norms also indicated that normal men and alcoholic men (r = .05) displayed different patterns of EPPS needs. Alcoholic women, were more similar to normal women (r = .81) than they were to normal (r = .39) or alcoholic men (r = .20). The latter findings contradict the hypothesis that alcoholic women are generally more masculine than nonalcoholic women, though the alcoholic women did have lower needs for affiliation and higher needs for heterosexuality and intraception than is customary for women in general.

Physiological Symptoms

The inability to adjust to anxiety is assumed to contribute to the development of various physiological syndromes. In a study in which they compared EPPS scores of sixteen obese men and women to a normative sample, Wunderlich, Johnson, and Ball (1973) found that the obese subjects had higher needs for aggression and heterosexuality and lower needs for endurance. Obese subjects averaged more than 25 percent overweight.

The scores of eighteen obese women who successfully completed group therapy were compared to the scores of nine women who didn't in Payne et al.'s (1970) study. Obese subjects were at least ten percent overweight. Successful participants, i.e. those who lost 10 pounds or more within a ten-week period, had higher needs for succorance and nurturance than a normative group, but unsuccessful participants did not differ from the normative group. As compared to unsuccessful group members, weight losers had a lower need for consistency, a finding that was replicated in a cross-validation study. As indicated by their checklist responses, women who did not lose weight seemed to be more satisfied with themselves. No scale was related to obesity or weight change in both studies, but different standards were used for defining obesity and comparison groups.

In one of the studies in which physiological measures were used to study anxiety, Shippman et al. (1970) found that palmar sweating was negatively correlated with endurance (r = -.51) and order (r = .40) and positively correlated with heterosexuality (r = .30); subjects with lowest frontalis muscle tension level tended to have high needs for achievement (r = .36). Subjects were male and female nonpsychotic outpatients of varying diagnoses. The authors interpret their results to indicate that reactivity of different muscles and autonomic functions are related to different personality characteristics — a conclusion that they failed to confirm in a subsequent reanalysis of their data (Shipman et al., 1970).

In their study of the relationship between blood pressure and personality characteristics of a sample of twelve male essential hypertensives, Pilowsky et al. (1973) found that deference and abasement were positively correlated and heterosexuality was negatively correlated with various cardiovascular measures. Their results were consistent with previous studies that showed that patients with hypertension were sexually inhibited and had self-abasive attitudes.

Three other studies have been attempts to identify character types that might contribute to certain physiological syndromes. Marshall (1960) found that male subjects who were prone to peptic ulcers described themselves as having lower needs for intraception and higher needs for order than did comparison groups exhibiting nongastrointestinal psychosomatic disorders or who were free from psychosomatic disorders.

Formicola et al. (1970) proposed that acute necrotizing ulcerative gingivitis (gum disease) might be precipitated by specific personality characerics which make it difficult for certain people to adjust to stressful situations. In their study of equal numbers of preflight trainees with and without the disease, they found that dominance (r = .25) and abasement (r = .26) were significantly correlated with various measures of gum disease. Schwartz, Dennerll, and Lin (1969) compared the EPPS scores of 199 men and women with epilepsy to those of nonepileptic respondents. They found no more than chance differences among their groups, suggesting that there were no common characteristics that contributed to an epileptic personality.

Again no EPPS scale was related to physiological symptoms or personality types in all of the studies in which such issues were investigated. If one examines the various studies concerned with physiological responses, circumstantial evidence suggests that need for heterosexuality may be a contributing factor for some of the disorders. Heterosexuality was high for severely overweight men and women, but negatively correlated with resting heart rate and diastolic blood pressure. If the Heterosexuality Scale measures acting out behavior, then it is possible that obese people act out by overeating, but that hypertensives have no suitable means for rebelling.

The Relationship of EPPS Scales to Other Inventories

Two personality measures have been intercorrelated with or factor analyzed in combination with the EPPS scales when psychiatric populations were the respondents. The MMPI, a measure of psychopathology, has been used in the intercorrelational studies. Cattell's 16 PF, a measure of personality traits, has been used in the factor analysis studies. Patient samples were psychiatric patients (Burton, 1971; Kear-Colwell, 1973; Gauron and Adams, 1966) and male vocational and educational counseling clients (Merrill and Heathers, 1956).

Looking first at the MMPI studies, Merrill and Heathers (1956) found substantial negative correlations (i.e. .40 or higher) between the following scale pairs: deference-Pd + K, Si-exhibition, Sc-dominance, Depresssion-dominance, F minus K-abasement, Pt-endurance, aggression-L, and F minus K-aggression. Substantial positive correlations were found between abasement-Pt, abasement-Sc + K, abasement-Si, and chg-Sc + K.

From their results, Merrill and Heathers (1956) concluded that since deference and dominance tended to be inversely related to the clinical scales, "clients who have accepted either a dominant, strong role or a more conforming, follower role in interpersonal relationships on the EPPS tend to be least like deviants as measured by the MMPI" (p. 313). On the other hand, their finding that abasement was clearly related to the clinical scales led the authors to conclude that "clients who rate their guilt and inadequacy feelings relatively high on the EPPS are most likely to be abnormal as measured by the MMPI" (p.313).

From their intercorrelational investigation of the MMPI and the EPPS scales, Gauron and Adams (1966) identified combinations of scales that they felt were related to mental health or mental illness or were unrelated to either of these dimensions. They speculated that the combination of elevations on the Deference, Order, and Endurance scales indicated a lack of or denial of pathology and suggested that significant depressions of these scales "might be considered indicative of the presence of psychological disturbance or pathology" (p. 207). They contended that deviantly high scores on the Succorance and Abasement scales indicated psychological sickness, particularly for male patients. (Deviantly high scores for many of their respondents were beyond the 85th percentile.) They found little evidence that needs for exhibition, autonomy, and intraception were related to any of the MMPI scales even though these scales were notably high among their population. A fourth grouping of scales, Heterosexuality, Change, and Aggression, Gauron and Adams explained as measuring a lack of conformity when elevated and suggested that such elevations were characteristic of personality disorders.

Two studies of the EPPS and the 16 PF exist. Burton identified several clusters from his linkage analysis of the factors summarized in Table 9-III.

An exclusively EPPS factor (Factor II) and cluster were represented by high

Table 9 - III

SUMMARY OF FACTOR ANALYTIC STUDIES
OF NONNORMAL POPULATIONS

Factor Names	No. EPPS Scales	EPPS[1] Scales	No. Other Test Scales	PF[4] Scales	Percent Variance	Total Scales
		[2]Burton's (1971) 16 PF Study				
1. Factor 1	1	-Aba	6	+C, +H, +L, -O, +Q₃, +Q₄	14.5	7
2. Factor 2	5	+Exh, +Aut, -Aff, -Nur, -End	0		10.6	5
3. Factor 3	4	+Ach, +Ord, +Aff, +End	3	-A, -F, +Q₂	8.9	7
4. Factor 4	2	-Dom, -Agg	2	+B, -N	7.8	4
5. Factor 5	1	+Nur	2	-C, +M	6.6	3
6. Factor 6	1	-Ach	1	+I	6.3	2
7. Factor 7	2	-Ord, +Chg	2	+Q₁, +Q₂	5.7	4
8. Factor 8	1	+Def	1	+G	4.9	2
9. Factor 9	3	+Int, +Dom, -Aba	0		4.8	3
10. Factor 10	3	+Suc, +Nur, -End	1	-N	4.4	4
11. Factor 11	2	-Ach, +Ord	2	+E, -H	3.4	4
		[3]Kear-Colwell (1973) 16PF Study (EPPS Alone)				
1. EPPS I	4	+Def, +Ord, +End, -Het	0			4
2. EPPS II	5	-Exh, -Aut, +Aff, +Nur, -Agg	0			5
3. EPPS III	2	+Aut, +Chg	0			2
4. EPPS IV	5	-Suc, +Dom, -Aba, +Agg	0			5
5. EPPS V	2	+Int, -Suc	0			2
6. EPPS VI	3	+Ach, -Aba, -Agg	0			3
		(EPPS and 16 PF)				
1. Factor I	3	-Def, -Exh, +Aba	5	-C, -H, +L, +O, +Q₄		8

Table 9 - III (continued)

Factor Names	No. EPPS Scales	EPPS[1] Scales	No. Other Test Scales	PF[4] Scales	Percent Variance	Total Scales
2. Factor III	3	+Def, +Ord, −Het	4	−E, −F, +G, −Q_1, +Q_4		7
3. Factor IV	3	−Aut, +Aff, +Nur	2	+G, −Q_2		5
4. Factor V	2	+Aut, +Chg	0			2
5. Factor VI	2	+Dom, +Agg	2	+E, +L		4
6. Factor VII	1	+Nur	6	+C, +G, +N, +Q_1, +Q_2, +Q_3		
7. Factor VIII	3	−Ord, +Int, −End	2	+I, +M		5
8. Factor IX	2	+Int, −Suc,	1	+Q_1		4
9. Factor X	2	+Ach, −Aut	0			2

[1]+ and minus signs equal direction of factor loading.

[2]data collected from English sample

[3]data collected from Scottish sample

[4]See appendix for test legends.

positive factor loadings on the needs exhibition, autonomy, and high negative loadings for needs affiliation, nurturance, and endurance. This factor may represent a self-aggrandizement versus group-focused dichotomy. Factor III he considers to be a measure of extroversion needs: achievement, order, affiliation, and endurance were the positively loaded EPPS scales constituting this factor and A (reserved), F (sober), and Q2 (self-sufficient) were the PF scales constituting Factor III.

Using a larger sample of psychiatric respondents than had Burton (1971), Kear-Colwell concluded that the two inventories had only limited relationship to one another; Factor I was labeled anxiety and consisted of EPPS Deference and Exhibition scales, which had negative factor loadings, and the Abasement Scale, which had a positive loading. Relevant PF scales were negatively loaded C (low emotional stability) and H (shyness) and positively loaded L (suspiciousness), O (depressive), and Q4 (tenseness). Factor III consisted of needs and personality traits, indicating a preference for a "carefully organized and socially diffident way of life" (p. 226). Negatively loaded variables were heterosexuality, E (assertive), F (impulsive), and Q1 (radicalism) and positively loaded variables were deference, order, G (stronger superego strength), and Q3 (controlled). Factor IV was an interpersonal factor with positive loadings for nurturance, affiliation, and G (stronger superego strength) and negative loadings for Q2 (group dependence) and need autonomy. Factor VIII possibly measures social sensitivity with positive loadings for I (sensitive), M (imaginative), and need intraception and negative loadings for order and endurance.

The combination of EPPS-PF scales that appeared in both the Burton (1971) and Kear-Colwell (1973) studies were need abasement in combination with loadings in the opposite direction for C (emotionally stable-emotionally unstable), H (shy-socially bold), and O (placid-apprehensive). This clustering of traits supports the idea that high need abasement may be related to psychopathology in psychiatric populations. While no exclusively EPPS factors occurred in both studies, the deference-order-endurance triad that appeared in the factor analytic studies using normal populations also appeared in Kear-Colwell's study of psychiatric patients. Thus, the dimension of need for social control may be a dimension inherent in the instrument rather than the population being measured.

Therapy Process and Outcome Variables

Studies in the area of therapy process and outcome have generally been designed to answer one of three questions: (a) Can therapy outcome be predicted from the patients' EPPS needs? (b) Is in-therapy behavior related to need scores? (c) Do the helpers resemble the helpees in terms of their psychological needs?

In general, the EPPS scales have not been demonstrated to have been of any use in predicting treatment outcome. Both Goss (1969) and Distefano and Pryer (1970) tested models to predict the vocational outcome of psychiatric patients. Goss, the developer of the model, claimed that high needs for affiliation, intraception, and nurturance and low scores on succorance would be characteristic of patients who made successful vocational adjustment. However, he found no confirming evidence. Distefano and Pryer were also unable to find any scales that could be used consistently to predict vocational outcome. As previously mentioned, Pryer et al.'s (1969) and Gross et al.'s (1973) attempts to identify need scales that would distinguish alcoholics who successfully completed treatment programs from those who did not were unsuccessful.

Lester et al. (1975) attempted to discover whether needs differed for ex-drug addicts who completed a vocational training program when compared to non-completers. They found no significant differences. Caditz (1959) compared the need scores of delinquent boys when they first entered a "training school" to their scores once they had been in the program for a minimum of two months. She found that their need for affiliation had decreased significantly while their need for aggression had increased. Neither of these changes could have been predicted from their initial scores nor by comparing them to those scores of nondelinquent boys of similar ages.

Regarding the question of in-therapy behavior, Grosz and Wagoner (1971) found that male psychiatric inpatients who had high need for order tended to initiate few verbal interactions whereas those with high need aggression tended to initiate verbal interactions. Grosz and Wagoner suggested that these needs might represent a defensiveness-gregariousness dichotomy among the patients who participated in group therapy.

Whether or not helpers (therapists) and patients resemble one another was addressed in a study by Tucker and Cantor (1975). They compared affiliation, succorance, nurturance, endurance, and aggression need levels for peer counselors, suicide attempters, people who thought frequently about suicide, and people who seldom thought about suicide. As compared to the attempters, the counselors had lower needs for affiliation, succorance, nurturance, and aggression and a higher need for endurance. Endurance seemed to be the need that best distinguished the groups, as attempters were likely to have their lowest score on this scale, low-suicide thinkers were likely to have the highest score on this scale of all groups, and peer counselors had intermediate scores on this scale.

Bare (1967) was concerned with the question of whether helper (counselor) and client need similarities were related to their perceptions of the counseling process. She found that greater counselor need for achievement was negatively related to clients' perceptions of the helpfulness of the counseling. Higher counselor need for exhibition contributed positively to perceptions of helpfulness, higher needs for order contributed to greater perceptions of empathy, and greater needs for aggression led to client's perceptions that counselors did not know them well. Large counselor-client differences in achievement affected the relationship positively and large differences in nurturance affected the relationship negatively. Counselor ratings of counseling outcome revealed that large differences in achievement were negatively correlated with counselor-perceived helpfulness and impressions of how well they got to know the client.

Perceived empathy was negatively related to differences in autonomy and aggression and positively related to large differences in order, abasement, and endurance. In other words, the more similar the counselor was to the client in her or his own needs for order, abasement, and endurance, the less likely he or she was to perceive that the various aspects of the counseling relationship had been positive. Likewise, the more similar his or her needs for autonomy and aggression were to the client's level of these needs, the more likely he or she was to evaluate the relationship factors negatively.

Perkins (1968) was curious about whether psychiatry residents could anticipate the EPPS hierarchies of five of their patients. Therapist-generated profiles were compared to those actually obtained by patients. Significant similarities between the two types of profiles were obtained for only two of fifteen patients. Therapist profiles generated one month later revealed two similarities. Perkins suggested that therapist stereotypes of the patients in which the therapists perceived patients as having higher needs for exhibition, succorance, order, dominance, and deference may have accounted for the absence of long-term correlations of any magnitude.

Bendig (1956) attempted a similar study with naive undergraduate students who ranked case histories for level of severity. Students were divided into groups on the basis of whether their rankings agreed with those of psychiatrists and psychologists. While he found tentative evidence for a relationship between high agreement and achievement and endurance, these relationships were not confirmed in a replication study.

Overall, the therapy process and outcome studies do not reveal any scales that can be used to reliably predict therapy-related behavior. Scales that may be eventually shown to have some merit in this regard are affiliation, endurance, order, and aggression.

Summary and Conclusion

Some EPPS need scales may be indicative of psychopathology singly or in combination with other scales. Single scales include Order, Abasement, Exhibition, Autonomy, Nurturance, Dominance, Affiliation, and Aggression. Whether it is depressions or elevations of these scales which should be of concern to the test user depends upon the sex and age of the person with whom she or he is working; men and women often varied in opposite directions on some of these scales typically in directions suggesting a failure to conform to societal sex role proscriptions. Scale combinations of some significance are Deference, Order, Endurance. Moderate elevations of these scales seem to be associated with mental well-being.

References

Bendig, A.W.: The personality of judges and their agreement with experts in judging clinical case histories. *Journal of Consulting Psychology, 20:*422, 1956.

Burton, D.A.: A factor analysis of the Edwards Personal Preference Schedule and 16 PF in a psychiatric population. *Journal of Clinical Psychology, 27:*248-251, 1971.

Caditz, S.B.: Effect of a training school experience on the personality of delinquent boys. *Journal of Consulting Psychology, 23:*501-509, 1959.

Distefano, M.K., Jr., and Pryer, M.W.: Predicting vocational outcome of psychiatric patients with the EPPS. *Journal of Applied Psychology, 54:*522-524, 1970.

Field, T.F., and Madigan, M.: Personality and social factors of college students involved in drug use. *College Student Journal, 8:*23-26, 1974.

Fitzgerald, B.J., Pasewark, R.A., and Tanner, C.E.: Use of the Edwards Personal Preference Schedule with hospitalized alcoholics. *Journal of Clinical Psychology, 23:*194-195, 1967.

Formicola, A.S., Witte, E.T., and Curran, P.M.: A study of personality traits and acute necrotizing ulcerative gingivitis. *Journal of Periodontics, 41:*36-38, 1970.

Gauron, E.F.: Changes in Edwards Personal Preference Schedule needs with age and psychiatric status. *Journal of Clinical Psychology, 21:*194-196, 1965.

Gauron, E.F., and Adams, J.: The relationship of the Edwards Personal Preference Schedule to the MMPI in a patient population. *Journal of Clinical Psychology 22:*206-209, 1966.

Gordon, L.V., and Sait, E.M.: Q-typing in the domain of manifest needs. *Educational and Psychological Measurement 29:*87-98, 1969.

Goss, A.: Edwards Personal Preference Schedule patterns in psychiatric populations. *Journal of Projective Techniques and Personality Assessment, 32:*173-176, 1968.

Goss, A., Morosko, T., and Sheldon, R.: Use of the Edwards Personal Preference Schedule with alcoholics in a vocational rehabilitation program. *Journal of Psychology, 68:*287-289, 1968.

Gross, W.F., and Nerviano, V.J.: The prediction of dropouts from an inpatient alcoholism program by objective personality inventories. *Quarterly Journal of Studies on Alcohol, 340:*514-515, 1973.

Grosz, H.J., and Wagoner, R.: MMPI and EPPS profiles of high and low verbal interactors in therapy groups. *Psychological Reports, 28:*951-955, 1971.

Heilizer, F.: An ipsative factor analysis of the ipsative EPPS. *Psychological Reports, 12:*285-286, 1963.

Heilizer, F., and Trehub, A.: Relationships of the EPPS need profile among eight samples. *Journal of Clinical Psychology, 18:*462-464, 1962.

Hoffman, H., and Miner, B.B.: Personality of alcoholics who became counselors. *Psychological Reports, 33:*878, 1973.

Hoffman, H, and Nelson, P.C.: Personality characteristics of alcoholics in relation to age and intelligence. *Psychological Reports, 29:*143-146, 1971.

Kear-Colwell, J.J.: The factor structure of the 16PF and the EPPS in acute psychiatric patients. *Journal of Clinical Psychology, 29:*225-228, 1973.

Kissinger, R.D.: The Edwards Personal Preference Schedule in a psychiatric setting. *Journal of Projective Techniques and Personality Assessment, 30:*149-152, 1966.

Klett, C.J.: Social desirability stereotype in a hospital population. *Journal of Consulting Psychology, 21:*419-421, 1957.

Krug, R.E., and Moyer, K.E.: An analysis of the F. scale: II. Relationship to standardized personality inventories. *Journal of Social Psychology, 53:*293-301, 1961.

Lester, D., Narkunski, A., Burkman, T.H., and Gandica, A.: An exploratory study of correlates of success in a vocational training program for ex-addicts. *Psychological Reports, 37:*1212-1214, 1975.

Manaugh, T.S., and Scott, E.M.: EPPS scores of male alcoholics: A review and cross-validation. *Journal of Clinical Psychology, 32:*197-199, 1976.

Marshall, S.: Personality correlates of peptic ulcer patients. *Journal of Consulting Psychology, 24:* 218-223, 1960.

Merrill, R.M., and Heathers, L.B.: The relation of the MMPI to the Edwards Personal Preference Schedule on a college counseling center sample. *Journal of Consulting Psychology, 20:*310-314, 1956.

Newman, J., and Wischner, G.J.: The performance of a hospitalized neuropsychiatric sample on the Edwards Personal Preference Schedule. *Journal of Clinical Psychology, 16:*99-100, 1960.

Nowicki, S., Jr.: Use of the EPPS in a psychiatric population. *Journal of Clinical Psychology, 23:* 361-362m 1967.

Pasewark, R.A., Davis, F.G., and Fitzgerald, B.J.: Utilization of the Edwards Personal Preference Schedule with disturbed adolescents. *Journal of Clinical Psychology, 24:*451, 1968.

Payne, I.R., Rasmussen, D.M., and Shinedling, M.: Characteristics of obese university females who lose weight. *Psychological Reports, 27:*567-570, 1970.

Perkins, C.W.: Patient manifest-need hierarchy and EPPS results compared. *Journal of Consulting and Clinical Psychology, 32:*221-222,1968.

Pilowsky, I., Spalding, D., Shaw, J., and Korner, P.I.: Hypertension and personality. *Psychosomatic Medicine, 35:*50-56, 1973.

Primavera, L.H., Simon, W.E., and Camisa, J.M.: An investigation of personality and caffeine use. *British Journal of Addiction, 70:*213-215, 1975.

Pryer, M.W., and Distefano, M.K.: Further evaluation of the EPPS with hospitalized alcoholics. *Journal of Clinical Psychology, 26:*205, 1970.

Reiter, H.H.: Some EPPS differences between smokers and nonsmokers. *Perceptual and Motor Skills, 30:*253-254, 1970.

Rosenberg, C.M.: Personality and obsessional neurosis. *British Journal of Psychiatry, 113:*470-477, 1967.

Schwartz, M.L., Dennerll, R.D., and Lin, Yi-Guang.: Similarity of personality trait interrelationships in persons with and without epileptogenic cerebral disfunction. *Journal of Abnormal Psychology, 74:*205-208, 1969.

Scott, E.M., and Manaugh, T.S.: Feminity of alcoholics women's preferences on Edwards Personal Preference Schedule. *Psychological Reports, 38:*847-852, 1976.

Sheppard, C., Ricca, E., Fracchia, J., and Merlis, S.: Psychological needs of suburban male heroin addicts. *Journal of Psychology, 87:*123-128, 1974.

Shipman, W.G., Heath, H.A., and Oken, D.: Response specificity among muscular and autonomic variables. *Archives of General Psychiatry, 23:*369-374, 1970.

Shipman, W.G., Oken, D., and Heath, H.A.: Muscle tension and effort at self-control during anxiety. *Archives of General Psychiatry, 23:*359-368, 1970.

Simon, W.E., Primavera, L.H., Simon, M.G., and Orndoff, R.K.: A comparison of marijuana users and nonusers on a number of personality variables. *Journal of Consulting and Clinical Psychology, 42:*917-918, 1974.

Tucker, S.J., and Cantor, P.D.: Personality and status profiles of peer counselors and suicide attemptors. *Journal of Counseling Psychology, 22:*423-430, 1975.

Van Evra, J.P., and Rosenberg, B.G.: Ego strength and ego disjunction in primary and secondary psychopaths. *Journal of Clinical Psychology, 19:*61-63, 1963.

Watson, R.L., Pasewark, R.A., and Fitzgerald, B.J.: Use of the Edwards Personal Preference Schedule with delinquents. *Psychological Reports, 26:*963-965, 1970.

Weatherley, D.: Some personality correlates of the ability to stop smoking cigarettes. *Journal of Consulting Psychology, 29:*483-485, 1965.

Wunderlich, R.A., Johnson, W.G., and Ball, M.F.: Some personality correlates of obese persons. *Psychological Reports, 32:*1267-1277, 1973.

SECTION IV

VOCATIONAL/EDUCATIONAL USAGE

Chapter 10

USING THE EPPS TO
ASSESS VOCATIONAL INTERESTS

A TTEMPTS to define the relationship of the EPPS needs to vocational interests have generally followed one of three formats: (a) the correlation or factor analysis of the EPPS plus some vocational interest measure (usually the Strong Vocational Interest Blank); (b) the identification of vocational types via multivariate analyses of some sort such as factor analysis or canonical correlation; and (c) the identification of need levels that are characteristic of particular occupation or subgroups within that occupation as well as comparisons of need levels across different occupations. Obviously, the first class of studies should provide information that permits a person's need levels to be used as an indicant of her or his general vocational interests. The second should help one to identify need patterns that lead one to select a particular occupation over another. The other two ideally provide information about which specific need levels are characteristic of different occupational choices and about how areas of specialization within an occupational category differ in terms of expressed needs. In this chapter, studies pertinent to the first two formats will be discussed; Chapter 11 will deal with the third type.

General Interests

Five articles (Atkinson and Lunneborg, 1968; Dunnette, Kirchener, and DeGidio, 1958; Kohlan, 1968; Wakefield and Cunningham, 1975; Suziedelis and Steimel, 1963) have included correlations between the EPPS and various personality and interest measures commonly used in vocational counseling. Four of these studies (Atkinson and Lunneborg, Dunnette et al., Kohlan, and Suziedelis and Steimel) used male samples and the other used a 70 percent female sample. The relationships between EPPS scales and other interest measures reported here have been condensed primarily from these five articles.

ACHIEVEMENT. Need achievement was found to be positively associated with verbal/linguistic career interests (e.g. advertising and law) high investigative interest (e.g. psychology, architecture, and engineering), and theoretical biological science interests (e.g. psychiatry and biology). Interests in skilled and outdoor trades, detailed office work, and business management, i.e. banking, mortician work, and pharmacology, correlated negatively with need achievement. Other EPPS needs that sometimes covaried with achievement were dominance, intraception, endurance, succorance, and exhibition.

DEFERENCE. Preferences for stable situations and for avoiding conflict were positively correlated with need deference. Males for whom deference was one of their two highest needs expressed interests typical of people employed in technical occupations, e.g. Holland's "Realistic" occupations, farming, aviation, and carpentry. Personal contact interests at both administrative and service levels were positively correlated with deference. Examples of administrative personal contact careers are school superintendent, personnel director, and YMCA director. Social science teacher, social worker, and minister are examples of social service occupations.

ORDER. As one of a person's two highest needs, order seems to indicate a lack of interests consistent with social service occupations. Interests consistent with Holland's Conventional theme appear to be characteristic of respondents with high need order. Since computational and clerical interests were positively associated with need order, relevant career interests were those of the accountant, banker, and office worker. Sales interests, i.e. sales managing, real estate sales, and life insurance sales, were negatively correlated with need order as were verbal/linguistic interests. Order sometimes covaried with needs abasement, deference, and endurance.

EXHIBITION. Need exhibition was positively associated with high political values and a preference for being active in groups. Sales (e.g. sales managing, real estate, and life insurance sales) and verbal/linguistics (e.g. law and advertising) interests were positively correlated with need exhibition while occupational interests in applied technical sciences, skilled trades, applied biological science, e.g. general medicine and osteopathy, and detailed office work were negatively correlated. However, as one of a person's two highest needs, need exhibition did not necessarily pertain to occupational interests.

AUTONOMY. Interests in human science (e.g. general medicine, osteopathy, and dentistry), theoretical technical science (e.g. physiology and mathematics), applied technical science (e.g. engineering and chemistry), and verbal/linguistic areas (e.g. law and writing) characterized people with high need autonomy. However, interests in social service, social administration, business management, business office work, e.g. accounting and purchasing, and sales negatively correlated with autonomy. Thus, need autonomy appears to be positively related to interests consistent with Holland's Investigative theme. Needs change, intraception, and deference sometimes covaried with need autonomy.

AFFILIATION. Need affiliation was found to positively relate to interests in business detail, e.g. accounting and office managing. When it was among a person's two highest needs, it also implied interests similar to social service workers. This need seems to describe people who are socially oriented, avoid conflict, prefer stable situations, and like to be active in groups. Interests in human science fields and theoretical technical science have been found to be negatively related to affiliation. Dominance and deference sometimes covaried with need affiliation.

INTRACEPTION. Need intraception appears to be an indicant of a social service orientation. When it covaries with need nurturance, need intraception clusters with the social theme and Social Status Scale of the Vocational Preference Inventory (VPI) and opposes the Investigative and Enterprising themes. Social workers', social science teachers', ministers', psychologists', psychiatrists', and biologists' interests appear to be correlated positively with need intraception. Business management interests correlate negatively with intraception.

SUCCORANCE. The Investigative theme and the Self-control Scale of the VPI correlate positively with need succorance. Technical/skilled/outdoor interests also appear to be positively related to succorance. Sometimes the Succorance Scale covaried with affiliation, heterosexuality, deference, achievement, and endurance. Thus, succorance appears to have a strong social component that does not necessarily relate to career interests, particularly when it is one of a person's two needs.

DOMINANCE. Need dominance appears to measure leadership interests. It has been found to be positively associated with preference for group activity and persuading or directing others. Sales (e.g., sales management and real estate), verbal/linguistic (e.g. advertising, law, and journalism), and social administration (e.g. working as a YMCA physical director, personnel director, or city school superintendent) interests are consistent with need dominance. Interests in applied technical and theoretical science and skilled and outdoor trades were negatively related to dominance. People with high need dominance could probably be categorized in either Holland's Social, Conventional, Enterprising, or Artistic (verbal expression) themes.

ABASEMENT. Need abasement seems to relate to a desire for structure and a lack of social service interests. Interests in skilled trades and outdoor occupations correlated positively with abasement as do interests in physical science, e.g. mathematics, physiology, engineering, and chemistry. Religious values also seem to be positively correlated with this need to some extent. Sales interests were negatively correlated with abasement. While occupational interests subsumed under Holland's Conventional and Realistic themes would appear to be consistent with high need abasement, verbal/linguistic interests were not consistent. Abasement sometimes covaried with the Nurturance, Deference and Order scales.

NURTURANCE. Need nurturance was positively correlated with preferences for working with ideas and for stable situations with an absence of conflict. Social service (e.g. Social work and social science teaching), production managing and applied biological science (e.g. dentistry and veterinary medicine) interests were positively correlated with nurturance while verbal/linguistic interests were negatively correlated. Need nurturance sometimes covaried with abasement, succorance, and intraception. As one of a person's two highest needs, it may not necessarily indicate occupational interests.

CHANGE. When change was one of a person's two highest needs, it was not necessarily associated with occupational interests, but, in general, need change seemed to share some dimensions of Holland's Investigative and Artistic themes. Verbal/linguistic interests appeared to be positively correlated with need change, while skilled trade and outdoor interests often were negatively correlated with this need.

ENDURANCE. Computational interests and a preference for detail characterized people with high need endurance. Occupational interests in business-related office work (e.g. accounting and purchasing), applied technical science (e.g. chemistry and engineering), production management and technical skilled, and outdoor trades (e.g., farming, police work, and painting) were positively correlated with need endurance. Interests in sales, e.g. sales managing and life insurance sales, and verbal/linguistic occupations were negatively correlated. Endurance has also been found to sometimes covary with the Achievement and Succorance scales.

AGGRESSION AND HETEROSEXUALITY. Neither aggression nor heterosexuality were consistently related to vocational interests. However, one study indicated that when heterosexuality was one of male students' two highest needs, it suggested a lack of social service and literary interests. Another single study indicated that aggression might be positively related to sales and verbal/linguistic interests and negatively related to technical, skilled, and outdoor interests.

Vocational Types

The term *vocational types* is used broadly to refer to both the studies in which authors have tested a specific *type* theory or model as well as those in which correlational techniques have been used to search for particular vocational dimensions.

OCCUPATIONAL STEREOTYPES. Two studies have had as their premise the question of whether people held definite stereotypes about certain occupations — teaching in both instances. In the first, Saltz (1960) asked thirty-seven middle-class women to complete the EPPS as they believed the typical teacher would. She then compared their stereotyped need levels with the measured levels of Jackson and Guba's (1957) women elementary and high school teachers.

For elementary teachers, she found that the women expected the teachers to be more achieving, orderly, dominant, and aggressive and less autonomous, affiliative, abasive, nurturant, and changing than the teachers' measured needs indicated that they were. Expected and measured levels of deference, exhibition, succorance, endurance, heterosexuality, and intraception did not differ.

As compared to their measured needs, high school teachers were expected to be more orderly, dominant, aggressive, and intraceptive, and less autonomous, affiliative, abasive, nurturant, and changing. Expected and measured levels of deference, exhibition, succorance, endurance, heterosexuality, and achievement did not differ.

Combining the stereotypes of the two groups, Saltz (1960) concluded in part that the stereotype of teachers that was evident was ". . . one of an ambitious, domineering, managing, fussy, tyrannical woman who has powers that enable her to see more of people's motives than they wish to reveal. She has few friends; she is not interested in people's problems; social mingling is not to her liking" (p. 109).

Wakefield, and Crowl (1974) were seeking a model for the ideal teacher of exceptional students. Using rankings of EPPS needs provided by college professors, superior special education students, and graduate and undergraduate students enrolled in special education programs, they found much consistency among the rankings of the groups. In general, it appeared that the cluster of needs judged most desirable for special education teachers were intraception, nurturance, endurance, and achievement. The second most desirable cluster was order, affiliation, and change. Least important or desirable needs were exhibition, heterosexuality, abasement, and aggression. Smith (1968) presented evidence that intraception, change, affiliation, and nurturance were among the top four measured needs of graduate students enrolled in a special education program.

The results of the Saltz (1960) and the Wakefield and Crowl (1974) studies support the notion that people have certain stereotypes of teachers and that these stereotypes may correspond to reality in some instances. Nevertheless, the teacher type that emerges is not a very favorable one and necessitates questions about how social stereotypes of occupations influence one's personal selection of an occupation.

VOCATIONAL MODELS. Two studies of occupational models have tested vocational models by administering the EPPS and the Strong Vocational Interest Blank to male subjects. Bailey (1971), in an attempt to verify Holland's typology using interest and personality measures, found minimal evidence that EPPS scales, selected by judges to represent the six types, significantly differentiated the types. Only the Enterprising type with positive correlations on the EPPS Dominance Scale and the SVIB Law/Politics Scale and a negative correlation on the Exhibition Scale conformed to judges' a priori formulations.

However, Bailey (1971) did discover six types roughly corresponding to the Holland types, which did not duplicate those anticipated by judges. The first type was characterized by positive loadings for EPPS needs dominance, aggression, change, and exhibition and negative loadings for deference, order, nurturance, and endurance. Relevant positively related SVIB general interest scales were Public Speaking, Law/Politics, Business Management, Adventure, Merchandising, Sales, and Recreational Leadership. Negatively loaded interest scales were Science and Mechanical. Bailey (1971) describes this person as an asocial business type who is concerned with control and manipulation of others and of her or his environment.

The second type consisted of positively loaded abasement, nurturance, deference, affiliation, and dominance needs and negatively loaded autonomy, heterosexuality, and intraception. Positively related interest scales were Religious Activities, Military Activities, Public Speaking, Business Management, Law/Politics, Merchandising, Recreational Leadership, and Social Service; negatively correlated scales were Art and Writing. This person is regarded as being similar to Holland's Social Type, exhibiting a positive but rather dependent social orientation.

Needs characteristic of Type III were endurance, order, and exhibition as contrasted against intraception, nurturance, and affiliation. Positive interests were math, military activities, mechanical things, and technical supervision; negative interests were public speaking, law/politics, social service, teaching, art, writing, and religious activities. Bailey (1971) views this person as one whose "values suggest a preference for asocial, achievement-oriented, concrete kinds of activities and preferences."

Type IV, similar to Holland's Realistic Type, had positively loaded needs for exhibition, autonomy, succorance, abasement, and change and negatively loaded needs for deference, order, intraception, and dominance. Nature, agriculture, and adventure interests opposed law/politics and mathematics interests.

The fifth type contrasted an enterprising orientation against a realistic one: affiliation, nurturance, and endurance against order, autonomy, and intraception. Positively loaded interests were business and sales; negatively loaded ones were military activities, nature, agriculture, and art.

The sixth and final canonical root identified by Bailey (1971) was labeled interests in music and teaching versus preference for adventure or risk taking. Positive correlations were found for order, change, teaching, and music. Negative correlations were found for office practices, adventure, abasement, heterosexuality, and aggression.

Armatas and Collister (1962) developed a model based on test takers' response styles to the SVIB. They speculated that male college freshmen who chose mostly "L" alternatives would be socially oriented; "D" responders would prefer to relate to objects instead of people; "I" responses would be characteristic of passive, apathetic individuals who were overwhelmed by their environment.

From their results, Armatas and Collister (1962) claimed partial support for their model. Males who indicated a disproportionately high number of like responses had high needs for heterosexuality, dominance, and aggression and low needs for succorance and exhibition. These needs were matched by high social service, business contact, and occupational level and low physical science interests. From these combinations, Armatas and Collister concluded that the L-type person is "warm and sociable, dominant and aggressive, enthusiastic and talkative, adventurous and thick-skinned, trustful and adaptable, experimenting and critical, phlegmatic and composed" (p. 153).

High dislike responders had high needs for aggression, succorance, and deference and high physical science, business contact, and occupation level interests. Low needs were heterosexuality and dominance; low interest was social service.

Their third type, males who selected the indifferent response alternative frequently, had low needs for aggression, dominance, and deference and low business detail and occupational level interests. Social service and physical science interests were high.

Results of the Bailey (1971) and the Armatas and Collister (1962) studies suggest that it eventually may be feasible to identify vocational types. However, there was very little overlap between the types identified in the two studies. The only remotely similar types were Bailey's Business Type and Armatas and Collister's L type. Both were characterized by high needs or positively loaded needs for dominance and aggression, but high or low needs for exhibition. Other attempts to identify types (Dunkleberger and Tyler, 1961) have not yielded more relevant needs than one would expect by chance.

VOCATIONAL DIMENSIONS. Cook and his associates (Cook, Lebold, Linden, 1963; Cook, Linden, and McKay, 1961) sought to identify the factors of the EPPS and the Guilford-Zimmerman Temperament Survey that typified education and engineering students. They identified four factors that were common to both groups; (a) social maturity (or dependency), (b) social drive (or avoidance), (c) intraception (or introversion-extroversion), and flexibility (or compulsiveness-conformity).

For teacher trainees the dependency factor has positive factor loadings for affiliation and nurturance and negative loadings for achievement and autonomy. Of these four needs, only nurturance was positively loaded for engineers. The authors concluded that for teachers "behaviors characteristic of this factor suggest a de-emphasis of competition and acceptance of relatively nondemanding life goals" (p. 871). For engineering students this factor was assumed to reflect an acceptance of "nondemanding life goals and need to provide for the welfare of others."

The compulsive conformity factor consisted of positive factor loadings for deference, order, and endurance for the teacher respondents. Renamed *flexibility* for the engineers, the factor consisted of negative loadings for deference, order, exhibition, and endurance; only heterosexuality was positively loaded. The authors theorize that the direction of needs exhibited by the teachers shows "an admission of dependency needs and a need to sustain oneself in a well structured and predictable environment without change" (p. 871). The other factors, avoidance-intraception, common to both groups were characterized by no more than one EPPS need; heterosexuality or dominance for the former and intraception for the latter.

An additional factor, "Authoritarianism, occurred for the teacher sample, but not for the engineering students. Relevant EPPS needs were negative loadings for succorance and abasement and positive loadings for dominance. Cook et al. (1961) interpret this factor as an expression of "needs for status and prestige and a desire to manipulate and control the behavior of others" (p.871).

Since common factors or dimensions were identified for both the engineering and teacher student groups, Cook et al. (1963) concluded that these factors were probably due to characteristics of the instruments. Nevertheless, they suggest that the direction of factor loadings may be due to personality differences between the groups tested.

The relationship between teacher attitudes and EPPS needs was the dimension of interest to Wakefield, Cunningham, and Edwards (1975). Using responses of teacher education students of unspecified sex, they identified a single dimension anchored by affiliation and abasement needs and acquiescence-to-teacher attitudes on one end and nurturance and heterosexuality needs, conflict between teachers and pupils, and belief in children's irresponsible tendencies attitudes on the other. They suggest that the continuum of interpersonal relations underlying the dimension ranges from hostile to cooperative relations.

Discussion and Summary

Considering that Edwards originally speculated that one of the ways in which the EPPS would be useful is as an adjunct to vocational counseling, surprisingly few studies have been undertaken with the goal of identifying motivational and general interest commonalities. When general interests have been the area of concern, investigators have tended to limit their samples to college students, mostly male. The obvious difficulty with such sampling is that one is limited in the generalizations that one can make to other types of samples.

It does appear that some areas would profit from future investigation. Personality and interest measures and the EPPS scales converge often enough to warrant a closer look. People share stereotypes of teachers, and these stereotypes may have some basis in reality. It would be interesting to discover whether there are also shared stereotypes of other occupations and whether one's occupational stereotype influences one's willingness to select a particular occupation. Specific vocational models have rarely been examined more than once. Given the prevalance of vocational theory, which suggests that a person's vocational type or cluster of personality characteristics determines occupational compatibility, identification of relevant need systems might provide a quick method of assessing occupational types.

References

Armatas, J.P., and Collister, E.G.: Personality correlates of SVIB patterns. *Journal of Counseling*

*Psychology, 9:*149-154, 1962.

Atkinson, G., and Lunneborg, C.E.: Comparison of oblique and orthogonal simple structure solutions for personality and interest factors. *Multivariate Behavioral Research, 3:*21-35, 1968.

Bailey, R.L.: Testing Holland's theory. *Measurement and Education in Guidance, 4,* 1971.

Cook, D.L., Lebold, W., and Linden, J.D.: Comparison of factor analyses of education and engineering responses to selected personality inventories. *Education and Psychological Measurement, 21:*865-872, 1961.

Dunkleberger, C.J., and Tyler, L.E.: Interest stability and personality traits. *Journal of Counseling Psychology, 8:*70-74, 1961.

Dunnette, M.D., Kirchener, W.K., and DeGidio, J.: Relations among scores on Edwards Personal Preference Schedule, California Psychological Inventory, and Strong Vocational Interest Blank for an industrial sample. *Journal of Applied Psychology, 42:*178-181, 1958.

Edwards, A.: *Edwards Personal Preference Schedule.* New York, Psychological Corporation, 1954.

Jackson, P.W., and Guba, E.G.: The need structure of in-service teachers on occupational analysis. *The School Review, 65:*176-192, 1957.

Kohlan, R.G.: Relationships between inventoried interests and inventoried needs. *Personnel and Guidance Journal, 46:*592-598, 1968.

Saltz, J.W.: Teacher stereotype: Liability in Recruiting? *School Review, 68:*105-111, 1960.

Suziedelis, A., and Steimel, R.J.: The relationship of need hierarchies to inventoried interests. *Personnel and Guidance Journal, 42:*393-396, 1963.

Wakefield, J.A., and Cunningham, C.H.: Relationships between the Vocational Preference Inventory and the Edwards Personal Preference Schedule. *Journal of Vocational Behavior, 6:*373-377, 1975.

Wakefield, J.A., Jr., Cunningham, C.H., and Edwards, D.D.: Teacher attitudes and personality. *Psychology in the Schools, 12:*345-347, 1975.

Wakefield, W.M., and Crowl, T.K.: Personality characteristics of special educators. *Journal of Experimental Education, 43:*86-89, 1974.

Chapter 11

COLLEGE MAJOR AND OCCUPATIONAL TYPES

S EVERAL authors have attempted to discover the need levels and/or patterns that characterize people pursuing specific college majors (or extracurricular activities) and/or occupations. The three strategies used in the majority of these studies have been (a) to compare the level of EPPS needs expressed by people involved in different occupational fields, (b) to compare subgroups within a field who differ on some personality or performance characteristic, or (c) to compare the specialists to some of the various EPPS norms or to some other specially identified comparison group. Of course, the goal underlying the first type of comparison is to determine whether motivation or needs differ across the selected fields; the second type attempts to find a link between the other personality or performance dimensions and the person's motivation; the specialist-norm comparisons are designed for the purpose of differentiating specific majors or occupations from people in general.

A large number of the studies in which occupational types were investigated have contained means for the groups under study. Since several of the studies have involved the same majors or occupations, another way of addressing the various questions raised about how need levels are related to occupational choice and performance is to factor-analyze the group means reported in the various studies using the groups as the factoring variables, a procedure known as Q typing.

Because of the large number of studies pertaining to the general area of vocational choice and because the needs of college students and employed persons may differ even if they are involved in similar fields, separate Q-type analyses were performed for the majors and the occupational groups.

To address the question of whether there were different subgroups within an area, the analyses were performed on groups whose needs theoretically should have been identical or quite similar. If the hypothesized similarity did exist, then one would expect all of the groups specializing in the same field to have comparable factor loadings on the same (ideally one) factors.

In the subsequent discussion, the results for the college majors and occupations are presented separately. Table 11-I sumarizes descriptive data for the original sources of the college (and high school) groups involved in the analyses; Table 11-III does the same for occupations. To define the factors, means of the groups having a positive factor loading greater than .40 on only one factor were used. These means are presented for majors and occupations in Tables 11-II and 11-IV, respectively. Percentiles reported in the tables in both cases were obtained by using the mean raw scores of the predominating sex (or

148

Table 11 - I

SUMMARY OF FACTORS DESCRIBING COLLEGE MAJORS
AND EXTRACURRICULAR ACTIVITIES PARTICIPANTS

<u>Nursing Students</u>

Author	Sample	N	Mean Age	I	II	III
1. Adams & Klein (1970)	Medical & psychiatric affiliates	50	19.5	.75	.64	
2. Bailey & Claus (1969)*	California sophomores	247	20.8	.92	.27	
3. Bailey & Claus (1969)*	Completers of professional sequence	55		.90	.37	
4. Bailey & Claus (1969)	Indiana sophomores	212		.84	.52	
5. Gardiner (1976)	Sophomores, juniors, seniors	164	20.8	.69	.66	
6. Gynther & Gertz (1962)*[1,2]	"poor" academic & clinical performers	43	20.07	.82	.36	
7. Gynther & Gertz (1962)	"good" performers	44	20.07	.88	.41	
8. Gynther & Gertz (1962)	Psychiatric nursing	222	20.17	.86	.45	
9. Psathas & Plapp (1968)*	Seniors	49		.26	.91	
10. Psathas & Plapp (1968)	Seniors (1963)	53		.52	.84	
11. Psathas & Plapp (1968)	Freshmen completers	49		.78	.56	

Table 11 - I (continued)

Author	Sample	N	Mean Age	Factor I	II	III
12. Psathas & Plapp (1968)	Dropouts	30		.78	.57	
13. Psathas & Plapp (1968)	Retested Dropouts	30		.70	.67	
14. Reece (1961)	Withdrawers	32		.83	.44	
15. Stein (1969)*	Sophomores (1962)	61		.91	.36	
16. Stein (1969)	Seniors (1965)	61		.41	.87	
17. Stein (1969)	Sophomores (1965)	131	19.60	.81	.56	
18. Stein (1969)	Seniors (1967)	93	21.60	.44	.86	
	Percent Variance			86	7	

Liberal Arts Majors

Author	Sample	N	Mean Age	Factor I	II	III
1. Edwards (1959)	College norms (M)	760		.76	.27	.55
2. Edwards (1959)*	College norms (F)			.21	.93	.20
3. Fletcher (1971)*[2]	Sports non-participants (M)	278		.26	.20	.86
4. Frank & Kirk (1970)	Forestry graduates (M)	114		.49	.06	.78
5. Hetlinger & Hildreth (1961)	College non-debaters (M)	28		.46	.36	.79
6. Hetlinger & Hildreth (1961)*	College debaters (M)	28		.85	-.26	.39
7. Hetlinger & Hildreth (1961)	College debaters (F)	23		.70	.52	.32
8. Hetlinger & Hildreth (1961)*	College non-debaters (F)	23		-.08	.96	.09
9. Hetlinger & Hildreth (1961)	High school debaters (M)	21		.66	-.04	.70

Table 11 - I (continued)

Author	Sample	N	Mean Age	Factor I	II	III
10. Hetlinger & Hildreth (1961)	High school non-debaters (M)	21		.64	.21	.59
11. Klett (1957)*	High school boys	799	17.1	.24	.37	.85
12. Klett (1957)*	High school girls	834	16.9	-.11	.96	.21
13. Penn & Baker (1976)	Graduating social workers	30		.56	.64	.16
14. Walsh & Palmer (1970)	Random university juniors & seniors (M)	35		.64	.34	.54
15. Walsh & Palmer (1970)	Prelaw students (M)	35		.94	.08	.18
16. Walsh & Palmer (1970)	First year law students (M)	35		.80	.09	.58
17. Walsh & Palmer (1970)	Third year law students (M)	35		.88	-.03	.40
	Percent Variance			64	19	6

Medicine Affiliated Specialties

Author	Sample	N	Mean Age	Factor I	II	III
1. Allen & Foreman (1976)	Speech therapists (F)	34	17.82	.13	.98	-.02
2. Allen & Foreman (1976)	Occupational therapists (F)	58		.02	.97	.20
3. Allen & Foreman (1976)	Physiotherapists (F)	57	18.21	.00	.98	.12
4. Allen & Foreman (1976)	Combined therapists (F)	149	18.10	.04	.99	.11
5. Manhold et al. (1963)	Freshmen dental classes	66	25.41	.89	.07	.22

Table 11 - I (continued)

Author	Sample	N	Age	I	II	III
6. Manhold et al. (1963)	Freshmen medical students	74	22.12	.80	.14	.55
7. McDonald & Gynther (1963)	Medical students	66	23.5	.79	-.00	.45
8. McDonald & Gynther (1963)	Achieving medical students	7		.77	.16	-.11
9. McDonald & Gynther (1963)	Low ability medical students	8		.81	.05	.54
10. McDonald & Gynther (1963)	Over-achieving medical students	6		.82	-.11	.34
11. McDonald & Gynther (1963)	Under-achieving medical students	6		.30	.25	.85
12. Parker (1958)[2]	Non-authoritarian medical students	74	22.12	.68	.29	.57
13. Parker (1958)[2]	Medium-authoritarian medical students			.70	.07	.67
14. Parker (1958)[2]	Authoritarian medical students			.83	-.14	.42
15. Stone et al. (1972)	Physician's extension	19		.31	.10	.81
16. Vineyard et al. (1962)	First year pharmacy students (M)	50		.56	.38	.32
	Percent Variance			56	24	6

Education Majors

Author	Sample	N	Age	I	II	III
1. Coody & Hinely (1967)	"Submissive" secondary student teachers	12		-.03	.95	

Table 11 - I (continued)

Author	Sample	N	Age	I	II	III
2. Coody & Hinely (1967)	"Dominant" secondary student teachers	12		.90	.17	
3. Gordon (1963)	Secondary volunteers for an experimental professional program (M)	28		.93	.13	
4. Gordon (1963)	Secondary interns (M)	30		.92	.19	
5. Gordon (1963)	Secondary volunteers for an experimental professional program (F)	57		.77	.52	
6. Gordon (1963)	Secondary interns (F)	41		.55	.79	
7. Gordon (1963)	Elementary volunteers for an experimental professional program (F)	53		.64	.68	
8. Medley (1961)	Elementary interns (F)	25		.54	.71	
9. Merrill (1960)	Freshmen-Sophomores (M)	781	20.4	.72	.41	
10. Scandrette (1962)	Elementary student teachers (F)	73		.24	.93	
11. Scandrette (1962)	Secondary student teachers (F)	89		.59	.75	
12. Vineyard et al. (1962)	Education juniors (M)	50		.67	.49	
	Percent Variance			71	14	
	Physically Active Majors					
1. Balazs & Nickerson (1976)	Olympic contenders (F)	24		.82	.43	
2. Fletcher (1971)	High school activity participants (M)	672		.27	.91	

Table 11 - I (continued)

Author	Sample	N	Age	I	II	III
3. Singer (1969)	Collegiate baseball players (M)	59		.26	.90	
4. Singer (1969)	Collegiate tennis players (M)	10		.12	.83	
5. Thorpe (1958)	Senior physical education majors (F)	100		.88	.18	
6. Thorpe (1958)	Graduate student physical education majors (F)	55		.92	.06	
7. Wendt & Patterson (1974)	Individual sports parti-cipants (F)	21		.76	.51	
8. Wendt & Patterson (1974)	Team sports participants (F)	21		.88	.22	
	Percent Variance			64	19	

[1]Groups with factor loadings $\geq$ .40 on only one factor are marked with astericks.

[2]Means estimated from author's T scores.

males when neither sex predominated), which were transformed using Edwards's college or adult norms as appropriate. Mean standard deviations are not reported in the tables because many of the original sources did not report standard deviations.

College Majors

Types of Nurses. A large number of studies (eighteen) were located in which nursing students were the subjects of interest and for which means for the various needs were reported. The Q-type analysis indicated that two factors accounted for 93 percent of the variance to be explained with Factor I accounting for 86 percent of that variance. The four groups used to define the first factor in descending order of their factor loadings were two groups of sophomore nursing students (Bailey and Claus, 1969; Stein, 1969), nursing students who completed their professional sequence (Bailey and Claus, 1969), and "poor" students as indicated by academic and clinical performance (Gynther and Gertz, 1962). Only one group, senior nursing students (Psathas and Plapp, 1968), defined the other factor. One might think of these groups as pure types.

Table 11 - II

SUMMARY OF OCCUPATIONAL FACTORS

Nurses

Author	Sample	N	Mean Age	I	II	III	IV
1. Edwards (1959)	Adult norms (F)	4932		.29	.92	.13	
2. Edwards (1959)	Adult norms (M)	4031		.19	.72	-.43	
3. Navran & Stauffacher (1957)[1]	"Intermediate" nurses	66	31.21	.53	.34	.68	
4. Reece (1961)[1]	Graduated nurses	55		.86	.37	.22	
5. Stauffacher & Navran (1957)[1]	VA psychiatric	196	32.48	.88	.17	.30	
6. Stauffacher & Navran (1957)[1]	"Best" nurses	64	31.44	.77	.21	.34	
7. Stauffacher & Navran (1968)	Affiliated nurses	263		.78	.39	.21	
8. Stauffacher & Navran (1968)	Inexperienced nurses	8		.53	.34	.68	
9. Stauffacher & Navran (1968)[1]	Surgical nurses	66		.90	.32	.14	
10. Stauffacher & Navran (1968)[1]	"Follow-up" nurses	263		.88	.36	.21	
11. Stauffacher & Navran (1968)	Community nurses	47		.83	.48	.13	
12. Stauffacher & Navran (1968)	Medical nurses	263		.77	.56	.20	
13. Stauffacher & Navran (1968)	Administrative/ teaching	10		-.14	.00	-.79	
14. Stauffacher & Navran (1957)	"Poorest" nurses	66	34.69	.67	.58	.09	

Table 11 - II (continued)

Author	Sample	N	Age	I	II	III	IV
15. Stauffacher & Navran (1968)	Psychiatric nurses	10		.91	-.06	-.14	
	Percent Variance			66	11	8	

Teachers

Author	Sample	N	Age	I	II	III	IV
1. Anderson (1969)	Environmentally "open" elementary teachers	71		.81	.00	.51	.16
2. Anderson (1969)	Environmentally "closed" elementary teachers	99		.82	.09	.44	-.03
3. Eberlein (1970)	Elementary teachers (F)	293		.94	.09	.26	-.08
4. Edwards (1959)	Adult norms (F)	4932		.78	-.24	.54	.05
5. Edwards (1959)[1]	Adult norms (M)	4031		.28	.28	.87	.02
6. Goldman & Heald (1967)	Veteran teachers (M)	48		.21	.40	.80	.05
7. Goldman & Heald (1967)	Veteran teachers (F)	221		.88	.05	.42	.09
8. Goldman & Heald (1967)	Experienced teachers (F)	127		.88	.42	-.05	.10
9. Goldman & (1967)[1]	Teachers with 1-3 years experience (F)	140		.89	.33	-.25	-.03
10. Goldman (1969)[1]	Urban elementary teachers (M)	36		.30	.93	.05	-.01
11. Goldman (1969)[1]	Urban secondary teachers (M)	133		.12	.94	.26	-.00
12. Goldman (1969)[1]	Urban elementary teachers (F)	369		.97	.13	.16	-.07
13. Gordon (1963)	"Mature" teachers (M)	53		.33	.71	.54	-.03

Table 11 - II (continued)

Author	Sample	N	Age	I	II	III	IV
14. Gray (1963)	Secondary teachers (M)	50		.40	.78	.17	.20
15. Jackson & Guba (1957)	Elementary teachers (F)	196	34.9	.96	.04	.22	.12
16. Jackson & Guba (1957)[1]	Teachers for 4-9 years (F)	72		.96	.02	.11	.13
17. Jackson & Guba (1957)[1]	Teachers for 0-3 years (M)	25		.07	.95	-.07	-.16
18. Jackson & Guba (1957)[1]	Elementary teachers (M)	27		.02	.98	.02	.06
19. Jackson & Guba (1957)[1]	Inexperienced teachers	47		.21	.92	-.20	-.18
20. Jackson & Guba (1957)[1]	Experienced teachers (M)	74		.10	.95	.15	.03
21. Jackson & Guba (1957)	Teachers for minimum of 10 years (F)	93		.82	-.03	.53	.08
22. Jackson & Guba (1957)[1]	Teachers with 0-3 yrs. experience (F)	79		.91	.19	-.13	.20
23. Jackson & Guba (1957)[1]	Teachers with 4-9 years	55		-.03	.90	.14	.15
24. Jackson & Guba (1957)[1]	High school teachers	91		.08	.91	.28	.14
25. Jackson & Guba (1957)[1]	Teachers with minimum 10 yrs. experience (M)			.18	.77	.34	.28
26. Kemp (1964)	Secondary teachers	45		.40	.32	.06	.78
27. Locke (1962)[1]	Secondary teachers (M)	81	35.31	.13	.88	.08	.37
28. Locke (1962)	Active coaches (M)	44	33.59	.36	.77	.15	.42
29. Merrill (1960)	"Mature" science teachers	53	34	.33	.71	.54	-.03

Table 11 - II (continued)

Author	Sample	N	Age	I	II	III	IV
30. Rincon & Ray (1974)[1]	Bilingual ethnic teachers (F)	7	21.71	.81	.35	.05	-.07
31. Rincon & Ray (1974)	Bilingual ethnic teaching aides (F)	7	39.75	.55	.25	.63	.11
32. Robertson & Haas (1970)[1]	Utah social studies teachers	62		-.07	.95	.12	.06
33. Thorpe (1958)[1]	"Successful" physical ed teachers (F)	100		.78	.37	.27	.31
34. Goldman (1969)	Urban secondary teachers (F)	119		.79	.58	-.00	.01
35. Jackson & Guba (1957)[1]	High school teachers (F)	52	34.9	.90	.11	.34	.12
	Percent Variance			57	25	8	3
Heterogeneous Occupations							
1. Bromer et al.(1962)	Craft foreman (M)	56	45.5	.31	.83	.11	.22
2. Campbell et al. (1962)	Nonsales personnel	93		.59	.70	.90	.36
3. Campbell et al. (1962)	Sales employees	50		.76	.33	.31	.35
4. Edwards (1959)	Adult norms (F)	4932		-.44	.78	.25	-.18
5. Edwards (1959)	Adult norms (M)	4031		.24	.92	.04	-.05
6. Ferrari (1965)	Psychiatric nursing assistants (M)			.45	.36	.34	-.03
7. Fry & Reinhardt (1969)	Navy pilots (M)			.92	-.16	.27	.12
8. Gray (1963)	Mechanical engineers	50		.93	.29	-.13	.11
9. Gray (1963)	Certified public accountants (M)	50		.95	.18	.02	.12

Table 11 - II (continued)

Author	Sample	N	Age	I	II	III	IV
10. Kemp (1964)	Secondary school principals	45		.21	.70	.13	.57
11. Kemp (1964)	Secondary school counselors	45		.18	.20	.87	.35
12. Kirchner (1962)	Retail sales applicants (M)	97		.77	.15	.41	.39
13. Kirchner (1962)	Industrial sales applicants (M)	66		.79	.17	.45	.30
14. Kirchner (1962)	Retail salesmen (M)	69		.84	.07	.38	.26
15. Kirchner (1962)	Industrial salesmen (M)	49		.81	.08	.46	.26
16. Merrill (1960)	School administrators (M)	32	38.4	.13	.70	.38	.50
17. Nevis & Parker (1961)	Job applicants & employees (M)	307		.69	.37	.47	.40
18. Novello & Youssef (1974a)	General aviation pilots (M)	170	33.3	.92	-.05	.30	-.01
19. Novello & Youssef (1974b)	General aviation pilots (F)	87		.44	.35	.70	-.24
20. Roemmich (1967)	Counselors (M)	39		.52	.02	.76	.26
21. Roemmich (1967)	Counselors (F)	20		.18	.22	.92	-.13
22. Rychlak (1963)	Management personnel (M)	84	29.15	.48	.02	-.01	.79
23. Sheppard et al. (1974)	Police officers (M)	33	33.8	.68	-.55	.28	.05
24. Tolor (1961)	Psychiatric aides (F)	40	43.33	-.31	.91	.18	-.08
25. Tolor (1961)	Psychiatric aides (M)	33	43.50	.23	.86	.20	.11
	Percent Variance			54	22	9	5

[1]Used to define factor

Factor I seems to measure the need to sacrifice one's self in the service of others. The five highest mean needs that defined this factor were intraception, nurturance, affiliation, abasement, and change; the five lowest needs were aggression, autonomy, order, succorance, and dominance. Thus the picture that develops is one of a group of women who are extremely concerned about the well-being and motivations of others and, perhaps, overcome their self-doubts by sacrificing themselves in the service of others' needs. They worry about them, take care of them, and are happiest when they find themselves in

Table 11 - III

MEANS USED TO DEFINE COLLEGE MAJOR FACTORS

Factors[1]

	Nursing Students				Liberal Arts					
	I		II		I		II		III	
Needs	M	P	M	P	M	P	M	P	M	P
	(G=4)		(G=1)		(G=2)		(G=3)		(G=2)	
Ach	11.95	47	11.43	45	18.12	74	12.36	47	15.19	50
Def	13.18	62	10.55	44	11.14	52	12.08	50	11.55	63
Ord	11.01	64	10.78	52	10.20	54	10.49	55	10.76	63
Exh	13.63	52	15.82	55	15.13	62	14.55	63	15.26	62
Aut	10.67	45	13.22	52	14.70	61	11.85	63	14.14	52
Aff	17.28	50	14.96	44	13.08	36	17.69	58	14.46	45
Int	18.44	58	18.39	51	16.66	57	16.60	49	14.00	39
Suc	11.90	51	12.47	49	10.80	58	13.01	59	11.08	58
Dom	11.91	36	12.55	45	19.24	63	12.93	42	14.14	27
Aba	16.73	66	14.49	48	11.04	45	16.91	66	14.80	75
Nur	18.34	66	15.80	49	13.60	55	16.95	58	13.38	46
Chg	16.66	52	16.41	48	12.86	33	17.23	52	16.35	57
End	14.73	69	10.80	47	12.20	51	12.53	57	14.84	69
Het	13.66	52	19.24	59	16.08	39	13.92	52	17.17	45
Agg ·	9.93	51	13.10	55	15.01	72	10.56	60	13.05	57

[1] Five highest means are single-underlined;

Five lowest are double-underlined.

[2] G equals the number of groups from which the means were calculated;

P equals percentile of mean (college norms).

Table 11 - III (continued)

	Medicine Affiliates			Education Majors		Physically Active Majors			
	I		II	I	II	I		II	
	M	P	M	M	M	M	P	M	P
	(G=7)		(G=3)	(G=3)	(G=1)	(G=3)		(G=3)	
Ach	16.01	51	12.45	15.55	13.8	13.32	58	16.62	66
Def	11.96	52	10.35	11.52	15.0	12.35	47	10.37	43
Ord	11.59	54	9.07	9.01	11.8	9.05	46	9.35	46
Exh	14.08	49	13.57	14.73	13.3	14.44	52	14.81	62
Aut	12.57	43	14.22	14.09	10.5	12.79	62	14.31	52
Aff	13.84	48	17.91	15.01	20.0	17.24	50	14.36	45
Int	16.38	50	16.82	17.24	20.0	17.81	58	15.00	45
Suc	9.91	48	14.09	10.55	14.9	12.61	59	10.87	58
Dom	16.32	38	10.35	17.40	9.2	13.87	51	16.58	38
Aba	12.82	61	14.02	11.45	16.4	15.49	58	13.92	67
Nur	14.92	63	18.34	14.15	16.4	16.67	58	13.31	46
Chg	14.14	41	18.27	16.21	15.9	17.93	59	14.89	50
End	15.86	75	12.77	12.14	12.9	12.99	57	13.29	57
Het	16.99	45	14.85	15.74	13.0	13.16	45	17.37	45
Agg	12.71	57	12.79	12.67	7.8	10.44	51	14.51	65

the midst of a cohesive group of them. Their pattern of needs also suggests that they are relatively invisible and nonassertive people, although the high need for change and the low need for order suggests that they might not be entirely pleased with the environment in which they find themselves. Concern for others or self-sacrificers may be appropriate names for this factor. All but one of the nursing student groups, senior nursing students (Psathas and Plapp, 1968), had factor loadings of at least .40 on the self-sacrificing dimension suggesting the presence of some level of those needs for most of the nursing students.

Factor II, represented by high needs for heterosexuality, intraception, change, nurturance, and exhibition and low needs for deference, order, endurance, achievement, and succorance, suggests a lack of conventionality. Women who score high on this factor want to be visible; they think about and care for others, but they reject structure in their environment and their per-

Table 11 - IV

SUMMARY OF MEAN NEEDS USED TO DEFINE OCCUPATIONAL FACTORS [1]

Nurses

Need	I (G=7)	P	II (G=3)	P	III (G=1)	P
Aba	15.22	51	15.93	58	17.5	74
Ach	12.81	58	14.56	64	15.7	79
Aff	16.80	50	17.09	50	16.3	41
Agg	11.17	60	11.24	60	10.7	60
Aut	11.47	45	12.74	62	9.9	36
Chg	16.54	42	14.95	35	13.7	28
Def	13.03	62	13.64	73	11.5	50
Dom	12.87	42	11.88	36	13.6	51
End	13.74	63	15.82	76	16.4	76
Exh	14.00	52	12.24	30	14.3	52
Het	14.48	52	9.61	24	12.5	45
Int	17.71	58	14.52	28	15.1	35
Nur	16.50	50	16.72	58	17.1	66
Ord	12.36	72	15.09	88	13.2	77
Suc	11.34	44	12.85	59	11.9	51

Teachers

Need	I (G=9) M	P	II (G=11) M	P	III (G=1) M	P
Aba	14.80	36	12.16	33	14.59	49
Ach	13.54	60	15.90	65	14.79	56
Aff	17.29	44	14.39	48	14.51	58
Agg	10.36	55	12.53	46	13.06	54
Aut	11.87	54	13.84	54	14.02	54
Chg	16.53	53	15.13	62	13.87	54
Def	14.50	46	13.74	52	14.19	52
Dom	12.27	71	17.35	69	14.50	50
End	14.79	39	14.77	37	16.97	52
Exh	13.38	70	14.20	66	12.75	57
Het	12.70	78	14.38	66	11.21	54
Int	17.16	70	16.11	69	14.18	53
Nur	16.36	31	13.50	40	15.67	55
Ord	12.60	30	12.04	33	14.69	55
Suc	12.14	46	9.61	50	10.78	58

[1] See notes at Table 11 - III.

Table 11 - IV *(continued)*

Heterogeneous Occupations

Need	I^2 (G=8) M^3	P	II (G=5) M	P	III (G=2) M	P
Aba	11.59	33	15.81	62	11.94	18
Ach	17.32	74	14.34	46	13.34	50
Aff	13.33	39	14.68	58	16.99	44
Agg	13.18	54	11.61	46	10.03	55
Aut	13.42	46	11.90	37	12.86	64
Chg	15.07	62	14.58	62	17.39	60
Def	12.34	32	15.20	62	14.66	56
Dom	18.30	75	13.41	44	15.14	85
End	15.97	44	17.40	52	14.26	32
Exh	14.81	75	12.04	47	13.96	78
Het	15.84	73	10.04	50	14.56	84
Int	14.19	53	15.87	69	19.52	89
Nur	12.45	26	16.40	55	15.04	24
Ord	12.52	40	15.59	63	10.92	19
Suc	9.45	42	10.86	58	16.99	44

2 G = number of groups defining factor; P = percentile of mean (adult norms).

3 Five highest raw score means are underlined; five lowest are double-underlined.

---

sonal lives. All but six of the nursing groups had positive loadings of at least .40 on this factor although it seems to be most characteristic of senior nursing students.

Further examination of the various groups that load heavily on this factor suggests that loadings on Factor II are associated with impending graduation, dropping out of programs, or heterogeneity of sampling. Acting out or rebels seems to describe the commonality inherent in Factor II. And the conflict between caring for others and caring for one's self seems to characterize the general style of nursing students.

LIBERAL ARTS MAJORS. Included in this group were the various norm groups of high school and college undergraduates of unspecified majors, students involved in extracurricular activities that are not elsewhere categorized, and those occupations for which limited data were available and/or whose area of emphases seemed to differ from the other more homogeneous groupings.

Because both sexes appear in this group and because a variety of occupations and activities are included, one would expect a larger number of factors to occur in this analysis, supporting the notion that diversity of occupation should be linked to diversity of needs. In fact, three factors did occur for the liberal arts group.

Factor I, defined by male college debaters (Hetlinger and Hildreth, 1961) and first-year law students (Walsh and Palmer, 1970), measures a need for social dominance. Highest means needs were dominance, achievement, intraception, heterosexuality, and exhibition; lowest needs were order, succorance, deference, abasement, and endurance. People scoring high on this factor are assertive and self-assured; they enjoy being the center of attention and having leadership roles; they reject conventional attitudes and behavior. Though they have a need to analyze and understand other people, they probably use this understanding as a means of getting ahead.

Groups who did not have significant loadings on this factor were female nondebaters, male nonparticipants in sports, Edwards' college female norms, and Klett's high school boys and girls. Since most of the norm or comparison nonmajor groups of both sexes do not load heavily on this factor and since only one of the norm groups has its highest loading on this factor, it is probably safe to conclude that the drive for social dominance is not a "people-in-general" characteristic.

Factor II, defined by female college students not involved in debating as an extracurricular activity, the EPPS female college norms, and high school girls, seems to measure "typical femininity." It is not unlike the self-sacrificing factor of the nursing groups in that high needs include affiliation, change, nurturance, abasement, and intraception. Yet, the relative level of the needs for the two groups appears to be different. The norm groups have a somewhat higher need to belong to a social group and to be noticed. They are less likely to respond positively to authority or structure as indicated by low needs for deference and order. However, they also tend to lack self-assurance and probably do not actively seek to satisfy their own needs. Besides the groups used to define the factor, only female college debaters and social workers had significant positive loadings on this factor.

Female social workers loaded substantially on Factors I and II, indicating the presence of a combination of instrumental and expressive needs. In her comparison of physical therapists and occupational therapists who worked with physically disabled people to social workers and occupational therapists who worked with psychiatric populations, Brollier (1970) found that the latter group had higher needs for autonomy and dominance, which is additional support for the idea that a heavy dose of instrumental characteristics may be needed if one is to become a social worker.

Judging from the groups who have high loadings on Factor III, all of the male samples and none of the female samples, it measures typical masculinity. Descriptive of this factor are high needs for heterosexuality, change, exhibition, achievement, and endurance and low needs for order, succorance, deference, nurturance, and intraception. Groups who load high on this factor have little concern for the well-being of others relative to their own needs. That heterosexuality is a high need suggests a concern for sexual and, perhaps, sex role issues. However, achievement and competition appear to be primary motivators. This factor seems to especially characterize young men's interests generally rather than vocational interests per se.

MEDICINE AFFILIATED SPECIALTIES. A diverse group of specializations compose this group, including four types of female therapy students and nine groups of male medical students and related specialists. The groups divided into three factors, one of which was entirely female and the other two of which were entirely male.

Factor I, one of the male factors, consisted of students who had high needs for heterosexuality, achievement, exhibition, intraception, and dominance and low needs for deference, order, autonomy, succorance, and change. Of those groups having exclusively significant loadings, dental students loaded highest and pharmacy students loaded lowest on the factor. A general need for social power and status summarizes this factor.

Parker's (1958) analysis of medical students with different levels of authoritarianism suggests that Factor I may reflect conflict over sexual issues, a predilection for the use of concrete procedures for helping people rather than for ephemeral relationship qualities.

Haley and Lerner (1972) factor analyzed male medical students' grades and responses to various personality measures and concluded that there were three types of academic performance, each of which seemed to be related to different personality characteristics. The first type, general course grades, required a person with a high need to please others (relevant EPPS needs were nurturance and affiliation). Intellectual people (relevant EPPS needs were consistency and abasement) and those with mathematical ability (relevant EPPS need was change) did not do as well in their general course work. Students who did well in courses requiring a great deal of memorization were technician types. Their intellectual ability was not high, instead they tended to "plug away at whatever is required to succeed." Relevant EPPS needs were high endurance, deference, order, and achievement and low autonomy, aggression, and exhibition. Successful performance in mathematically oriented courses and behavioral science courses was characteristic of students whose orientation was humanitarian as opposed to authoritarian.

Kole and Matarazzo's (1963) study in which they found high needs for achievement and endurance and low needs for succorance and abasement imply an interpretation similar to Haley and Lerner's (1972), whereas Yufit et als'. (1969) study suggests that the medical specialty one chooses during medical training may be linked to different need levels. As compared to the college norms, they found that of the fourteen freshmen medical students with an internal medicine preference, 64 percent had high needs for heterosexuality, 57 percent had high needs for nurturance, and 64 percent had low needs for order; of those fourteen students selecting surgery, 78 percent had high need for aggression, 64 percent had high need for autonomy, and 71 percent had low needs for succorance and heterosexuality. Needs for nurturance and intraception tended to be highest among students who chose pediatrics.

Heist's (1960) study of dental students reported findings that were not particularly consistent with the loading of dental students on Factor I. He reported high needs for deference, order, and endurance and low needs for autonomy, change, and dominance. Thus, his sample tended to be conservative in attitude and typical of what one would expect theoretically of an authoritarian personality. More studies are needed of dental students.

Factor II is composed of Australian physiotherapists, occupational therapists, speech therapists, plus the three groups combined. This group of women shows a pattern of strong needs to care for others (nurturance, affiliation, and intraception), flexibility (change), sexuality or sex role issues and a lack of interest in status (dominance), achievement, or structured personal relationships and environments (order, deference, and endurance). However, Crane's (1962) study of occupational therapists indicated that need for order was positively correlated with grade point average and need for change was negatively correlated.

Using supervisors' evaluations of student performance in different clinical specialties, Lind (1970) found that performance in general medicine and surgery was partially predicted by endurance; psychiatry was partially predicted by dominance and nurturance; pediatrics performance was partially predicted by succorance; and performance in physical disabilities was partially predicted by order. Thus, it is possible that many needs are relevant to quality of performance depending upon the situation.

Among employed occupational and physical therapists (who worked with physically disabled clients), Brollier (1970) found average needs for achievement, autonomy, deference, nurturance, and dominance and a high average need for intraception and a low need for order. Those therapists who worked with psychiatric populations showed similar patterns of needs although they had higher needs for dominance and autonomy. Thus, her results seem to confirm the pattern of needs revealed by the factor analysis.

EDUCATION MAJORS. Two factors describe the ten groups of education majors. The "pure" groups comprising Factor I were male secondary education majors who volunteered for an experimental education program (Gordon, 1963), male secondary interns (Gordon, 1963), and student teachers of unspecified sex whose supervising teachers reported that they were extremely dominant (Coody and Hinely, 1967).

Factor I members were characterized by high needs to direct and to understand others' motives, a liking for novel situations, and a dislike for structured situations or conventional attitudes; they tended to be self-sufficient and self-confident and to reject nurturing from others. All of the education groups except "submissive" student teachers had substantial loadings on Factor I.

Factor II is represented by one pure group, Coody and Hinely's (1967) student teachers who were described as being submissive by their supervisors. Characteristic of this factor is an other-orientation, marked by a strong concern for others' well-being and a lack of self-confidence, which may cause the person to be inhibited and self-effacing. All of the groups of female education majors and one of the groups of male majors had significant loadings on Factor I as well as on Factor II, though females loaded heavier on Factor II than I; the reverse was true of the male group.

Cangemi, Harryman, Coan, and Kesler's (1974) attempt to manipulate leadership needs of education majors indicates that a brief training module was effective in increasing the needs for aggression and reducing the needs for deference and abasement to a statistically significant (though perhaps not practically significant) extent. Needs for autonomy, intraception, succorance, and dominance were not influenced by their training program. Cangemi et al.'s findings suggest that it might be possible to modify some of the characteristics of submissive teachers in a more healthful direction, but probably not to any appreciable extent.

PHYSICALLY ACTIVE MAJORS. The samples contained in this grouping consist of men and women who participate in physical activities either as a major or as an extracurricular activity. Again two factors explained most of the variance for this specialty area.

Loading heavier on Factor I were female graduate student and senior physical education majors (Thorpe, 1958) and female team sports participants (Wendt and Patterson, 1974). Women loading heavily on this factor seem to be involved in physical activities primarily as a means of satisfying strong needs for novel situations and social relationships. Although they do not value structured environments and deferential relationships, they are likely to be neither self-assertive nor self-expressive.

Factor II consists of college men who participated in high school activities (Fletcher, 1971), male college baseball players, and tennis players. This group is characterized by a high concern for sex or sex role issues combined with a need to achieve by leading others. They reject the conventional and prefer the novel. Caring for or being cared for by others are low among their hierarchy of needs.

While it is tempting to think of Factors I and II as separate physically active female and male dimensions, it is notable that several of the samples of female athletes, e.g. olympic competitors, had substantial loadings on both factors, though the same was not true for males.

Studies that have involved attempts to differentiate sports types on the basis of individual need differences have generally indicated an absence of consistent differences. In three studies (Higgs, 1972; Wendt and Patterson, 1974; Singer, 1969) no significant differences were reported for highly competitive as compared to average competitive female physical education majors and female and male individual versus team sports competitors, respectively. Harris (1963) compared female physical education majors differing in level of physical fitness and found that the "fit" group had significantly higher needs for endurance and intraception. Fletcher (1971) found small significant correlations between six EPPS needs and male college freshmen's participation in intramural sports. Positive correlations were reported for order, affiliation, dominance, and heterosexuality; negative correlations were reported for achievement and autonomy. The small size of the correlations caused the author to question the practical significance of his findings.

Studies in which samples involved in sports were compared to normative groups also suggest the absence of a definitive sports personality. Most of the studies have involved female samples. From her comparison of successful physical education teachers, graduate students and seniors to the college norms, Thorpe (1958) concluded that the physical education group had higher needs for deference, order, intraception, dominance, and endurance and lower needs for autonomy, succorance, nurturance, heterosexuality, and aggression.

Dayries and Grimm (1970) found that women intercollegiate athletes had a higher need for intraception and a lower need for order than the norm group. Using a sample of Olympic competitors, Balazs and Nickerson (1976) found that the mean profile for the women revealed high needs for achievement and autonomy and low needs for affiliation, intraception, dominance, exhibition, and change. However, neither the high nor the low needs was much beyond the normal range. Williams, Hoepner, Moody, and Ogilvie (1970) reported that champion level fencers only had higher than average needs for achievement.

Occupations

NURSING FACTORS. The thirteen nursing samples represented among the nursing factors were abstracted from Stauffacher and Navran's (1968) five-year follow-up samples of nurses and various subspecialties of which the follow-up sample was composed. Veterans' hospital psychiatric nurses whose job performance was rated best, poorest, or intermediate (Stauffacher and Navran, 1957) by their supervisors were included in this grouping as were Reece's (1961) subgroup of nursing students who successfully completed a three-year nursing program.

All of the nursing samples but two had significant positive loadings on Factor I. "Empathic social interest, liking for novelty, and self-abasiveness versus passivity" seem to be appropriate names for the poles characterizing this factor. Relative to their other needs, women who load heavily on this factor have a need to understand others, to belong to a close knit group, and to care for others. They have little need to express themselves verbally or to satisfy individualistic needs. The presence of a relatively high abasement score among their constellation of needs suggests that their social concern and lack of positive self-concern may mask an underlying lack of self-confidence.

Factor II seems to measure normative characteristics. As the pure samples for this factor were the EPPS male and female adult norms and a group of nurses who had had little work experience since their graduation five years before (Stauffacher and Navran, 1968). Concern for others and self-sacrifice versus invisibility describe the dimensions of this factor. A theme of martyrdom seems to run through the preeminent needs of this factor. People who load heavily on this factor want to belong to a social group and, perhaps, they ensure their belonging by nurturing others and being steadfast and reliable. Their individual needs are likely to remain unsatisfied as they eschew roles that would cause them to be the center of attention. Few of the other nursing samples (community nurses, "poorest" nurses, and medical nurses) loaded substantially on Factor II.

None of the samples loaded exclusively in a positive direction on Factor III. However, administrative nurses who loaded minimally on Factors I and II loaded substantially, albeit in a negative direction on Factor III. Therefore, the means for these nurses were used to define the factor and are reported in Table 11-IV. Administrative nurses were nurses who had been involved in teaching or administration for at least two years following graduation. These nurses are characterized by strong self-doubt and guilt feelings that they attempt to resolve through achievement and persistence. They are not likely to be assertive, independent, or confident in their relationships with members of the opposite sex. None of the other nursing samples loaded substantially in a negative direction on Factor III, suggesting that it is not characteristic of nurses with other specialties. Whether it is characteristic of teaching and administrative nurses in different settings requires further investigation.

TEACHERS. The teachers sample was composed of thirty-three samples of teachers (and the female and male adult norms). Four factors explained 92 percent of the variance prior to rotation.

Factor I is primarily descriptive of women elementary and high school teachers with less than ten years of experience. These teachers are characterized by relatively high need to be involved in warm relationships with others and to understand them psychologically. They like novelty and dislike the staid; they are unlikely to be assertive in expressing their own wishes and needs. All of the female groups load substantially on Factor I and none of the male teachers do. What distinguishes the female teachers from the women's norm group is that the latter approaches a meaningful negative loading on Factor II and loads positively on Factor III. Therefore, it is likely that women and men who enter teaching possess different motivations.

The various male teaching groups load heavily on Factor II. These men have a need to lead and direct others. They are interested in understanding other people, but primarily as a source of satisfying their own achievement needs. Neither the desire to help nor to be helped is high among their needs. They seek novelty and resist structured environments, but can persist at tasks in order to achieve their own ends. These teachers are relatively self-assured though they are not likely to speak their mind.

Only the adult male, college norm group loaded exclusively on Factor III. Adult men as represented by the norm group are *conventional achievers*. Although they have a strong need to achieve, they do so by persisting at tasks that they prefer to perform in structured environments. They nurture others but do not expect such care from others. They are somewhat self-abasive and are no longer unduly concerned with sex role or sexual issues. Self-expression is not high among their needs. As shown in Table 11-II, there is a tendency for older, more experienced teachers of both sexes and for teachers' aides to load significantly on Factor III. Thus, it seems to represent a combination of the effects of the aging process and less skilled workers.

Factor IV could not be defined because of an absence of pure occupations. The two samples with noticeable loadings on the factor were male high school coaches and secondary teachers of unspecified sex. It is possible that this factor measures some aspect of needs of active teachers.

HETEROGENEOUS OCCUPATIONS. As was the case with the college majors, there were a number of occupations for which only few exemplars were available. These occupations were combined in a single factor analysis. Again, if it is true that different need patterns represent different occupations, then one would expect the appearance of several factors and/or that certain occupations might not load substantially on any of the factors.

Four factors, representing 85 percent of the variance, were extracted and rotated. The occupations used to define Factor I seem to reflect business and action interests. People who load heavily on Factor I are characterized by high average needs to lead others and to achieve. Although they enjoy environmental variety, they are willing to persist at concrete tasks as a means of reaching their goals. Except for their concern for sexual or sex role issues, they are characterized by a low level of social needs. They like neither to be cared for nor to care for others, they indulge in little introspection, and they resist hierarchical relationships and structured environments. *Dominant Achievers vs. Asociability* seems to describe this factor, and the occupations that load heavily on it seem to be characteristic of Holland's Realistic and Enterprising Types.

In support of the heavy loadings of business people on Factor I, Hornaday and Bunker (1970) reported high achievement and autonomy needs for male entrepreneurs. Morrison and Sebald (1974) who compared female executives to nonexecutives found that executives had higher needs for dominance and lower social needs (i.e. affiliation and nurturance).

It is hard to determine the commonality among the three occupations, craft foremen and male and female psychiatric aides, with exclusively high loadings on Factor II. These occupations are joined by the adult male and female norms. It is possible that this factor represents unskilled or blue collar labor. Factor II occupational members are *nurturant plodders.* They take on tasks and persist at them in an orderly fashion, possibly, as a means of satisfying the needs of others; they are prone to self-abasiveness and do not expect others to succor them; they are unlikely to make known their own needs and opinions. Pulos, Nichols, Lewinsohn, and Koldjeski (1962) investigated the relationship between supervisor performance evaluations and new male and female psychiatric aides' EPPS scores. They found a positive relationship between autonomy and efficiency scores, which seems to contradict the loading of experienced aides on Factor II. It is possible that high autonomy need dissipates if one remains in the occupation.

It is noticeable that police officers are the only group with a high negative loading on Factor II, suggesting a personality pattern that is the antithesis of the nurturant plodders. Although only one sample of police officers was included in the present study, two other studies have reported differences between officers' mean needs and the EPPS norms, which are consistent with their heavy loading on Factor I. Simon, Wilde, and Cristal (1973) found that they had higher needs for exhibition, change, heterosexuality, and aggression and lower needs for order, affiliation, abasement, nurturance, and endurance. Matarazzo, Allen, Saslow, and Wiens (1964) reported that successful police force applicants had higher needs for achievement, exhibition, intraception, dominance, endurance, and heterosexuality and lower needs for autonomy, succorance, nurturance, and aggression.

Factor III reflects high school counselor characteristics since the samples used to define this factor were employed counselors. Characteristics of these groups were high needs to understand the motivations of others (intraception) and themselves and a desire to belong to social groups (affiliation) and to be a leader among the people with whom they affiliate (dominance). They like to care for others (nurturance), but not to be cared for (succorance). Mental flexibility (change) seems to be indicative of these counselors who resist an orderly environment, but do not appear to need excessive independence or self-expression.

Among rehabilitation counselors, Patterson (1962) found that males and females had high average intraception needs; women had low average abasement needs and men had high average deference and nurturance needs. It seems likely that some combination of elevated intraception, affiliation, and nurturance will appear among the hierarchy of counselor needs.

No group had an exclusive loading of .40 or better on Factor IV and, therefore, it could not be defined. However, the high loadings of business and school administrators on this factor suggest that it might measure characteristics of managers or leadership-related occupations. Further studies are needed to define further the relevant characteristics.

Summary and Discussion

A variety of interest areas have been examined for their contribution to differential need levels — some areas more so than others. Nursing majors (but not nurses) and teachers (but not education majors) are two groups that have been excessively popular among researchers.

Given that the nursing student samples have been selected from numerous settings and have had a multitude of characteristics, it can be stated with some confidence that women who enter nursing will show a pattern of needs characteristic of self-sacrificers and/or rebellion depending somewhat upon their class level.

On the other hand, because the sampling of employed nurses has been restricted to only a few settings, it is difficult to decide whether the factors discovered in this analysis are typical of nurses in general or only of the particular nurses in the cited investigations. However, the empathic social interest factor among employed nurses is essentially equivalent to the "concern-for-others" factor among students and suggests a commonality of needs among those women interested in nursing, represented by elevated needs for nurturance, intraception, affiliation, abasement, and change and depressed needs for aggression, autonomy, order, succorance, and dominance or achievement.

Means for thirty-five samples of male and female secondary and elementary teachers were factor analyzed. The results of this analysis indicated that the pattern of needs characteristic of female teachers regardless of specialization tends to be different from the pattern of needs of male teachers. It is also apparent that the needs of teachers differ from the needs of potential teachers, although this last observation must be tempered because of the limited number and variety of education major samples.

A number of occupations and majors could stand further investigation. Some of the majors in need of such investigation are included in the liberal arts cluster; some of the occupations are included among the heterogeneous occupations. With such studies, whether or not the factors identified for these samples accurately represent the need patterns of people with like interests could be more precisely determined.

In any case, two main points stand out in this chapter: (a) It is important to examine need levels relative to one another, i.e. within a person or group, rather than totally relying on a comparison to the norms, and (b) patterns of needs may be more important in determining relevant motivation than single scale scores. Most of the need levels for the different occupations fell within the normal range when compared to the norms, and needs that, according to other sources, should have differed in level between different occupational groupings occasionally were similar in pattern.

References

Adams, J., and Klein, L.R.: Students in nursing school: Considerations in assessing personality characteristics. *Nursing Research, 19:*362-366, 1970.

Allen, L.R., and Foreman, P.E.: Norms on EPPS for female Australian therapy students. *Perceptual and Motor Skills, 42:*1233-1234, 1976.

Anderson, D.D.: Personality attributes of teachers in organizational climates. *Journal of Educational Research, 62:*441-443, 1969.

Bailey, J.T., and Claus, K.E.: Comparative analysis of the personality structure of nursing students. *Nursing Research, 18:*320-326, 1969.

Balazs, E., and Nickerson, E.: A personality needs profile of some outstanding female athletes. *Journal of Clinical Psychology, 32:*45-49, 1976.

Brollier, C.: Personality characteristics of three allied health professional groups. *American Journal of Occupational Therapy, 24:*500-505, 1970.

Bromer, J.A., Johnson, J.M., and Sevransky, P.: Validity information exchange, No. 15-20. *Personnel Psychology, 15:*107-109, 1962.

Campbell, J.T., Otis, J.L., Liske, R.E., and Prien, E.: Assessments of higher-level personnel: II. Validity of the overall assessment process. *Personnel Psychology,* 63-74, 1962.

Cangemi, J., Harryman, E., Coan, D.L., and Kesler, T.: Leadership training for teacher education majors. *College Student Journal, 8:*63-67, 1974.

Caputo, D.V., and Hanf, C.: The EPPS pattern and the "nursing personality." *Educational and Psychological Measurement, 25:*421-435, 1965.

Coody, B.E., and Hinely, R.T.: Validity study of selected EPPS subscales for determining need structure of dominant and submissive student teachers. *Journal of Educational Research, 61:*59-61, 1967.

Crane, W.J.: Screening devices for occupational therapy majors. *American Journal of Occupational Therapy, 16:*131-132, 1962.

Dayries, J.L., and Grimm, R.L.: Personality traits of women athletes as measured by EPPS. *Perceptual and Motor Skills, 30:*229-230, 1970.

Eberlein, E.L.: EPPS need structure of in-service elementary school teachers. *Journal of Educational Research, 64:*112-114, 1970.

Edwards, A.: *Edwards Personal Preference Schedule.* New York, Psychological Corporation, 1954.

Ferrari, L.M.: Some personality characteristics of male psychiatric nursing assistants in one facility. *Perspectives on Psychiatric Care, 3:*39-41, 1965.

Fletcher, R.: Correlations of EPPS personality traits and intramural particpation. *Perceptual and Motor Skills, 32:*242, 1971.

Frank, A.C., and Kirk, B.A.: Forestry students today. *Vocational Guidance Quarterly, 19:*119-126, 1970.

Fry, G.E., and Reinhardt, R.F.: Personality characteristics of jet pilots as measured by the Edwards Personal Schedule. *Aerospace Medicine, 40:*484-486, 1969.

Gardiner, H.W.: Performance of student nurses on the Edwards Personal Preference Schedule. *Journal of Psychology, 94:*297-300, 1976.

Goldman, H.: Differential need patterns: Implications for principals. *The School Review,* September-December, 266-275, 1969.

Goldman, H., and Heald, J.E.: Teachers' need patterns and the administrator. *NASSP bulletin,* December, 93-103, 1967.

Gordon, I.J.: Personality patterns of volunteers for an experimental professional education program. *Journal of Experimental Education, 32:*115-121, 1963.

Gray, J.T.: Needs and values in three occupations. *Personnel and Guidance Journal, 42:*238-244, 1963.

Gynther, M.D., and Gertz, D.: Personality characteristics of student nurses in South Carolina. *Journal of Social Psychology, 56:*277-284, 1962.

Haley, J.V., and Lerner, M.J.: The characteristics and performance of medical students during pre-clinical training. *Journal of Medical Education, 47:*446-452, 1972.

Harris, D.V.: Comparison of physical performance and psychological traits of college women with high and low fitness indices. *Perceptual and Motor Skills, 17:*293-294, 1963.

Heist, P.: Personality characteristics of dental students. *Educational Records, 41:*240-252, 1960.

Hetlinger, D.F., and Hildreth, R.A.: Personality characteristics of debaters. *Quarterly Journal of Speech, 47:*398-401, 1961.

Higgs, S.L.: Personality traits and motor ability associated with observed competitiveness in women physical education majors. *Perceptual and Motor Skills, 34:*219-222, 1972.

Hornaday, J.A., and Bunker, C.S.: The nature of the entrepreneur. *Personnel Psychology, 23:* 47-54, 1970.

Kemp, C.G.: A comparative study of the need structure of administrators, teachers, and counselors. *Journal of Educational Research, 57:*425-427, 1964.

Kirchner, W.K.: "Real-life" faking on the Edwards Personal Preference Schedule by sales applicants. *Journal of Applied Psychology, 46:*128-130, 1962.

Klett, C.J.: Performance of high school students on the Edwards Personal Preference Schedule. *Journal of Consulting Psychology, 2:*68-72, 1957.

Kole, D.M., and Matarazzo, J.D.: Intellectual and personality characteristics of medical students. *Journal of Medical Education, 38:*138-139, 1963.

Lind, A.I.: An exploratory study of predictive factors for success in the clinical affiliation experience. *American Journal of Occupational Therapy, 24:*222-226, 1970.

Locke, L.F.: Performance of administration oriented male physical educators on selected psychological tests. *Research Quarterly, 33:*418-429, 1962.

Manhold, J.H., Shatin, L., and Manhold, B.S.: Comparison of interests, needs, and selected personality factors of dental and medical students. *Journal of the American Dental Association, 67:*601-605, 1963.

Matarazzo, J.D., Allen, B.V., Saslow, B., and Wiens, A.N.: Characteristics of successful policemen and firemen applicants. *Journal of Applied Psychology, 40:*123-133, 1964.

McDonald, R.L., and Gynther, M.D.: Non-intellectual factors associated with performance in medical school. *Journal of Genetic Psychology, 103:*185-194, 1963.

Merrill, R.M.: Comparison of education students, successful science teachers, and educational administrators on the Edwards PPS. *Journal of Educational Research 54:*38-40, 1960.

Morrison, R.F., and Sebald, M.: Personal characteristics diffentiating female executive from female non-executive personnel. *Journal of Applied Psychology, 59:*656-659, 1974.

Navran, L., and Stauffacher, J.C.: The personality structure of psychiatric nurses. *Nursing Research, 5:*109-114, 1957.

Nevis, E.C., and Parker, J.W.: The use of published norms in the in the industrial setting. *Personnel Psychology, 14:*59-65, 1961.

Novello, J.R., and Youssef, J.I: Psychosocial studies in general aviation: 1, Personality profiles of male pilots. *Aerospace Medicine, 45:*185-188, 1974.

Novello, J.R., and Youssef, J.I.: Psychosocial studies in general aviation: 2, Personality profile of female pilots. *Aerospace Medicine, 45:*292-297, 1976.

Parker, S.: Personality factors among medical students as related to their predisposition to view the patient as a whole man. *Journal of Medical Education, 33:*736-744, 1958.

Patterson, C.H.: Test characteristics of rehabilitation counselor trainees. *Journal of Rehabilitation, 28:*15-16, 1962.

Penn, N.E., Baker, F., and Schulberg, H.C.: Community mental health ideology and personality preferences of social work students. *Journal of Community Psychology, 4:*292-297, 1976.

Psathas, G., and Plapp, J.: Assessing the effects of a nursing program: A problem in design. *Nursing Research, 17:*336-342, 1968.

Pulos, L., Nichols, R.C., Lewinsohn, P.M., and Koldjeski, T.: Selection of psychiatric aides and prediction of performance through psychological testing and interviews. *Psychological Reports, 10:*519-520, 1962.

Reece, M.M.: Personality characteristics and success in a nursing program. *Nursing Research, 10:* 172-176, 1961.

Rincon, E., and Ray, R.: Bilingual ethnic teachers: An answer to illiteracy and drop-out problems. *Reading Improvements, 11:*34-46, 1974.

Robertson, J.R., and Haas, J.D.: Teacher personality and the new social studies. *The Journal of Educational Research, 64:*133-138, 1970.

Roemmich, H.: The need structure of public school counselors. *The Journal of Educational Research, 61:*24-26, 1967.

Rychlak, J.F.: Personality correlates of leadership among first level managers. *Psychological Reports, 12:*43-52, 1963.

Scandrette, O.: Differential need patterns of women elementary and secondary level student teachers. *Journal of Educational Research, 55:*376-379, 1962.

Sheppard, C., Bates, C., Fracchia, J., and Merlis, S.: Psychological need structues of law enforcement officers. *Psychological Reports, 35:*583-586, 1974.

Simon, W.E., Wilde, V., and Cristal, R.M.: Psychological needs of professional police personnel. *Psychological Reports, 33:*313-314, 1973.

Singer, R.N.: Personality differences between and within baseball and tennis players. *Research Quarterly, 40:*582-588, 1969.

Stauffacher, J.C., and Navran, L.: The predication of subsequent professional activity of nursing students by the Edwards Personal Preference Schedule. *Nursing Research, 17:*256-260, 1968.

Stein, R.F.: The student nurse: A study of needs, roles, and conflicts, Part 1. *Nursing Research 18:*308-315, 1969.

Stein, R.F.: The student nurse: A study of needs, roles, and conflicts, Part 2. *Nursing Research, 18:*433-440, 1969.

Stone, L.A., Bassett, G.R., Brousseau, J.D., Demers, J., and Stiening, J.A.: Psychological test characteristics associated with training success in a MEDEX (physician's extension) training program. *Psychological Reports, 32:*231-234, 1973.

Thorpe, J.A.: Study of personality variables among successful women students and teachers of physical education. *Research Quarterly of the American Association for Health, Physical Education, and Recreation, 29:*83-92, 1958.

Tolor, A.: The personality need structure of psychiatric attendants. *Mental Hygiene, 46:*218-222, 1962.

Uhlinger, C.A., and Stephens, M.W.: Relation of achievement motivation to academic achievement in students of superior ability. *Journal of Educational Psychology, 51:*259-266, 1960.

Vineyard, E.E., Drinkwater, R., and Dickison, W.L.: Teacher education and pharmacy students: A comparison of their need structures. *Journal of Teacher Education, 13:*409-413, 1962.

Walsh, W.B., and Palmer D.A.: Some personality differences between law-and non-law-oriented students. *Vocational Guidance Quarterly, 19:*11-15, 1970.

Wendt, D.T., and Patterson, T.W.: Personality characteristics of women in intercollegiate competition. *Perceptual and Motor Skills, 38:*861-862, 1974.

Williams, J.M., Hoepner, B.J., Moody, D.L., and Ogilvie, B.C.: Personality traits of champion level female fencers. *Research Quarterly, 41:*446-453, 1970.

Yufit, R.I., Pollock, G.H., and Wasserman, E.: Medical specialty choice and personality: Initial results and prediction. *Archives of General Psychiatry, 20:*89-99, 1969.

Chapter 12

ACADEMIC ACHIEVEMENT AND THE
EPPS SCALES

ONLY one of the EPPS scales, Achievement, was specifically designed to measure a person's drive toward achievement. Heilbrun (1963) summarizes achievement as the need "to accomplish successfully tasks of social and personal significance." Naturally, a number of studies have been inspired by authors' desires to assess the validity of this particular scale. Fortunately enough, however, since there is no obvious theoretical reason for supposing that the other EPPS scales should be related to the Achievement Scale, many investigators have not limited themselves to the exclusive investigation of the Achievement Scale, but also have sought an answer to the question of which, if any, of the fifteen scales relate to a person's achievement. For the most part, achievement has been operationally defined as scholastic achievement, though such a meaning is not necessarily inherent in Edwards's definition of the need as presented in the manual.

Single Scale Studies

Most studies of the EPPS Achievement Scale have involved efforts to assess the convergent validity of the scale by correlating it with other measures also assumed to measure achievement. These other measures have included projective techniques, other objective measures, academic performance variables, as well as various miscellaneous techniques assumed to relate to achievement in some manner.

PROJECTIVE TESTS. The projective tests that have been correlated with need achievement most often are McClelland's TAT and French's achievement test. As shown in Table 12-I, these two measures have not been shown to correlate significantly with the EPPS Achievement Scale at more than a chance level. Thus, it is likely that if achievement is measured by both types of tests, then it is a nonoverlapping aspect of achievement that each measures.

OBJECTIVE TESTS. A few other objective tests have been intercorrelated with achievement. However, the variety of measures used has been too great to permit any definite conclusions, although two of the studies reported in Table 12-I (Hickson and Driskill, 1970; Weinstein, 1969) lend credence to the supposition that the California Psychological Inventory may measure a type of achievement similar to that of the EPPS.

ACADEMIC PERFORMANCE. The results obtained by correlating EPPS

Table 12 - I

SUMMARY OF MEASURES CORRELATED
WITH EPPS NEED ACHIEVEMENT

Projective Tests

Study	Samples[1]	Measures of N Ach		r
1. Weiss et al. (1959)	60 psych students (M)	a.	TAT	.26*
2. Shaw (1961)	18 high school achievers (M)	a.	TAT	.12
		b.	French	.51*
	20 high school under- achievers (M)	a.	TAT	-.03
		b.	French	.26
	21 high school achievers(F)	a.	TAT	.14
		b.	French	-.15
	19 high school under- achievers (F)	a.	TAT	-.23
		b.	French	-.13
3. Wortruba & Price(1975)	65 business majors (?)		TAT	-.17
4. Marlowe (1959)	44 fraternity undergrads (M)		TAT	.05
5. Weinstein (1969)	198 dorm residents (M)	a.	TAT	.10
		b.	French	.00
		c.	doodles	.16*
6. Himelstein (1958)	298 air force academy freshmen (M)	a.	TAT	.00
		b.	French	.02
7. Bendig (1957)	136 (M) and 108 (F) psych students		TAT	.11
8. Melikian (1958)	84 Arabic psychology students (?)		TAT	.16
9. Uhlinger & Stephens (1960)	72 merit scholars (?)		incomplete sentences	.19
10. Shaw (1961)	18 achievers (M)		French	.51

Table 12 - I (continued)

Study	Samples	Measures of N Ach		r
		Academic Performance		
1. Weiss et al. (1959)	60 psych students (M)	a.	aptitude test	.18
		b.	GPA	.42*
2. Wortruba & Price (1975)	65 business majors (?)		GPA	.28*
3. Hickson & Driskell (1970)	70 honors & non-honors undergrads (?)		GPA	.36**
4. Gibbs (1966)	72 Australian students (F)		exam performance	.45**
5. Dunham (1973)	161 (M) & 142 (F) college students		GPA	.11
6. Bendig (1958a)	164 psych students (M)		GPA	.23
7. Bendig (1958b)	110 psych students (M)	a.	GPA	.17
		b.	psych grade	.13
8. Izard (1962)	53 undergrads (F)	a.	GPA	.17
	33 undergrads (M)	b.	GPA	.28**
9. Morgan (1975)	135 (M) & 82 (F) psych students	a.	GPA	-.02
		b.	psych grade	-.03
10. Bachman (1964)	37 psych students (M)	a.	GPA	.28
		b.	psych grade	.41*
		c.	SAT	.30
	24 psych students (M)	a.	GPA	.19
		b.	psych grade	.45*
		c.	SAT	.50*
		Objective Tests		
1. Wortruba & Price (1975)	65 business students (?)	a.	Herman's	.22
		b.	Mehrabian	.22

Table 12 - I (continued)

Study	Samples	Measures of N Ach		r
2. Hickson & Driskell (1970)	70 honors & non-honors undergrads (?)	a. CPI-ach		.39**
		b. sensation-seeking		.14
3. Weinstein (1969)	198 dorm residents (M)		ach scale	-.04
			Sherwood	.11
		a. CPI-conformance		-.12
		b. CPI-independence		.28**
4. Bendig (1957)	136 (M) & 108 (F) psych students		anxiety	-.05
5. Farley (1966)	66 trade apprentices (M)		introversion	-.21
6. Uhlinger & Stephens (1960)	72 merit scholars (?)		need for recognition	.33**
7. Bendig (1959)	73 psych students (M&F)		temperament	.26*
	Miscellaneous Measures			
1. Marlowe (1959)	44 fraternity members (M)		peer ratings	.09
2. Hickson & Driskell (1970)	70 honors and non-honors undergrads (?)		honors participation	.34**
3. McFall & Schenkein (1970)	48 college students (F)		concealed figures	.07
4. Bendig (1959)	73 psych students (M&F)		rod & frame	.27
			puzzle solving	-.05
5. Gavurin & Murgatroyd (1974)	163 psych students (F)		anagram solving	.13
	83 psych students (M)		anagram solving	.02

[1](M) = males; (F) = females; (?) = unspecified

*p < .05

achievement with course grades and cumulative grade point average have been somewhat more promising. Of the nineteen correlations reported in Table 12-I, 42 percent were significant at at least the .05 level of significance.

OTHER MEASURES. Of the various other single scale studies (reported in Table 12-I) in which EPPS achievement was correlated with various measures, only one reported a significant correlation. Participation in a university honors program was related in the Hickson and Driskill (1970) study.

Where academic performance is concerned, various authors have investigated the relationship between others of the EPPS scales and achievement. Lublin (1965) tested the effects of need autonomy on academic achievement, defined as scores on a criterion test, after the sample of college students had participated in a programmed learning course. She divided program participants into three groups, high, medium, or low, on the basis of their autonomy needs. Her results indicated that the high autonomy group had lower scores on the dependent measure than the low autonomy group. The level of performance of students with a medium autonomy need was between that of the other two groups, but different from both.

Bernhardt (1960), Muchinsky and Hoyt (1973), Johnson (1973), and Hamilton (1970) investigated the relationship of specific EPPS scales to grades of students who were majoring in particular subject areas. In his investigation of need intraception, Bernhardt (1960) tested his assumption that the scale scores and medical students' freshmen and sophomore grades in their psychiatry courses were positively correlated. Surprisingly, for his predominantly male sample, he found a significant negative correlation ($r = -.275$) between the two measures for their freshmen year and no relationship ($r = .022$) for their sophomore year.

Focusing on graduated engineering students of unspecified sex, Muchinsky and Hoyt (1973) examined the relationships between the Achievement and Affiliation scales and four measures of grade point average. They found no significant correlations between need achievement and grade point, but affiliation was significantly correlated with cumulative grade point ($r = -.24$) and grade point in core engineering courses ($r = -.18$). Nonsignificant correlations between GPA and exhibition ($r = -.15$), nurturance ($r = -.05$), change ($r = -.16$), and intraception ($r = -.03$) were reported for Gallessich's (1970) sample of engineering students.

Johnson (1973) found that intraception was positively correlated with the performance of fifty-three practical nursing students in four different courses. Correlations ranged from .40 to .45.

For various subsamples of English university students, Hamilton (1970) found that examination performances was related to different EPPS needs. For instance, for males majoring in the college of letters (liberal arts), succorance ($r = -.368$) and heterosexuality ($r = -.431$) were negatively correlated with performance; for females, achievement ($r = .292$) and nurturance ($r = -.354$) were correlated with exam performance in opposite directions.

Together, the investigations of the Achievement Scale suggest that it is weakly related to behavioral indices of academic achievement other than personality tests. However, the small absolute size of the correlations of the scale with other criteria plus the lack of a consistent relationship with other measures of need achievement raise the possibility that academic achievement may not be an area that is best tapped by the EPPS Achievement Scale.

As for the other single scales that have been investigated for their effects on academic performance, the results have been intriguing but inconclusive. Most of the needs that have been investigated correlated negatively with performance. In the case of autonomy and intraception, the behavior of male respondents was in a direction opposite to that which was expected by the investigators, but for female nursing students intraception was positively correlated. In the case of engineering students, it appears that too much of a social need may be a hindrance to successful academic achievement.

ABILITY LEVELS. In some studies authors have divided students into performance categories, e.g. overachieving versus underachieving, on the basis of some combination of scores on a test of general aptitude and obtained undergraduate grade point average. Unfortunately, many of these studies have been characterized by authors' failures to discard profiles with consistency scores of less than ten; instead, they have used the consistency score as an additional variable in their analyses. The consequence of such a procedure is that a number of random profiles probably have been fortuitously combined with non-random profiles, thus mitigating the chances of discovering legitimate profile characteristics.

Only a few of the studies in which ability levels have been manipulated have revealed EPPS scale differences. Considering one extreme of academic ability, scholastically weak college students, Merrill and Murphy (1959) divided students into overachieving (passing) and achieving as expected (failing) groups by comparing their first semester college grade point to their predicted grade point average and found that overachievers (grade point ⁶1.50) had higher needs for deference, dominance, and endurance and lower needs for exhibition, autonomy, affiliation, and change than did those who were achieving as expected.

Looking at the other extreme, honors students, Palmer and Wohl (1970) reported that "for both sexes, honors students score higher [than students enrolled in a basic psychology course] on autonomy, and both sexes are lower on the affiliation and abasement scales of the EPPS" (p. 107). They also found that honors females had higher needs for achievement.

O'Shea (1970) found that among bright (IQ⁴112) junior high school boys, high achievers had greater needs for achievement, deference, endurance, dominance, and aggression. Low achievers had greater needs for autonomy and heterosexuality. Haas (1963) compared EPPS needs of twenty-five upper class undergraduate students with a grade point average of 3.60 or better on a 4-point system to the EPPS norms. They found no significant differences among means, although male "superior" students did have a higher than average deference need.

In one study involving academically strong students, achievement variables other than grade point were used. Kennedy, Cottrell, and Smith (1964) selected adolescent subjects of unspecified sex who were mathematically gifted.

They reported that the group had high needs for achievement and autonomy and low needs for order, deference, and succorance.

Using a wider variety of ability levels (achievers, underachievers, overachievers, and nonachievers) of a combined sample of male and female students, Demos and Spolyar (1961) found no significant differences between the achievers as compared to the underachievers or between the overachievers as compared to the nonachievers. In an earlier study, Gebhart and Hoyt (1958) compared three ability levels of male freshmen engineering students and arts and sciences students, high ability, average, and low ability, and two levels of achievement, over- and underachievers. They reported that "(a) overachievers scored significantly higher on the following scales — Achievement, Order, Intraception, and Consistency . . ." and "(b) underachievers scored significantly higher on the following scales — Nurturance, Affiliation, and change" (p. 126).

They also reported that high ability respondents (as determined by their predicted grade point average) had higher needs for achievement, exhibition, autonomy, dominance, and consistency. While low ability students scored significantly higher on the Deference, Order, Abasement, and Nurturance scales. Obvious problems with Gebhart and Hoyt's data are that the high ability and high achievement groups had higher mean consistency scores than the comparison groups. Since the profiles of those students whose consistency scores were less than adequate were not eliminated, Gebhart and Hoyt (1958) were, in essence, comparing somewhat valid (i.e. higher ability) to less valid responses (i.e. lower ability) profiles; consequently, their results may be questioned.

Bhatnagar (1969) was the only investigator to consider that age of test takers might relate to obtained grades. In his study, he used 261 Indian high school boys who were administered a Hindi version of the EPPS in addition to an intelligence test and a socioeconomic questionnaire. Bhatnagar found that if one disregarded the topic area of the courses taken by his subjects, then different needs were correlated with grades for this three different age groups when the effects on intelligence were eliminated. Boys whose ages were between 15.5 and 17.5 years exhibited significant correlations between nurturance ($r = .332$) and endurance ($r = .235$) and academic performance. For boys in the age range from 13.5 to 15.5 years, dominance ($r = .198$), nurturance ($r = .421$), and endurance ($r = .221$) were the significant needs, whereas for boys aged 11.5 to 13.5 years, achievement ($r = -.256$) and affiliation ($r = .255$) were significant.

Obviously, the relevant needs were not synonymous across age groups. Differences between age groups were further accentuated when he compared achievement in arts courses to achievement in science courses. Nurturance ($r = .314$) was significantly correlated for the arts courses and achievement ($r = .375$) for the science courses when the oldest subjects were used as the classification groups. For the group whose mean age was 12.5 years, endurance

(r = .389) and aggression (r = -.386) were correlated for arts courses and nurturance (r = -.331) and aggression (r = .378) were correlated for science courses.

Bhatnagar's data illustrate the merit of examining demographic indicants of intellectual achievement as well as test scores. It would be interesting to see the results of a similar study using an American sample.

When ability levels have been manipulated, the needs that appear most often as being descriptive of the higher ability groups are high needs for achievement, deference, dominance, endurance, and autonomy. The only need that shows up with any consistency for the lower ability groups is a high need for affiliation.

CROSS-VALIDATION STUDIES. Some of the studies in which ability level has been a manipulated factor have been intentionally designed as replications of Goodstein and Heilbrun's (1962) correlational analysis of the EPPS and semester grade point average when level of intelligence was partialed out. Their investigation involved separate analyses of the male (206 respondents) and female (151 respondents) samples. For the total groups of males, elimination of the effects of intelligence only resulted in one significant correlation involving achievement (r = .24). For the total group of women, none of the EPPS scales were significantly correlated with grade point.

Dividing the respective groups into low ability, middle ability, and high ability groups using respondents' scores on a vocabulary test, Goodstein and Heilbrun (1962) found that different scales were related to academic achievement for different groups. Autonomy (r = -.27) and nurturance (r = -.21) were significantly correlated for low ability male groups and abasement (r = -.38) and nurturance (r = -.29) were significantly correlated for the low ability female group. Significantly correlated needs for the middle ability groups were achievement (r = .29), endurance (r = .48), affiliation (r = -.26), intraception (r = -.25), nurturance (r = -.24), and change (r = -.21) for males. No scales were significantly correlated for the middle ability female group. The only significantly correlated needs were aggression (r = -.22) and intraception (r = .33) for high ability male and female groups, respectively.

In his attempted replication of Goodstein and Heilbrun's (1962) study, Hakel (1966) divided 102 male subjects into the three ability groups using aptitude test scores. Besides quarter-grade point average, he also used grades in core liberal arts courses as his criteria. Although he found a percentage of significant partial correlations equivalent to that of the parent study, only the Achievement, Endurance and Aggression scales were significantly correlated in both studies. The correlation involving quarter grade-point and achievement was r = .27 for the total group in Hakel's study. Endurance was significantly correlated with Goodstein and Heilbrun's (1962) semester grade point (r = .48) and with Hakel's quarter grade-point (r = .39) for the middle ability group. Hakel also found a significant correlation between aggression (r

= -.37) and core grade point among the high ability group.

Significant scales unique to Hakel's (1966) study that correlated with both of his grade point criteria for the group with ability level unspecified were the Order and Endurance scales. Correlations with quarter and core grade point were r = .21 and r = .20 (order) and r = .33 and r = .29 (endurance), respectively. Using just the low ability group, the correlations between endurance and quarter and core grade points were r = .44 and r = .36. None of the correlations were significant for the middle ability group. Order was significantly correlated with quarter (r = .58) and core (r = .55) grade point in the high ability group.

Hakel (1966) carried his analysis further by testing the stability of his results when heterogeneous groups were formed by randomly assigning subjects to group membership. Ideally, random assignment should have worked against correlations that were differentially significant because of group membership. However, he did find a number of group-related significant correlations of a higher magnitude than those obtained using ability-related grouping procedures.

Kazmier (1961) attempted a cross-validational study in which he used a mixed sex sample of 140 subjects. He divided his sample into experimental and cross-validation groups. The former was used to identify the EPPS scales that best predicted points on course exams and the latter was used to test the validity of the obtained weightings. He found that the best combination of predictors for the experimental group was change, succorance, and heterosexuality (R = .345), but that the predictive utility of this combination disappeared when it was used with the cross-validation group (R = -.058).

In a subsequent replication of the Goodstein and Heilbrun (1962) and Hakel (1966) studies, Morgan (1976) did separate sex analyses of eighty-two female and 135 male undergraduates. He found no scales that were common across studies for female subjects. For male average ability subjects, Morgan found a significant correlation between achievement (r = .24) and semester grade point as had Goodstein and Heilbrun. For high ability groups, he found that aggression was significantly related (r = .41) as had Hakel (1966) for his two measures and Goodstein and Heilbrun for their one. Achievement (r = .20) was the only significant scale that Hakel found that was significant for the total group regardless of ability across all three studies.

Varieties of Academic Achievement

Just as various definitions of ability levels have been used to assess the relevance of EPPS needs, various definitions of achievement have been used as well. The latter definitions include faculty ratings (Lang, Sferra, and Seymour, 1962), grades in a one semester introductory psychology course (Bendig, 1958), academic persistence (Zaccaria and Creaser, 1970), reading improvement (Morton, 1959), completion of a teacher preparation program (Belcastro, 1975), and teaching evaluations (Wink, 1970).

In one of the few studies in which both adequate consistency scores and separate sex analyses were evident, Lang, Sferra, and Seymour (1962) found significant positive correlations between faculty ratings of academic achievement and female freshmen's needs for achievement and dominance and a significant negative correlation between nurturance needs and ratings of achievement. Men students' need for order was correlated positively with their faculty-perceived academic achievement, whereas their need for dominance was negatively correlated. Their analysis of the EPPS variables without regard to sex indicated that need for achievement was positively correlated and nurturance and deference were negatively correlated. On the other hand, Wink (1970) who used supervising teachers' evaluations of music student teachers of unspecified sex found that high achievers had high needs for deference, order, and affiliation and low need for autonomy.

Bendig (1958) found some evidence that for combined samples of men and women college students, deference, autonomy, abasement, and change showed small negative (average $r = -.19$) correlations with introductory psychology grades.

In their study of academic persistence of urban commuter college students, Zaccaria and Creaser (1971) classified women and men students as graduates, achieving withdrawers, nonachieving withdrawers, or failures on the basis of GPA and degree status. They found four EPPS scales (deference, aggression, order, and intraception) that differentiated the four male persistence groups and six scales (deference, heterosexuality, succorance, change, and order) that differentiated the female groups. Those males who withdrew in spite of satisfactory academic achievement had a significantly lower need for deference and a higher need for aggression than did the graduates. Those who flunked out had higher needs for order than the graduates and achieving withdrawers and lower needs for intraception than the achieving withdrawers.

For the female students, achieving withdrawers had higher needs for heterosexuality than the graduates, but lower needs for deference. The achieving withdrawers had higher needs for succorance than the failing withdrawers and the failures. The failing (or nonachieving) withdrawers had higher needs for autonomy and change than the achieving withdrawers and a lower need for order than those women who failed.

Whether or not men and women college undergraduates successfully completed a teacher preparation program was the academic behavior of interest to Belcastro (1975). To predict program completion, he used combinations of grade point average, EPPS scales, and SVIB scales with his samples of 207 women and eighty-eight men analyzed separately. He found eight predictive items for women: grade point, heterosexuality, consistency, artist, librarian, English teacher, life insurance salesman, and the feminity-masculinity scale.

Fourteen predictive items were identified for males: grade point, autonomy, affiliation, succorance, nurturance, change, heterosexuality, architects, physician, veterinarian, printer, industrial arts teacher, physical therapist, and occupational level. Because of the small sample size that he used, Belcastro recommended cross-validation of his results. Morton (1959) found that male postal workers' reading improvement was positively correlated with their achievement need negatively correlated with their succorance need.

Studies of learning as an active process have yielded contradictory results as well. Worell (1960) used the Achievement Scale and found that high achieving females (beyond the 79th percentile) and high achieving males (beyond the 74th percentile) performed better on a paired associated learning task than low achievers, but Hart (1967) found that male high and low need achievers didn't differ in performance on an addition task. However, Gavurin and Murgatroyd's (1974) findings with male and female psychology students suggest that other scales might be better for predicting task performance. They found that exhibition, affiliation, and succorance were significantly positively correlated and endurance was negatively correlated with the number of anagrams solved by male participants. Only succorance and nurturance were positively correlated for females.

Patterns of Achievement

The purpose of this small group of studies has been to determine whether combinations of the EPPS scales might be more efficacious predictors of academic achievement than single scales.

Heilbrun (1963) used a configural categorization system modeled after Hathaway's procedures for coding the MMPI. His intention was to identify those patterns that would distinguish academic achievers from nonachievers when academic aptitude was controlled. Table 12-II summarizes his results. Because the number of differentiating patterns was less than one would expect by chance, he concluded that, for the most part, "multiple scale interpretation of the PPS in predicting college achievement holds very limited promise" (p. 266-267). His one exception to this gloomy prediction was that female nonachievers as compared to achievers more frequently exhibited high autonomy need in combination with low deference, intraception, or abasement (and possibly order). Heilbrun's analysis of the scales that distinguished nonachieving women implies that assertive, aggressive, and independent behavior might not be rewarded when exhibited by women in an academic setting.

Lunneborg and Lunneborg (1967) examined five of the EPPS scales, Achievement, Exhibition, Intraception, Abasement, and Aggression, to determine whether scale combinations would yield higher correlations and better predictive utility. They divided EPPS scale scores into categories of high (H), medium (M), or low (L) on the basis of whether scores fell in the first, second,

Table 12 - II

HIGHEST POINT (HTP), HIGH POINT (HP),
LOWEST POINT (LTP), AND LOW POINT (LP)

FREQUENCIES OF EPPS SINGLE SCALE CODES
WHICH DISTINGUISH ACHIEVERS (A) FROM NON-ACHIEVERS (NA)
FOR MALE AND FEMALE COLLEGE STUDENTS

	Males								Females							
	HtP		HP		LtP		LP		HtP		HP		LtP		LP	
EPPS Scales	A	NA	A	NA	A	NA	A	NA	A	NA	A	NA	A	NA	A	NA
Achievement	42	26														
Exhibition									14	29	26	52				
Autonomy											29	50				
Intraception															27	42
Abasement													10	25	18	41
Nurturance			11	34					44	25						
Change							41	35								
Endurance	38	24	58	47											28	42
Aggression									15	28	28	42				

Note. N's in the four achievement groups are: male A = 233, male NA = 316, female = 206, female NA = 222.

Reproduced from Heilbrun (1963). Copyright <u>Personnel and Guidance Journal</u>.

third, or fourth quartile of a normative group. The need combinations for males that contributed most to prediction of grade point were high achievement-high intraception, high achievement-medium abasement, low achievement-high abasement, and high intraception-low abasement. The best predictive combinations for women were high achievement-low abasement, high intraception-low abasement and high achievement-medium abasement, high abasement-low aggression, and medium abasement-low aggression, all of which were negatively related to grade point.

In a subsequent study, Lunneborg (1970) did not find any patterns that correlated significantly with university grade point. In combination with aptitude measures, patterns consisting of high achievement-low abasement, high achievement-high exhibition, and high intraception-low succorance were about as predictive as aptitude tests alone.

Dixon, Fukuda, and Behrens (1971) factor analyzed the EPPS scores of 169 graduating high school seniors in combination with a variety of aptitude and teacher evaluation measures. They identified six factors that included some of the EPPS scales. Factors with relevant EPPS loadings were as follows: intellectual introversion (affiliation [-.37], intraception [.31] change [.37], heterosexuality [-.40], and consistency [.37]); dependence (intraception [.37], change [-.31], succorance [.82], and nurturance [.33]); superego strength (intraception [.36], deference [.86], order [.80], abasement [.46], and endurance [.86]); independent orientation (autonomy [.68], change [.74], and heterosexuality [.68]); ego strength (exhibition [.74], dominance [.69], abasement [-.35], and endurance [.31]); verbal aggression (affiliation [-.79], nurturance [-.48], aggression [.61], and consistency [-.45]).

Although the three configural analyses cited have each reported some combinations of scales, which appeared to be at least tenuously related to academic achievement as indicated by cumulative grade point average, these patterns have not been substantiated across studies nor have they demonstrated that the use of EPPS scales improve the predictions one could make by using aptitude measures alone.

Personality Characteristics

An issue of some interest has been to what extent personality characteristics influence psychological needs and academic achievement. Usually studies in this area have involved comparisons between groups who were categorized on the basis of their responses to other personality inventories, particular behaviors assumed to be influenced by personality, and physical characteristics theoretically related to personality variables. In each of these types of studies, a significant question is how or whether the selected variables affect academic achievement as variously defined.

PERSONALITY INVENTORIES. Hamachek and Mori (1964) administered the California Test of Personality, the EPPS, and an Academic Self-Concept Questionnaire to male and female secondary education and female elementary majors to determine how the groups compared to one another. On the EPPS variables, women secondary and elementary majors had higher needs for affiliation, succorance, nurturance, and change than the male majors. The elementary majors also had a lower need for achievement. Male students had higher needs for dominance, aggression, and autonomy. Thus, the groups differed from one another in directions that were consistent with male-female sex roles.

Responses to the California test indicated that whereas male respondents felt more self-reliant than the female groups, the female groups felt more capable and attractive, had more faith in their future, and (in the case of the elementary students) felt that they had greater personal freedom than did the male group. The only significant finding regarding academic self-concept was that the elementary majors reported a lower academic self-concept, i.e. self-perception of scholastic abilities, than the other two groups.

Though the authors did not report correlational analyses, they did report comparisons to the EPPS norms. It appears that, for their groups, perceived academic security and self-worth were associated with being similar to the norms and not deviating significantly in a gender atypical direction. Although, with regard to this last statement, males did demonstrate a level of need intraception higher than that of the same sex norm group, but women demonstrated higher heterosexuality and lower deference than the norm group.

In an attempt to discover the academically related personality characteristics of black students, Brazziel (1964) administered the Allport-Vernon-Lindsay Scale of Values and the EPPS and collected grade point averages of 100 black, lower socioeconomic college students of unspecified sex. As compared to the EPPS norms, he found that the black college students had lower needs for deference and succorance and higher needs for autonomy, dominance, heterosexuality, and achievement. Correlations between the six values scales and the EPPS scales revealed positive associations between theoretical values and achievement, succorance, exhibition, endurance, autonomy, intraception, and nurturance; aesthetic values and achievement and affiliation and intraception; social values and affiliation and intraception; political values and endurance; religious values and affiliation; political values and abasement and succorance; and economic values and aggression.

Grade point average was positively correlated only with EPPS needs for autonomy ($r = .31$) and succorance ($r = .33$). The Theoretical Value Scale allegedly measures a cognitive search for truth; the Political Scale measures "a quest for power." Although Brazziel's sample was not particularly deviant (as compared to the norm group) on these scales, the direction of the correlations between measures suggests that the succorance scale may be positively related to a cognitive aspect of achievement and negatively related to activistic tendencies for black students.

However, Wen and McCoy (1975), who correlated the two-quarter grade point averages and EPPS needs of 164 male and 202 female black college students from rural, depressed environments, found negative correlations for achievement ($r = -.26$), deference ($r = -.30$), order ($r = -.33$), exhibition ($r = -.26$), autonomy ($r = -.21$), affiliation ($r = -.31$), intraception ($r = -.23$), succorance ($r = -.35$), dominance ($r = -.22$), abasement ($r = -.29$), nurturance ($r = -.28$), change ($r = -.26$), endurance ($r = -.30$) for the male sample. This combination of variables yielded a significant multiple correlation ($R = .53$). The only significant correlation for women was between intraception and grade point ($r = .15$), but the multiple correlation was not significant ($R = .30$). Only two of the significant correlations between scales and grade point that Wen and McCoy found involved the same scales reported by Brazziel (1964) — autonomy and succorance — for male subjects, but the correlations were in opposite directions.

The sample sizes were rather small for the number of variables investigated in both the Brazziel (1964) and Wen and McCoy (1975) studies. Nevertheless, they suggest that the EPPS variables were not particularly potent predictors of academic achievement as indicated by grade point average, particularly for black women.

Academic Behaviors and Personality Characteristics

Three studies have identified academic behaviors that hypothetically related to personality variables. The academic behavior of interest to Tukey (1964) was the social as contrasted to the intellectual orientation of upper level college undergraduate women. After dividing women into groups according to whether they were campus leaders (social orientation) or gifted intellectually (intellectual orientation), she found that the latter group had higher mean needs for achievement, exhibition, and autonomy and the former had higher needs for deference. Her rank ordering of the women's needs indicated that autonomy ranked No. 1 for the intellectual group and No. 13 for the social group.

Test performance under stress was the academic behavior with which Mogar (1962) was concerned. In one study, he compared same sex groups of women and men whose performance on a block design task was either facilitated, i.e. facilitators, or inhibited, i.e. nonfacilitators, by their being required to perform the task in a competitive situation. For male facilitators and non facilitators, there were no significant differences on the EPPS scales. Women facilitators had higher succorance and dominance needs than same-sex non facilitators. In a second study in which he examined the relationship between the EPPS scales and course examination scores once intelligence had been partialed out, Mogar found a significant correlation with succorance ($r = .34$), dominance ($r = .33$) and abasement ($r = -.46$) for women.

The act of seeking counseling was the behavior that Lunneborg and Lunneborg (1966) used to identify a subject pool. They were particularly concerned about the usefulness of personality variables, including the Strong Masculinity-Femininity Scale and various biographic information for predicting the cumulative grade point of counseling clients. Only the two scales Achievement ($r = .17$) and Exhibition ($r = -.31$) were significantly related to grade point for their 300 male counseling clients. Intraception ($r = .12$), Abasement ($r = .15$), and Aggression ($r = .11$) scales were significantly related for their 300 female counseling clients.

The three studies in which academic performance was defined in terms of specific behaviors do not reveal that fluctuations on any of the scales are definitely common to various types of academic performance.

Physical and Psychological Correlates

The belief that a person's overall body type influences her or his behavioral and temperament development has long been one focus of certain personality theorists. However, the two EPPS studies pertaining to this area have had specific functions of the body as their focus.

In the first, Becker (1965) examined the possibility that visual acuity is related to EPPS needs. Comparing ametropes (near and farsighted) males to emmetropes (normal-sighted males), he found that the former had lower needs for autonomy and greater needs for affiliation and nurturance. A combined sample of normal-sighted and mild myopes had greater needs for achievement and lower needs for affiliation and nurturance than ametropes; mild myopes as compared to severe myopes had greater needs for intraception.

Becker (1965) found that for ametropes need achievement correlated positively with dominance, endurance, and order and negatively with autonomy, but for emmetropes need achievement correlated negatively with dominance, endurance, and order and positively with autonomy. Becker concluded that ametropes "tend to be more socially dependent and emotionally attached" (p.280) people who "achieve 'via' more social and systematic factors" whereas emmetropes "achieve 'via' Independence" (p.281).

In the second study of the relationship between physical function, personality characteristics, and academic achievement, Sanders, Mefferd, and Bown (1960) used urinary analyses obtained from male college students as their physiological measure. They report that certain metabolic attributes are associated with psychological state. For example stress level is indicated by such factors as sodium/potassium ratio, uric acid/creatinine ratio, etc. Comparing male college students who were divided into groups who had high verbal and high quantitative aptitude (VQ), high verbal and low quantitative aptitude (Vq), or low verbal and high quantitative aptitude (vQ), they found that VQ had higher needs for dominance than vQs and Vqs had higher needs for autonomy than VQs and less of a need for endurance than VQs and vQs.

Combining the EPPS, the Holtzman Ink Blot, the Q-check test results, grade and grade point analyses, plus the various urinary analyses, Sanders et al. generated the following descriptions of their academic groups: " The VQ individuals on the average were capable and performed well in any course attempted. . . . They characterized themselves as being decisive and able to chart the course of their own college careers with little help from superiors. They saw themselves as needing only moderate degrees of either autonomy or affiliation. Although they were willing to accept authority, they had strong desires to become effective leaders and organizers. . . . Many of these expressed needs were verified by the scholastic performance of VQ individuals. . . . The norepinephrine/epinephrine ratio was significantly low in these subjects. Such ratios have been reported to indicate individuals who are more or less passive in their emotional displays. This might indicate that they tended to be emotionally mature. . . ." (p. 500).

"The Vq individuals can be characterized from the data as being somewhat idealistic, subjective, imaginative, and intuitive. They describe themselves as being independent and aloof from higher authority. Although they felt neither need for affiliation nor for conformity to custom and convention, they indicated their need to be the center of attention where they could gain individual recognition. They expressed high levels of aspiration but felt they could achieve these goals with little need for perseverance. Their grade points indicated the fallacy of this belief. Their low preference for physical activity was reflected in the psychological tests and was made quite evident by the low excretion rates of almost all urinary constituents. . . ." (p. 501).

"Individuals in the VQ group were inclined to be introspective, objective, systematic, perseverant, and factual and to perceive of themselves being significantly more ambivalent and dependent on higher authority and group affiliation than either of the other two groups. . . . The VQ students participated actively in group sports such as football which, in part, accounts for their elevated creatinine excretion rates (index of muscular activity). . . ." (p. 502).

Though limited in number, the studies of the relationship between personality, academic, and physiological functions suggest that there may be some correspondence between these elements. Need for autonomy, for instance, emerged as a significant contributor to achievement in both studies despite the different definitions of achievement. Physical types who hypothetically should have been more introspective tended to express a need for higher or lower autonomy than comparable groups. The generality and importance of such deviations remains to be seen.

Discussion and Summary

As one examines the studies of achievement and the EPPS scales, two general issues call out for attention. The first is the poverty of definitions of achievement. With few exceptions most authors have chosen to define achievement as academic achievement and usually in terms of grade point average. Yet, as a criterion grade point is notoriously fallible since any number of extraneous factors can intercede to attenuate any correlations between it and other variables.

This fallibility is evident within institutions; it becomes even more exaggerated if one intends to make comparisons across institutions. Also, recall that Heilbrun (1963) suggested that the EPPS Achievement Scale referred to accomplishments that were personally meaningful to the test taker. None of the studies of academic variables have considered whether or not participating subjects believed that the selected academic variables were meaningful. Yet, studies such as Bhatnager's and Muchinsky and Hoyt's would suggest that personalized critieria lead to more readily interpretable results.

The second compelling issue is methodological in nature. Typically, considerable care has been used to define intellectual aptitude and academic performance variables, but such care has been missing in the identification of EPPS variables. Rarely did authors eliminate profiles because of inadequate consistency scores even though the lack of such a procedure probably increased the randomness of the EPPS data. Likewise, it was the rule rather than the exception that male and female subjects were mixed indiscriminantly, even though it is customary for them to perform differently on achievement related variables. The difference between Achievement Scale scores for the EPPS norm groups is a clear example of this difference. Therefore, for many of the studies discussed in this section, it is not surprising that unstable correlations were often found.

Given the numerous methodological deficiencies previously discussed, is there anything substantive that can be said about the EPPS scales and academic achievement? Well, tentatively, the need for achievement is related to actual achievement. This conclusion stems from the observation that of the many studies in which achievement was a variable of import, more than 80 percent reported significant relationships with the academic criterion. Nevertheless, these relationships were of small absolute size ranging from .20 to .42.

In no case did the scale offer a marked improvement over exclusive use of aptitude measures. Therefore, if the test user has aptitude measures at hand, he or she should certainly rely on these for predictions about academic achievement. If such measures are not available, then the direction of a person's scores on the Achievement Scale could be used to decide whether or not it would be advantageous to collect additional achievement information. Other scales on which fluctuations occurred often enough to suggest that they might be related to the Achievement Scale under some circumstances were Deference, Dominance, Autonomy, Affiliation, and Endurance.

References

Bachman, J.G.: Prediction of academic achievement using the Edwards need achievement scale. *Journal of Applied Psychology, 48:*16-19, 1964.

Becker, G.: Visual acuity, birth order, achievement versus affiliation, and other Edwards Personal Preference Schedule scores. *Journal of Psychosomatic Research, 9:*277-283, 1965.

Belcastro, F.P.: Use of selected factors as predictors of success in completing a secondary teacher preparation program. *Educational and Psychological Measurement, 35:*957-962, 1975.

Bendig, A.W.: Manifest anxiety and projective and objective measures of need achievement. *Journal of Consulting Psychology, 21:*354, 1957.

Bendig, A.W.: Objective measures of needs and course achievement in introductory psychology. *Journal of General Psychology, 59:*51-57, 1958.

Bendig, A.W.: Comparison of the validity of two temperament scales in predicting college

194 *A Practitioner's Guide to the Edwards Personal Preference Schedule*

Bendig, A.W.: Predictive and postdictive validity of need achievement measures. *Journal of Educational Research, 52:*119-120, 1958.

Bendig, A.W.: Personality variables related to individual performance on a cognitive task. *Journal of General Psychology, 60:*265-268, 1959.

Berndhardt, H.E.: Intraception test score and psychiatry grade as a freshman and a sophomore medical student: A validational study of sub-scale of the EPPS. *Educational and Psychological Measurement, 20:*365-379, 1960.

Bhatnagar, R.P.: A study of some EPPS variables as factors of academic achievement. *Journal of Applied Psychology, 53:*107-111, 1969.

Brazziel, W.F.: Correlates of southern Negro personality. *Journal of Social Issues, 20:*45-52, 1964.

Demos, G.D., and Spolyar, L.J.: Academic achievement of college freshmen in relation to the Edwards Personal Preference Schedule. *Educational and Psychological Measurement, 21:*473-479, 1961.

Dixon, P.W., Fukuda, N.K., and Berens, A.E.: A factor analysis of EPPS scales, ability, and achievement measures. *Journal of Experimental Education, 39:*31-41, 1971.

Dunham, R.B.: Achievement motivation as predictive of academic performance: A multivariate. *Journal of Educational Research, 67:*70-72, 1973.

Farley, F.H.: Introversion and achievement motivation. *Psychological Reports, 19:*112, 1966.

Gallessich, J.: An investigation of correlates of academic success of freshmen engineering students. *Journal of Counseling Psychology, 17:*173-176.

Gavurin, E.I., and Murgatroyd, D.: Personality correlates of anagram problem solving. *Journal of Psychology, 85:*97-101, 1974.

Gebhart, G.G., and Hoyt, D.P.: Personality needs of under- and overachieving freshman. *Journal of Applied Psychology, 42:*125-128, 1958.

Gibbs, D.N.: Cross-cultural comparison of needs and achievement of university freshmen. *Personnel and Guidance Journal, 44:*813-816, 1966.

Goodstein, L.D., and Heilbrun, A.B.: Prediction of college achievement from the Edwards Personal Preference Schedule at three levels of intellectual ability. *Journal of Applied Psychology, 46:*317-320, 1962.

Haas, K.: Personality needs of academically superior students and their parents. *Journal of Educational Research, 56:*389-390, 1963.

Hakel, M.D.: Prediction of college achievement from the Edwards Personal Preference Schedule using intellectual ability as a moderator. *Journal of Applied Psychology, 50:*336-340, 1968.

Hamachek, D.E., and Mori, T.: Need structure, personal adjustment, and academic self-concept beginning education students. *Journal of Educational Research, 58:*158-162, 1964.

Hamilton, V.: Noncognitive factors in university students' examination performance. *British Journal of Psychology, 61:*229-241, 1970.

Hart, J.J.: Assessing individual differences in motivation and their effect on performance on number faculty. *Psychological Reports, 20:*55-59, 1967.

Heilbrun, A.B.: Configural interpretation of the Edwards Personal Preference Schedule and the prediction of academic performance. *Personnel and Guidance Journal, 42:*264-268, 1963.

Hickson, R.H., and Driskill, J.C.: Needs for achievement: difference between honors and non-honors students. *Journal of Experimental Education, 38:*37-38, 1970.

Himelstein, P., Eschenbach, A.E., and Carp, A.: Interrelationships among three measures of achievement. *Journal of Consulting Psychology, 22:*451-452, 1958.

Izard, C.E.: Personality characteristics (EPPS), level of expectation, and performance. *Journal of Consulting Psychology, 26:*394, 1962.

Johnson, D.M.: Relationships between selected cognitive and noncognitive variables and practical nursing achievement. *Nursing Research, 22:*148-153, 1973.

Kazmier, L.J.: Cross-validation groups, extreme groups, and the prediction of academic achievement. *Journal of Educational Psychology, 52:*195-198, 1961.

Kennedy, W.A., Cottrell, T.B., and Smith, A.H.: EPPS norms for mathematically gifted adolescents. *Psychological Reports, 14:*342, 1964.

Lang, G., Sferra, A.G., and Seymour, M.: Psychological needs of college freshmen and their academic achievement. *Personnel and Guidance Journal, 41:*359-360, 1962.

Lublin, S.C.: Reinforcement schedules, scholastic aptitude, autonomy need, and achievement in a programmed course. *Journal of Educational Psychology, 56:*295-302, 1965.

Lunneborg, C.E., and Lunneborg, P.W.: EPPS patterns in the prediction of academic achievement. *Journal of Counseling Psychology, 14:*389-390, 1967.

Lunneborg, P.W.: EPPS patterns and academic achievement in counseling clients. *Educational and Psychological Measurement, 30:*393-398, 1970.

Lunneborg, P.W., and Lunneborg, C.E.: The utility of EPPS scores for prediction of academic achievement among counseling clients. *Journal of Counseling Psychology, 13,* 241, 1966.

Marlowe, D.: Relationships among direct and indirect measures of the achievement motive and overt behavior. *Journal of Consulting Psychology, 23:*329-332, 1959.

McFall, R.M., and Schenkein, D.: Experimenter expectancy affects need for achievement and field dependence. *Journal of Experimental Research in Personality, 4:*122-128, 1970.

Melikian, L.H.: The relationship between Edwards' and McClelland's measures of achievement motivation. *Journal of Consulting Psychology, 22:*296-298, 1958.

Merrill, R.M., and Murphy, D.T.: Personality factors and academic achievement in college. *Journal of Counseling Psychology, 6:*207-210, 1959.

Mogar, R.E.: Competition, achievement, and personality. *Journal of Counseling Psychology, 9:*168-172, 1962.

Morgan, R.R.: Prediction of college achievement. *Education and Psychological Measurement, 35:*387-392, 1975.

Morgan, R.R.: Utilization of levels of intellectual ability as a control variable in studies of nonintellectual factors in academic achievement. *Education and Psychological Measurement, 36:*465-472, 1976.

Morton, J.: An investigation into the effects of an adult reading efficiency course. *Occupational Psychology, 33:*222-237, 1959.

Muchinsky, P.M., and Hoyt, D.P.: Predicting college grades of engineering graduates from selected personality and aptitude variables. *Educational and Psychological Measurement, 33:*935-937, 1973.

O'Shea, A.J.: Low-achievement syndrome among bright junior high school boys. *Journal of Educational Research, 63:*257-262, 1970.

Palmer, A.B., and Wohl, J.: Some personality characteristics honors students. *College Student Journal, 4:*106-111, 1970.

Sanders, E.M., Mefferd, R.B., Jr., and Bown, O.H.: Verbal quantitative ability and certain personality and metabolic characteristics of male college students. *Educational and Psychological Measurement, 20:*491-503, 1960.

Shaw, M.C.: Need achievement scales as predictors of academic success. *Journal of Educational Psychology, 52:*282-285, 1961.

Tukey, R.S.: Intellectually oriented and socially oriented superior college girls. *National Association of Women Deans and Counselors Journal, 27:*120-127, 1964.

Uhlinger, C.A., and Stephens, M.W.: Relation of achievement motivation to academic achievement in students of superior ability. *Journal of Educational Psychology, 51:*259-266, 1960.

Weinstein, M.S.: Achievement motivation and risk preference. *Journal of Personality and Social Psychology, 13:*153-172, 1969.

Weiss, P., Wertheimer, M., and Groesbeck, B.: Achievement motivation, academic aptitude, and college grades. *Educational and Psychological Measurement, 19:*663-666, 1959.

Wen, S., and McCoy, R.E.: Relationships of selected nonacademic and academic variables to the grade point average of black students. *Educational and Psychological Measurement, 35:*935-939, 1975.

Wink, R.L.: The relationship of self-concept and selected personality variables to achievement in music student teaching. *Journal of Research in Music Education, 18:*234-241, 1970.

Worrell, L.: EPPS in achievement and verbal paired-associate learning. *Journal of Abnormal and Social Psychology, 60:*147-150, 1960.

Wortruba, T.R., and Price, K.F.: Relationships among four measures of achievement motivation. *Educational and Psychological Measurement, 35:*911-914, 1975.

Zaccaria, L., and Creaser, J.: Factors related to persistance in an urban commuter university. *Journal of College Student Personnel, 12:*286-291, 1971.

SECTION V

BEHAVIOR CORRELATES

Chapter 13

BEHAVIORAL AND ATTITUDINAL
SCALE CORRELATES

WHAT the studies summarized in this chapter have in common is that they represent someone's efforts to discover how specific attitudes and/ or behaviors are influenced by the personality characteristics measured by the various EPPS scales. The issues that have been investigated can be divided into two broad categories: (a) behaviors elicited by social or interpersonal factors and (b) behaviors that are intrapersonal or self-motivated.

Socially Influenced Behaviors

In general, social influence studies attempt to determine whether certain personality characteristics predispose the person to react differently to the pressures exerted by her or his social environment. Such pressure may be exerted via either group or one-to-one interactions.

Group Pressure

To investigate individuals' responses to group pressure situations, investigators have typically used some version of the Asch (1956) or Crutchfield (1955) conformity-inducing paradigms. The basic Asch paradigm involves showing naive subjects lines of varying lengths and asking them to match a standard after they have observed group members make a wrong choice. Conformity or susceptibility is assumed to have occurred if the naive subject also chooses or makes errors in the direction of the erroneous stimulus selection. The Crutchfield paradigm is similar except that the experimenter exerts pressure by manipulating lights in such a way as to lead the subject to believe other subjects are participating in the experiment when, in fact, they are not.

Using a version of the Asch paradigm, Appley and Moeller (1963) found that conforming behavior was positively correlated with women college students' needs for abasement ($r = .33$, $p < .05$). Gisvold (1958) investigated the relationship of the Autonomy and Deference scales to the conformity scores of a combined sample of male and female subjects. He found a significant negative correlation between autonomy and conformity ($r = -.54$, $p < .02$), but not between deference and conformity ($r = .17$). Another study (Bernadin and Jessor, 1957) in which subjects had been divided into groups of independents and dependents on the basis of the combination of their autonomy and deference scores revealed no differences between groups on the Asch conformity measure.

Of the four studies in which responses to a version of the Crutchfield paradigm were correlated with needs, Endler (1961) found no significant EPPS scale correlates using male college students, but Phelps and Meyer (1966) found that aggression was correlated for males (rho = .44), heterosexuality (rho = -.45) was correlated for women, and autonomy was correlated for the combined sample (rho = -.28). Tuddenham (1959) found that for male subjects, nurturance was positively correlated with yielding (r = .59) and negatively correlated with heterosexuality (-.51), order (-.54), and autonomy (r = -.41); for females, achievement (r = -.68) and dominance (r = -.59) were negatively correlated while order (r = .59), change (r = .50), autonomy (r = .43), and exhibition were positively correlated.

Sistrunk and McDavid (1965) used patterns of the achievement and affiliation scores to examine male and female students' responses to pressure. They found that people low on achievement (scores ≤ 13), but high on affiliation (scores ≥ 14) conformed more than low achievement-low affiliation people. On the other hand, people who were high in affiliation and achievement conformed less than those who were high in affiliation and low in achievement. Thus, yielding to group pressure seemed to occur in response to high affiliative need, but was counterindicated by high achievement need particularly on easy tasks.

Regardless of the model used to investigate conformity behavior, none of the single EPPS scales appear to be consistently correlated. The effect of patterns of needs has received little attention, although the few studies in this area offer some promise.

PERSUASIBILITY. Social pressure to conform can also be exerted in one-to-one interactions. When susceptibility to this type of social pressure involves attitudes or opinions it is often referred to as the person's level of persuasibility. Aspects of persuasibility as variously defined have been examined in some studies.

Rodgers (1974), Lang and Lazovik (1962), and Finch, Rickard, and Wilson (1970) investigated what might be called *passive* persuasibility. That is, in their studies of the hypnotic susceptibility of subjects, they were concerned with behaviors that typically are not actively controlled by the person, e.g. body sway. Rodgers found only one significant EPPS correlation, abasement (r = .41, $p < .05$) was positively related to susceptibility for college volunteers of unspecified sex, and Finch et al. found that none were related for their mixed sex sample. The only significant correlates that were identified in the earlier study was between affiliation and total scores on the Stanford Hypnotic Scale for combined sex sample (r = .36) and between deference (r = .50) and affiliation (r = .50) and the postural sway item for male volunteers. No significant correlates were reported for the female volunteers.

Active resistance to persuasion might be expected to occur in situations in which one person attempts to change another's behavior. Hypothetically, resistance to change should be incited by certain personality characteristics. Speculating that high autonomy scores might be a defense against one's tendency to acquiesce, Ward (1963) compared high need to low need autonomy in junior college students. He found that the high autonomy subjects changed their own opinions in the direction advocated by an expert to a greater extent than low autonomy subjects. On the other hand, for his predominantly male sample, Abraham (1962) found that respondents high on autonomy minus deference need were less likely to change their opinions on a paper-and-pencil measure. Likewise, Izard (1960) found that resistance to change was positively associated ($r = .38$) with need for autonomy for male college students. Dominance ($r = .38$) and order ($r = -.53$) were also significantly correlated for males, but no needs were significantly correlated for females.

The Ward (1963) and Izard (1960) studies dealt with individuals' willingness to change their opinions about inanimate situations. However, Carrier (1963) questioned whether people's acceptance of an expert's evaluation of them was related to their psychological needs. He found that males who willingly accepted a bogus interpretation of their personality had high needs for achievement, deference, intraception, and abasement as expected, but low need for endurance, contrary to his prediction.

Conditionability is the term often used to refer to the process in which individuals learn a different manner of expressing an old behavior at another's indirect behest. The more one changes, the more conditionable one is.

Using *mm-hmmms* to reinforce male college students' production of dependent and aggressive words, Cairns and Lewis (1962) found that highly dependent subjects (deference[6]70th percentile; autonomy[5]50th percentile) emitted a high number of dependent words when not being reinforced, but increased their production of aggressive words when being reinforced for doing so. Independent subjects decreased the number of the kinds of responses reinforced by the experimenter.

When male subjects were in charge of reinforcing themselves, Bartol and Duerfeldt (1970) found that different levels of dependency (as indicated by deference and autonomy scores) didn't differ in their rate of self-reinforcement. Although their criteria for defining dependency were less stringent than Cairns and Lewis's (1962), their results may indicate that dependency behaviors are elicited by social interactions.

Using a similar definition of dependency, Gerson (1974) found that dependency statements were influenced by the type of social interaction in which the person found her- or himself. Interacting with an experimenter who used dependent rather than independent statements led to subjects using more dependency statements.

Two studies have involved attempts to manipulate conditioned responses of psychiatric patient populations. Vestre (1962) attempted to condition hospitalized schizophrenic patients to use pronouns. He found that the conditionable subjects as compared to the nonconditionable subjects had lower needs for achievement, autonomy, and dominance and higher needs for deference, affiliation, abasement, and order.

Brady et al. (1962) conditioned the button-pushing behavior of eleven male inpatients who had been diagnosed as acute schizophrenic reaction. They found that variability of responding within or between sessions was correlated with deference, order, nurturance, or heterosexuality; response delay during a session was positively correlated with achievement, exhibition, succorance, nurturance, or aggression. Endurance negatively correlated with response delay and heterosexuality negatively correlated with rate of responding.

Normal Group Behavior

Although most group studies have emphasized the relationship between need levels and social conformity, a few have involved interactive behaviors when no overt group pressure was involved. Bennis, Burke, Cutter, Harrington, and Hoffman (1957) found that none of the needs predicted the group behavior of participants in a human relations group.

Scheidel, Crowell, and Shephard (1958) divided undergraduates into groups of effective and ineffective group member discussants on the basis of their classmates' ratings. Effective discussants in terms of their individual preeminence had greater need for dominance and lesser need for affiliation than ineffective group members. As compared to the norms, effective discussants had higher need for dominance and lesser need for succorance and abasement.

SOCIAL PERCEPTION. A person's style of behavior may influence how he or she is perceived by others as well as how he or she perceives others. In a study of others' perceptions, a sample of nursing students were asked to nominate the ones of their peers who were rebellious, submissive, conformist, or dependent (Zuckerman, 1958). As compared to the submissive nominees, the rebellious nurses were less deferent and had a lower dependency ratio, (deference + succorance + abasement) (autonomy + dominance + aggression). Their needs for autonomy, dominance, and autonomy were higher. As compared to the conformist nominees, rebellious nurses had higher autonomy, dominance, and aggression needs and lower deference, succorance, and abasement needs. The same set of low needs distinguished rebellious from dependent nominees. Autonomy was the only high need that distinguished the two groups. Overall, Zuckerman concluded that abasement and autonomy were the most effective scales for distinguishing the various groups.

How the person is perceived may be influenced by the way in which she or he communicates with others. Tutko and Sechrest (1962) found that a person's tendency to conceptualize her or his environment via "public, communicable concepts" was significantly correlated with their needs for nurturance (r = .28), affiliation (r = .19), and intraception (r = -.21).

Rezler (1965) studied the influence of students' EPPS needs on their perceptions of their male teachers. He reported that male students who believed that they were liked by their teacher had lower needs for abasement and higher needs for exhibition and dominance than those male students who believed their male teacher did not know them; females who believed that they were liked had higher needs for dominance. Nurturance, exhibition, heterosexuality, and dominance needs positively influenced male students' evaluations of their teacher. Their needs for succorance, heterosexuality, and exhibition negatively influenced female students' evaluation.

JOB PERFORMANCE. Others' perceptions often influence the quality of another's work. Three studies have used job performance or work samples as the behavior presumably influenced by psychological needs. Comparing successful to less successful business executives, Rawls and Rawls (1968) found that the former had higher needs for deference and order. Success was defined in terms of salary level, company job title, and former superiors' ratings.

Identification of personality factors involved in more socially focused occupations has yielded mixed results. Using a variety of behavioral and test measures including role plays of situations that nursing students were likely to encounter on the job, Caputo, Plapp, Hanf, and Anzel (1965) could identify no EPPS variables that were significantly related to work-related behavior. However, Steinkamp (1966) found that dominance and intraception were positively correlated and succorance and change were negatively correlated with effective interviewer behavior. Amount and type of information elicited by interviewers determined their degree of effectiveness.

Self-Influenced Behaviors

Self-influenced behaviors are those characteristics that develop out of the individual's own psychological processes. They are, in a sense, one's his manner of responding to and/or organizing one's environment. Studies of the EPPS scales have sought an answer to the question of whether certain needs could be used to predict a person's manner of behaving.

ALTRUISTIC BEHAVIOR. Perhaps the most social of self-influenced behaviors is the willingness to help others when there is no extrinsically obvious reward to the person for doing so, i.e. altruistic behavior. The aspect of altruism that has concerned social scientists is whether EPPS scales could be used to differentiate people who volunteer to participate in experiments from those who do not.

The evidence regarding this issue has been mixed. When a mixed sex sample of students were asked to volunteer for a leaderless group discussion experiment, the volunteer group did not differ from the nonvolunteers on any of the EPPS needs (Frye and Adams, 1959). Cairns and Lewis (1962) did find that more of the male freshmen whom they had categorized as highly dependent (i.e. high deference-low autonomy) did appear for an interview. However, Waters and Kirk (1969) found no difference between need levels of mixed sex volunteers who appeared or did not appear for experiments dealing with various topics.

Although the manner of soliciting subject participation is not clearly described in Frye and Adam's (1959) presentation, it is possible that the level of self-assertion required to refuse a request may determine when volunteer and nonvolunteer groups will differ. Student nurses who volunteered via responses to a mailed questionnaire had a significantly higher dependency ratio, (deference + succorance + abasement) (dominance + autonomy), and a higher need for order than nonresponders. They also tended to have higher needs for deference, succorance, achievement, and nurturance. Nonresponders, on the other hand, had a higher need for aggression and tendencies toward greater needs for dominance, autonomy, and intraception.

Edwards (1968a; 1968b) suggested that social orientation might distinguish volunteers from nonvolunteers. He reported that nursing students who volunteered for a sleep and hypnosis experiment had lower autonomy and dominance needs. Based on their responses to a number of personality measures, he classified the volunteers and nonvolunteers into groups representing their social role orientations. The two groups in which all members volunteered, which he called analytic orientation and instrumental orientation, when visually compared to the group that had no volunteers, appear to have had higher needs for exhibition and succorance. The non-volunteer group had higher needs for autonomy, intraception, and dominance.

Because one volunteers for an experiment does not mean that he or she will be able to successfully complete it. Hull and Zubek (1962) explored the relationship of needs to successful completion of a social isolation experiment, male college students were exposed to continuous lights and noise; in the other, they were exposed to darkness and silence. Those who were successful in the light experiment tended to have lower needs for intraception prior to participating than those who were unsuccessful. Those who were successful at remaining in the dark had significantly lower needs for abasement and tendencies toward higher succorance and lower change needs.

Taylor, Altman, Wheeler, and Kushner (1969) found that successful male boot camp trainees, participating in a lighted-room, social isolation study, had lower preisolation need for heterosexuality than riot aborters and aborters and lower aggression needs than riot aborters.

Thus, a certain social "neediness" may characterize people who volunteer to participate in experiments varying along the dimension of potential social interaction, but there also may be no differences between people who agree to participate in an experiment and those who do not depending upon how their agreement was elicited. However, those who eventually do actually participate as contrasted to those who do not may be more socially dependent and these socially dependent needs may interact with the experimental treatment.

CONCEPTUAL PROCESSES. Personality needs that influence how an individual learns about and communicates with her or his world has received minimal attention. Two studies (Bernadin and Jessor, 1957; Lipetz and Milton, 1962) have used finger mazes to study respondents learning behavior under stressful conditions. The first indicated that the quality of dependent subjects' (i.e. those who exceeded the 70th percentile in their need for deference and were below the 50th percentile in their need for autonomy) performance on the learning task was poorer if they were exposed to negative verbal reinforcement while they were attempting to learn. Dependent subjects were also likely to ask the experimenter for help more often.

In the Lipetz and Milton (1962) study, the EPPS Autonomy Scale items were reworded to refer to independence from authorities and from peers, and either an authority or a peer administered the negative verbal reinforcement. They found a significant negative correlation between EPPS autonomy (r = -.45) and finger-maze performance in the presence of a peer and concluded that their results did not confirm Bernadin and Jessor's (1957). The two sets of authors have since engaged in a written debate attempting to explain why their results were inconsistent (Lipetz, 1963; Jessor, 1963). However, to complicate the matter further, Cairns and Lewis' (1962) finding that low dependent subjects (high autonomy-low deference) evaluated verbal stimuli less positively than high dependents suggests that negative verbal reinforcement may have differential impact regardless of the content of the verbalization (and perhaps who delivers it).

Attitudes about one's self and one's environment are another dimension of a person's conceptual processes and have been examined by some investigators. Questions about the person's attitudes about her- or himself appeared in three studies. Tolor and Murphy (1967) examined men and women's self-projected life expectancy. He divided his sample into "self-directed" (i.e. the sum of the Deference, Affiliation, Intraception, Succorance, Abasement, Nurturance, and Change scales) and "outer-oriented" (i.e. the sum of the Achievement, Autonomy, Dominance, Heterosexuality, and Aggression scales) patterns and compared them to actuarial data. He found that regardless of their orientation, women accurately estimated their expectancy. Men who were high in self-direction needs or low in outer-oriented needs accurately estimated their life expectancy whereas men who were high outer-oriented or low self-directed overestimated their life expectancy.

The extent to which personal expectations were congruent with reality was of concern to Izard (1962) and Renzaglia, Henry, and Rybolt (1962). Izard asked male and female college students to anticipate their performance on future course examinations. For females, there were no correlations between expected performance and EPPS scales, but achievement (r = .33), dominance (r =

.33), change (r = .32), and nurturance (r = -.48) were significantly correlated with actual performance. For males, endurance was correlated with the expected level of performance and achievement (r = .40) and abasement (r = -.70) were significantly correlated with actual performance.

Examining reactions to the environment, Levy (1962) attempted to determine whether a person's expectancies for technological change, institutional change, and a combination of both were correlated with EPPS needs. He concluded that "the person with a high expectancy for change is somewhat introspective and detached socially (high in intraception [r = .23]), not likely to become involved in interpersonal power struggles (low in deference [r = -.22] and dominance [(r = -.35]), but one who seeks new experiences and attempts to avoid the routine or humdrum in his [sic] life (high in change [r = .29]) . . ." (p. 355). Change expectancies were defined in terms of the person's willingness to believe in innovations that had not yet happened.

Reiter (1965) developed a current events questionnaire and used it in combination with the EPPS to determine which personality characteristics were related to actual knowledge about the environment. He found correlations between knowledge and achievement (r = .368), consistency (r = .265), affiliation (r = .312), and aggression (r = -.260). However, his use of the consistency scale as a predictor suggests that he did not eliminate subjects with invalid responses.

A small cluster of studies have examined how need levels relate to a person's selection of products from the environment. Kuehn (1963) reanalyzed Evans's (1959) data to show that the difference between a person's dominance and affiliation needs could be used to predict Ford car ownership. Ford owners tended to have higher levels of dominance minus affiliation scores than Chevy owners.

Alpert (1972) showed that different dimensions influencing male business students' choice of residence were correlated with different personality needs. For instance, the dimension he calls *anti-social personality* consisted of high needs for exhibition, autonomy, and achievement and low needs for deference and affiliation combined with a choice of residence that was convenient to school, had large rooms, and nonfriendly atmosphere, and was private.

In his attempt to discover whether people's esthetic preferences were related to EPPS needs, Christensen (1961) reported no significant relationships between needs and the color and design preferences of college students of unspecified sex.

Summary and Discussion

Behaviors (and attitudes) examined in this chapter were arbitrarily characterized as either socially influenced or self-motivated. In the former category are those studies focusing primarily on social conformity and susceptibility to persuasion (including conditionability as a subtype of persuasion). Self-motivated behaviors investigated have included altruism (usually defined as willingness to participate in psychology experiments), conceptual processes, and consumer behavior.

Studies in each of these areas have varied considerably in the manner in which characteristics have been defined and assessed. In the face of non-significant results, the typical reaction has been to move toward using less vigorous measures and definitions, which is tantamount to changing the yard-stick to fit the yard.

With this caveat in mind, a few suppositions seem to emerge from the studies presented in this chapter. It appears that needs may be classifiable as either affiliative, e.g. deference and affiliation, or self-centered, e.g. achieve-ment, autonomy, and aggression. Affiliative needs may contribute to behavioral compliance whereas self-centeredness may lead to rebellion, par-ticularly in situations requiring a response to social pressure.

Others' perceptions of one's behavior may also be more favorable if one ex-hibits a level of affiliative or self-centered needs that is characteristic of the set-ting in which one is functioning, and one's capacity to exercise personal choice may be positively correlated with self-centered needs. More research is needed, however, to determine where the various needs lie along the affiliative-self-centeredness dimension and to discover whether such a dimension is more useful in predictng social behaviors than the individual needs taken separately.

References

Abraham, H.L.: The suggestible personality: A psychological investigation of susceptibility to persuasion. *Acta Psychologica, 20:*167-184, 1962.

Alpert, M.I.: Personality and the determinants of product choice. *Journal of Marketing Research, 9:* 89-92, 1972.

Appley, M.H., and Moeller, G.: Conforming behavior and personality variables in college women. *Journal of Abnormal and Social Psychology, 66:*284-290, 1963.

Asch, S.E.: Studies of independence and conformity: I. A minority of one against a unanimous majority. *Psychological Monograph, 70 (9, Whole No. 416),*1956.

Bartol, G.H., and Duerfeldt, P.H.: Self-reinforcing behavior: The effects of base rate and de-pendency. *Journal of General Psychology, 83:*151-161, 1970.

Bennis, W., Burke, R., Cutter, H., Harrington, H., and Hoffman, J. A.: Note on some prob-lems of measurement and prediction in a training group. *Group Psychotherapy, 10:*328-341, 1957.

Bernadin, A.C., and Jessor, R.: A construct validation of the Edwards Personal Prefer-ence Schedule with respect to dependency. *Journal of Consulting Psychology, 21:*63-67, 1957.

Brady, J.P., Thornton, D.R., Pappas, N., and Tansig, T.N.: Edwards Personal Preference Schedule correlates of operant behavior. *Journal of Clinical Psychology, 18:*224-226, 1962.

Cairns, R.B., and Lewis, M.: Dependency and the reinforcement value of a verbal stimulus. *Journal of Consulting Psychology, 26:*1-8, 1962.

Caputo, D.V., Plapp, J.M., Hanf, C., and Anzel, A.S.: The validity of the Edwards Personal Preference Schedule (EPPS) employing projective and behavioral critieria. *Educational and*

*Psychological Measurement, 25:*829-848, 1965.

Carrier, N.A.: Need correlates of "gullibility." *Journal of Abnormal and Social Psychology, 66:*84-86, 1963.

Christensen, C.M.: Use of design, texture, and color preferences in assessment of personality characteristics. *Perceptual and Motor Skills, 12:*143-150, 1961.

Crutchfield, R.S.: Conformity and character. *American Psychologist, 10:*191-198, 1955.

Edwards, C.N.: Characteristics of volunteers and nonvolunteers for a sleep and hypnotic experiment. *American Journal of Clinical Hypnosis, 11:*26-29, 1968.

Edwards, C.N.: Defensive interaction and the volunteer subject: A heuristic note. *Psychological Reports, 22:*1305-1309, 1968a.

Endler, N.S.: Conformity analyzed and related to personality. *Journal of Social Psychology, 53:*271-283, 1961.

Evans, F.B.: Psychological and objective factors in the prediction of brand choice: Ford versus Chevrolet. *Journal of Business, 22:*340-369, 1959.

Finch, K., Rickard, H.C., and Wilson, W.: Personality variables and sexual status in observer performance. *Psychological Reports, 26:*676-678, 1970.

Frye, R.L., and Adams, H.E.: Effect of the volunteer variable on leaderless group discussion experiments. *Psychological Reports, 5:*184, 1959.

Gerson, A.R.: Subject's satisfaction with a task as a function of E's communication style and S's dependency. *Psychological Reports, 34:*463-466, 1974.

Gisvold, D.: A validity study of the autonomy and deference subscales of the EPPS. *Journal of Consulting Psychology, 22:*455-457, 1958.

Hull, J., and Zubek, J.P.: Personality characteristics of successful and unsuccessful sensory isolation subjects. *Perceptual and Motor Skills, 14:*231-240, 1962.

Izard, C.E.: Personality characteristics associated with resistance to change. *Journal of Counseling Psychology, 24:*437-440, 1960.

Izard, C.E.: Personality characteristics (EPPS) level of expectation and performance. *Journal of Counseling Psychology, 26:*394, 1962½.

Jessor, R.: On studying autonomy — without deference. *Psychological Reports, 12:*132-134, 1963.

Kuehn, A.A.: Demonstration of a relationship between psychological factors and brand choice. *Journal of Business, 36:*237-241, 1963.

Lang, P.J., and Lazovik, D.: Personality and hypnotic susceptibility. *Journal of Consulting Psychology, 26:*317-322, 1962.

Levy, L.H.: Age and personal need correlates of expectancy for change. *Perceptual and Motor Skills, 15:*351-356, 1962.

Lipetz, M.E.: Further comments on the prediction of autonomy behavior from the EPPS in autonomy scale. *Psychological Reports, 12:*737-738, 1963.

Lipetz, M.E., and Milton, G.A.: Prediction of autonomy behavior from situations modifications of the EPPS autonomy scale. *Psychological Reports, 11:*487-493, 1962.

Lubin, B., Levitt, E.E., and Zuckerman, M.: Some personality differences between responders and nonresponders to a survey questionnaire. *Journal of Consulting Psychology, 26:*192, 1962.

Phelps, R.E., and Meyer, M.E.: Personality and conformity, and sex differences. *Psychological Reports, 18:*730, 1966.

Rawls, D.J., and Rawls, J.R.: Personality characteristics and personal history data of successful and less successful executives. *Psychological Reports, 23:*1032-1034, 1968.

Reiter, H.H.: Four personality correlates of current events awareness. *Psychological Reports, 17:*350, 1965.

Renzaglia, G.A., Henry, D.R., and Rybolt, G.A., Jr.: Estimating and measurement of personality characteristics and correlates of their congruence. *Journal of Counseling Psychology, 9:*71-78, 1962.

Rezler, A.G.: The influence of needs upon the student's perception of his instructor. *Journal of*

*Educational Research, 58:*282-286, 1965.

Rodgers, C.W.: Prediction of hypnotic susceptibility from the Edwards Personal Preference Schedule: Negative finding. *Psychological Reports, 34:*406, 1974.

Scheidel, T.M., Crowell, L., and Shephard, J.R.: Personality and discussion behavior: A state of possible relationships. *Speech Monograph, 25:*261-267, 1958.

Sistrunk, F., and McDavid, J.W.: Achievement motivation, affiliation motivation, and task difficulty as determinants of social conformity. *Journal of Social Psychology, 66:*41-50, 1965.

Steinkamp, S.W.: Some characteristics of effective interviewers. *Journal of Applied Psychology, 50:* 487-492, 1966.

Suinn, R.M.: Limited sensory and social deprivation and operant control of affiliation and deference responses. *Journal of Projective Techniques and Personality Assessment, 33:*535-538, 1969.

Taylor, D.A., Altman, I., Wheeler, L. and Kushner, E.N.: Personality factors related to response to social isolation and confinement. *Journal of Consulting and Clinical Psychology, 33:*411-419, 1969.

Toler, A., and Murphy, V.M.: Some psychological correlates of subjective life expectancy. *Journal of Clinical Psychology, 23:*21-24, 1967.

Tuddenham, R.D.: Correlates of yielding to a distorted group norm. *Journal of Personality, 27:*272-284, 1959.

Tutko, T.A., and Sechrest, L.: Conceptual performance and personality variables. *Journal of Consulting Psychology, 26:*481, 1962.

Vestre, N.D.: The relationship between verbal conditionability and the Edwards Personal Preference Schedule. *Journal of Clinical Psychology, 18:*513-515, 1962.

Walsh, R.P.: The effect of needs on responses to job duties. *Journal of Counseling Psychology, 6:*194-198, 1959.

Ward, W.D.: Persuasability as related to need autonomy. *Psychological Reports, 13:*357-358, 1963.

Waters, L.K., and Kirk, W.E.: Characteristics of volunteers and nonvolunteers for psychological experiments. *Journal of Psychology, 73:*133-136, 1969.

Weinstein, M.S.: Achievement motivation and risk preference. *Journal of Personality and Social Psychology, 13:*153-172, 1969.

Zuckerman, M.: The validity of the Edwards Personal Preference Schedule in the measurement of dependency-rebelliousness. *Journal of Clinical Psychology, 14:*379-382, 1958.

Chapter 14

NEEDS FOR RELATIONSHIPS

T WO theoretical positions compete as explanations for why people befriend or marry the people that they do. The first suggests that people are attracted to people who are or who they perceive are similar to themselves and is variously referred to as balance theory, e.g. Heider (1958), or the homogamy position (Murstein, 1967). The second hypothesis, proposed by Winch (1955), to explain mate selection, stresses that people select partners who are opposites of themselves regarding certain needs. These two positions have been investigated using the EPPS variables as measures of needs and friendship or marital relationships as the interpersonal relationships of concern.

Selecting Friends

PERCEIVING OTHERS. One reason why people select the friends that they do may be because their own needs lead them to perceive other people in certain limited ways. Two studies explored this possibility (Chance and Meaders, 1960; Abate and Berrien, 1967). Chance and Meaders asked male undergraduates to predict the responses of male interviewees to the Autonomy and Succorance scales of the EPPS. They found that accurate judges had lower needs for aggression, succorance, and intraception and higher needs for affiliation and dominance than did inaccurate judges. In addition, they found that judges who assumed that the interviewee were quite similar to them, i.e. high assumed similarity, as contrasted to those who assumed that the interviewees were quite dissimilar, i.e. low assumed similarity, had higher needs for deference, affiliation, succorance, and order and lower needs for exhibition, autonomy, and dominance. Both high and low assumed similarity judges tended to be inaccurate predictors of others' responses.

Abate and Berrien (1967) used the EPPS scales to assess the similarity between cross-national stereotypes. They compared American college students' and Japanese college students' self-descriptions, descriptions of members of the other country, and the degree of agreement between actual EPPS responses and stereotypes. The Japanese students' stereotype of Americans was more accurate than the Americans' stereotype of Japanese as measured by correlations between *measured* personality traits of the two groups as well as between measured needs of Americans and the Japanese's estimates of the descriptiveness of the traits. However, only the correlation for American males was statistically significant. Americans' stereotypes of themselves and Japanese stereotypes of Americans correlated highly, but only moderate correlations were discovered between Japanese stereotypes of themselves and Americans' stereotypes of Japanese, whereas both correlations for American males and females as related to Japanese stereotypes for Japanese women was significant.

In a subsequent report, Berrien (1967) noted that the Japanese viewed themselves as having characteristics that were opposite of Americans. In terms of measured personality needs, in order of decreasing rank, intraception, nurturance, affiliation, change, and heterosexuality were the top five needs for American women; autonomy, succorance, nurturance, endurance, and abasement were the top five needs for Japanese women. For American men, heterosexuality, dominance, change, achievement, and intraception were the top five needs; nurturance, autonomy, endurance, succorance, and abasement were the top five needs for Japanese men.

These two studies suggest that when accuracy of social perception requires entering another's frame of reference, that different needs may be relevant for American male and female perceivers. High needs for affiliation and dominance and low needs for aggression, succorance, and intraception may promote accuracy as far as males are concerned, whereas for women some combination of high needs for intraception, nurturance, affiliation, change, and heterosexuality and low needs for aggression, order, deference, endurance, and dominance may contribute to social accuracy. In two of the studies cited, only intraception, affiliation, aggression, and dominance appeared to be relevant for both sexes, but not necessarily in the same direction.

FRIENDSHIP SIMILARITY. Do friendship pairs share similar needs? To address this question, Mehlman (1962) asked very best friends, friends, and best enemies to take the EPPS and to rate the other person's level of possession of the EPPS attributes. The results revealed two significant correlations between needs for best friends: nurturance ($r = .78$) and heterosexuality ($r = .57$); four significant need correlations for friends were revealed: succorance ($r = .24$), abasement ($r = .26$), heterosexuality ($r = .38$), and aggression ($r = .55$). Only heterosexuality was significant for more than one relationship type.

Analyses of perceptual ratings indicated that best friends agreed moderately in their perceptions of one another's dominance ($r = -.52$) and aggression ($r = -.59$); friends showed some agreement in their perceptions of each other's achievement ($r = -.79$) and order ($r = -.35$), but they disagreed in their evaluations of each other's endurance ($r = .53$). Enemies agreed in their evaluations of achievement ($r = -.79$), but disagreed in their evaluations of order ($r = .75$), autonomy ($r = .49$), abasement ($r = .55$), nurturance, ($r = .46$), endurance ($r = .46$), and heterosexuality ($r = .60$). Mehlman's results suggested that friends and enemies were actually similar to each other to about the same extent, but that friends shared common perceptions of one another to a greater extent than did enemies.

Izard (1960) searched for profile similarities between best friends as well as similarities between friends' specific needs. As compared to randomly paired dyads, mutual best friends' overall profiles were found to be significantly more similar. Specific needs that were shared by friends were deference ($r = .44$), exhibition ($r = .39$), and endurance ($r = .47$). Random pairs shared no common needs. Izard interpreted the results as substantiating the similarity of needs position.

Bowerman and Day (1956) examined differences in need levels between engaged couples and their same-sex friends. They found that the male and female members of the couple differed from one another in traditionally sex-typed directions, but the friends did not differ on most of the mean needs. Although Bowerman and Day found no support for either the complementarity or the homogamy hypothesis, they did conclude that individuals select same-sex friends and opposite-sex friends who possess different needs and need combinations.

Winch's (1955) original statements of the complementarity hypothesis had two postulates: (a) a person high in one need would be attracted to a person who was low in the same need and (b) a person who had a high need would be attracted to a person who had a high opposite or complementary need. Reilly, Commins, and Stefic (1960) tested both versions of the hypothesis using five pairs of women enrolled in a Catholic college. They found no significant correlations between friends' measured needs nor between those of randomly matched pairs. Neither did they find significant correlations between friends' need when opposite need pairs were correlated. They did find significant correlations, however, between measured needs and friends' predictions of needs for the following: achievement ($r = .24$), deference ($r = .25$), exhibition ($r = .22$), autonomy ($r = .31$), affiliation ($r = .20$), succorance ($r = .19$), abasement ($r = .35$), nurturance ($r = .30$), heterosexuality ($r = .32$), and aggression ($r = .29$). Again it appeared that better knowledge of one's friend rather than actual need characteristics distinguished friends from random pairs. Poe and Mills (1972) also reported that undergraduate sorority women more accurately predicted the measured need patterns of close rather than distant peers.

FRIENDSHIP CHARACTERISTICS. Perhaps the friendship process involves two distinct phases: the initial attraction followed by the subsequent commitment. Although most studies of friendships have focused on characteristics of friends once the relationship has been established, a few have examined characteristics that contribute to the initial attraction.

Two studies suggest that type of personal involvement may be related to different needs. Rychlak (1965) found that male telephone company employees with high need for order preferred employers with a *low* need for change, but preferred neighbors with a *high* need for change.

For Markey's (1973) sorority sample, their needs for nurturance and aggression were negatively related to their social/emotional friends' needs, but nurturance and abasement were negatively correlated with the needs of the person whom they chose as an intellectual-task companion. These needs were not consistent across different types of measures, i.e. peer and self-ratings. Examination of these other types of need measures led Markey to conclude that subjects did not perceive themselves as their peers did, but their peers perceived that the subjects' friends and social companions were similar with respect to their needs.

Wright (1968) contended that one reason why inconsistent support for either the homogamy or complementarity hypothesis has been found is that people who have different levels of particular needs may be differentially receptive to similar others. Seyfried and Hendrick's (1973) study in which male and female college students with different levels of nurturance and succorance reacted to a standard stranger seems to support Wright's position to some extent. They found that highly nurturant male and female subjects were attracted to a stranger whom they believed was highly nurturant, but highly nurturant males were also attracted to a stranger who they believed was highly succorant.

In general, the friendship studies suggest that friends are probably no more similar than nonfriends, but that they seem to share a common perception of one another or of their relationship. It is also possible that the relevant needs may depend upon the roles that the respondent and his or her friend play with respect to one another. Nevertheless, it should be noted that one methodological difficulty with the friendship studies has been that they have used heterogeneous dyads of unspecified sex proportions in most cases. Therefore, obtained results may have been tempered by investigators' failure to filter out variability due to the sex variable.

Mate Selection

PERCEPTIONS OF THE OTHER. One postulate of balance or similarity theory is that people perceive positive traits in the people they like. Generalizing this postulate to engaged couples, Centers (1971) speculated that needs for abasement, affiliation, aggression, autonomy, deference, dominance, intraception, nurturance, and succorance would influence a person's perception of her or his mate. Using a modified version of the EPPS, he found that females and males high in affiliation, nurturance, deference, intraception, dominance (for males), succorance, and abasement as opposed to those low in these needs evaluated their mates more positively. Females high and low in dominance did not differ in the manner in which they evaluated their mates. Males low in aggression and females low in aggression rated their mates more positively than men and women who had a high need for aggression.

Murstein (1967) proposed an alternative way of looking at the issue of how one's perceptions are related to couple's needs. He suggested that the degree to which couples satisfied the members' role expectations, rather than need levels per se, would influence mate selection. To test his prediction, he compared actual EPPS scores of each partner to the desired or ideal characteristics desired by the other partner. He also compared each partner's perception of her or his mate's actual characteristics to her or his perceptions of an ideal mate. The consistency between these two types of scores as considered to be an indicant of role compatibility; Murstein called the first a measure of intraperceptions and the second a measure of interperception.

Subjects in the study were ninety-nine couples who were dating or going steady. As compared to randomly matched couples, Murstein found that actual couple's interperception scores, i.e. ideal spouse behavior as compared to actual EPPS needs, tended to be less discrepant. For the male members of the couples, the needs showing less discrepancy were intraception, dominance, nurturance, change, endurance, and aggression; for the female members of the couple, less discrepant needs were achievement, exhibition, affiliation, nurturance, change, endurance, heterosexuality, and aggression. The difference between women's actual succorance needs as compared to men's ideal succorance need for their spouses was greater for the actual couples than it was for the randomly matched couples. Intraperception scores were more consistent for actual couples than for random couples for all needs suggesting that actual couples are likely to perceive their mates as conforming to their ideals more than they actually do.

COUPLE CHARACTERISTICS. Winch (1967) speculated that there were two dimensions underlying the needs that linked members of a couple, nurturance-receptivity and dominancy-submissiveness. Defining *receptivity* in terms of deference, affiliation, succorance, and abasement and *dominance* in terms of needs for achievement, exhibition, autonomy, dominance, and aggression, Saper (1965) found a negative correlation between wife's receptivity and husband's dominance, which was contrary to what would be predicted by a complementarity position. Spouses' aggression needs were positively correlated ($r = .49$). Couples in Saper's study had been married a median of 5.8 years.

A series of investigations have involved direct or indirect comparisons of the complementarity/similarity hypotheses as they relate to couple characteristics. In a direct comparison, Katz, Glucksberg, and Krauss (1960) also used a modified version of the EPPS to discover whether need complementarity or need homogamy was related to couple member's perceptions of her or his spouse's capacity to satisfy the spouse's needs. They found that the profiles of the couples who had been married a median of five years were not significantly more similar than those obtained from randomly paired couples. Significant positive associations were found between abasement, autonomy, and nurturance, indicating that spouses tended to be similar in their level of these needs. Husband's succorance and wife's nurturance were negatively associated.

In terms of level of satisfaction, highly satisfied wives as compared to less satisfied wives were significantly more similar to their husbands. Husbands of high satisfaction as compared to husbands of low satisfaction were less similar to their spouses in their needs for achievement and succorance. The relationship between husband's succorance and wife's nurturance was greater for high satisfaction husbands. Husbands' own needs for nurturance and succorance were positively related to satisfaction. Wives' total satisfaction was positively associated with husbands' need for achievement. Husbands' total satisfaction was related to their own need for affiliation and their wives' needs for succorance and nurturance; it was negatively related to their wives' need for autonomy and dominance.

In a second part of his study, Murstein (1967) compared data relating to three positions: complementarity needs, homogamy, and role theory. This latter position suggests that couples have role expectations for themselves as well as for their spouses, and the extent to which these expectations are met influences couple satisfaction (Ott, 1950). Using intreparceptions (a spouse's perceptions of how well her or his spouse matches her or his ideal and the spouse's perception of mate similarity), he found greater evidence for the role compatibility position although spouses did tend to perceive that they were similar to each other as opposed to complementary. There was a statistically nonsignificant tendency for actual EPPS scores as compared to ideals (interperception) to support the superiority of the role complementarity and similiarity positions, respectively. Measured needs that were similar for couples were order ($r = .22$), nurturance ($r = .24$), change ($r = .25$), endurance ($r = .22$), heterosexuality ($r = .26$), and aggression ($r = .21$).

Becker's (1964) and Reiter's (1970) studies represented indirect tests of the complementary/similarity positions. Becker attempted to discover whether engaged couples who differed in dominance need also differed in other EPPS needs. If a complementarity hypothesis were accurate, one might expect couples who showed high differences in their dominance scores to likewise differ on other needs relating to Winch's (1967) dominance-receptivity dimensions.

His results indicated that for the female member in a couple in which the difference between dominance need was low (low dominance difference), needs for succorance, dominance, heterosexuality, and aggression were greater and needs for deference, intraception, and abasement were less as compared to the high dominance-difference women. Males in the low difference couple had greater need for heterosexuality and less of a need for intraception than males in the high dominance-difference group. When the combination of high and low dominance-differences couples was compared to couples of medium difference, males in the medium couple had higher need for achievement and less need for affiliation and nurturance. Women in the medium couple had more need for autonomy and less need for nurturance.

If one uses the needs that Saper (1965) used to measure receptivity-dominance, then it appears that women, who are involved in couples who are similar with respect to dominance have comparatively low needs for succorance (i.e. receptivity), dominance, and aggression (i.e. dominance). In other words, their needs consistently reflect neither dominance nor receptivity.

Among engaged college students, Reiter (1970) found that the male half of the couple had higher scores in needs for achievement, dominance, and endurance whereas the women had higher scores on needs for abasement, nurturance, affiliation, and succorance. Reiter interprets these differences as supportive of the notion that people select mates who complement their own needs. However, the elevated means that he found are typical of the sex for which they were found.

The overall results of the need complementarity-homogamy studies offer little support for the complementarity hypothesis when the EPPS scales are used to measure couples' needs. There is at least some support for small, but significant, similarities among mates with regard to specific needs. However, Winch's (1968) criticism of the use of correlations to assess couple similarity or dissimilarity applies to many of the investigations in this area.

MARITAL DISCORD. Practitioners have recommended different strategies for comparing couples' need levels as a means of exploring marital discord. Araoz (1975), for example, has suggested that EPPS profiles can be used beneficially in counseling couples by examining pairs of needs that he states should be inversely related (deference-dominance, order-change, exhibition-intraception, autonomy-affiliation, succorance-nurturance, and abasement-aggression), plotting mates' profiles on the same sheet, looking for instances in which the needs of the two vary in directions that could reflect·conflict, and then encouraging the partners to discuss how they go about getting their needs met.

Drewery (1969) and his associate have developed a statistically more sophisticated manner of assessing spousal incongruence. Their procedure involves correlating spouses' responses to the EPPS under instructions to describe: "Myself as I am," "My spouse as I see him/her," and "Myself as I think my spouse sees me."

Using the interpersonal patterns technique, they.(Rae and Drewery, 1972) found that in alcoholic couples in which the wives' MMPI Pd scores were above the median, the partners were more likely to disagree about the male's masculine characteristics than was true of controls. Men saw themselves as having greater levels of feminine needs than did their wives whereas wives saw the men as having higher levels of masculine needs than did the men.

In a second study (Drewery and Rae, 1969) of male alcoholic patients and their wives who were compared to nonalcoholic couples, they found that the longer the marriage lasted, the more the control wives "understood" (i.e. shared their husband's perceptions) of the husband. For patients, the longer the relationship, the less the wife understood the husband. Husbands' perceptions of wives did not agree with the wives' perceptions in either the alcoholic or nonalcoholic groups.

Murstein's (1973) approach for studying neurotic courtships uses a modified form of the EPPS with which couples describe self, ideal self, their perception of their current partner, and their ideal spouse. These ratings are intercorrelated. Although Murstein's strategy has been used primarily as a research tool, he reported that neurotic couples appeared to have conflicting perceptions (negatively correlated) whereas nonneurotic couples had uncorrelated perceptions.

Summary and Discussion

Whether considering friendships, premarital relationships, or marriages, most of the studies in which the EPPS needs have been used to test the homogamy/complementarity hypotheses have obtained evidence that has tended to support the notion that friends and mates are more similar than they are different with respect to certain needs. Unfortunately, the specific needs for which similarity has been demonstrated have differed across studies. In criticizing researchers' attempts to replicate his original findings, Winch (1967) decried the use of *grab samples*, samples who have little in common and do not relate to his theoretical position as he stated it. His complaint about the lack of specificity of samples is well taken. It is possible that authors' failure to find relevant needs that are similar (or dissimilar) across studies may be due to the fact that similar samples have not been used across studies.

In addition, it appears that a role compatibility explanation of mate and friendship relationships may offer more directions for the future. Although this particular position has been investigated directly in only one EPPS study (Murstein, 1967), indirect evidence, i.e. friends and mates' perceptions that they are similar, suggests that how a person is perceived more than her or his actual characteristics may determine the nature of a relationship. In marriages, it may be particularly important for the wife to share the husband's self-perception.

It is also possible that similarities or differences with respect to certain needs are more important than others. Need for aggression stands out as an important need whether friends or mates are being considered. A low need for aggression seemed to be related to more accurate and more positive interpersonal perception and the level of aggression tended to be positively correlated across a variety of couples.

Efforts to determine the clinical usefulness of the EPPS have been relatively minimal. Nevertheless, a couple of strategies appear to offer some promise for the usefulness of the EPPS in marital counseling and/or diagnosis.

References

Abate, M., and Berrien, F.K.: Validation of stereotypes: Japanese versus American students. *Journal of Personality and Social Psychology, 7*:435-438, 1967.

Araoz, D.T.: The Edwards Personal Preference Schedule in couple therapy. *Journal of Family Counseling, 3*:46-51, 1975.

Becker, G.: Complementary-needs hypothesis, authoritarianism, dominance, and other Edwards Personal Preference Schedule scores. *Journal of Personality, 32:*45-56, 1964.

Berrien, F. K.: Familiarity, mirror imaging and social desirability in stereotypes: Japanese versus Americans. *International Journal of Psychology, 4:*207-215, 1969.

Bowerman, C. E., and Day, B. R.: A test of the theory of complementary needs as applied to couples during courtship. *American Sociological Review, 21:*602-605, 1956.

Centers, R.: Evaluating the loved one: The motivational congruency factor. *Journal of Personality, 39:*303-318, 1971.

Chance, J. E., and Meaders, W.: Needs and interpersonal perception. *Journal of Personality, 28:*200-209, 1960.

Drewery, J.: An interpersonal perception technique. *British Journal of Medical Psychology, 42:*171-181, 1969.

Drewery, J., and Rae, J. B.: A group comparison of alcoholic and nonalcoholic marriages using the interpersonal perception technique. *British Journal of Psychiatry, 115:*287-300, 1969.

Heider, F.: The psychology of interpersonal relations. New York, Wiley, 1958.

Izard, C. E.: Personality similarity and friendship. *Journal of Abnormal Social Psychology, 61:*47-51, 1960.

Katz, I., Glucksberg, S., and Krauss, R.: Need satisfaction and Edwards PPS scores in married couples. *Journal of Consulting Psychology, 24:*205-208, 1960.

Markey, V. K.: Psychological need relationships in dyadic attraction and rejection. *Psychological Reports, 32:*111-124, 1973.

Mehlman, B.: Similarity in friendships. *Journal of Social Psychology, 57:*195-202, 1962.

Murstein, B. I.: Empirical tests of role, complementary needs and homogamy theories of marital choice. *Journal of Marriage and the Family, 29:*689-696, 1967.

Ott, R. S.: A study of role conflicts as related to happiness in marriage. *Journal of Abnormal and Social Psychology, 45:*691-699, 1950.

Poe, C. A., and Mills, D. H.: Interpersonal attraction, popularity, similarity of personal needs and psychological awareness. *Journal of Psychology, 81:*139-149, 1972.

Rae, J. B., and Drewery, J.: Interpersonal patterns in alcoholic marriages. *British Journal of Psychiatry, 120:*615-621, 1972.

Reilly, M. S., Commins, W. D., and Stefic, E. C.: The complementarity of personality needs in friendship choice. *Journal of Abnormal and Social Psychology, 61:*292-294, 1960.

Reiter, H. H.: Similarities and differences in scores on certain personality scales among engaged couples. *Psychological Reports, 26:*465-466, 1970.

Rychlak, J. F.: The similarity, compatibility, or incompatibility of needs in interpersonal selection. *Journal of Personality and Social Psychology, 2:*334-340, 1965.

Saper, B.: Motivational components in the interpersonal transactions of married couples. *Psychiatric Quarterly, 39:*303-314, 1965.

Seyfried, B. A., and Hendrick, C.: Need similarity and complementarity in interpersonal attraction. *Sociometry, 36:*206-220, 1973.

Winch, R. F.: The theory of complementary needs in mate selection: Final results on the test of the general hypothesis. *American Sociological Review, 20:*52-56, 1955.

Winch, R. F.: Another look at the theory of complementary needs in mate selection. *Journal of Marriage and the Family, 29:*756-762, 1967.

Wright, P. H.: Need similarity, need complementarity and the place of personality in interpersonal attraction, *3:*126-135, 1968.

Chapter 15

THE COUNSELING PROCESS

EFFORTS to understand the personality characteristics of counselors, clients, or both have inspired a small number of EPPS studies. The largest number of these studies has had the identification of pertinent counselor characteristics as their emphasis. A small number have addressed issues of how client characteristics interact with the counseling process. In general, efforts to obtain conclusive results in either of these areas have been hampered by researchers' tendencies to subject massive numbers of variables collected from extremely small numbers of subjects to various correlational analyses. The guiding philosophy seems to have been to toss everything into a pot to see what, if anything, bubbles to the top; the survivors are then assumed to represent dimensions relevant to the counseling process. Of course, the problem with such an approach is that any significant findings in one study may simply represent error particularly if the same variables do not appear in subsequent replication attempts.

Counselor and Other Helper's Characteristics

PROFESSIONALS. Are there EPPS needs that are characteristic of helpers? Various approaches have been used to investigate this question. Mills, Chestnut, and Hartzell (1966) did a component analysis of counselors' needs (n = 37) and identified five counselor styles, which they labeled (a) social service need, (b) masculinity, (c) nondirective, (d) false aggression, and (e) unnamed. The social service need consisted of positive component loadings on intraception and negative loadings on order, succorance, and abasement. It accounted for 46 percent of the variance, and thirty-five of the counselors had significant loadings on this component. Masculinity consisted of positive loadings for achievement, dominance, and aggression and of negative loadings for deference and affiliation. This component accounted for 10 percent of the variance, and high scores on the positively related variables were characteristic of male counselors. Positive loadings on deference, autonomy, and intraception and negative loadings on affiliation, succorance, and dominance were characteristic of the nondirective component. False aggression was characterized by positive loadings on deference, intraception, heterosexuality, and aggression and negative loadings on change and endurance. The authors view this component as reflecting a maturity-immaturity dimension. The fifth component, unnamed, consisted of negative loadings for order and succorance and positive loadings for exhibition, dominance, and endurance. This component appears to include persuasion or leadership as a crucial element.

In the only other study to use experienced counselors, Mills and Abeles (1965) investigated the relationship between affiliation and nurturance and counselors' liking for clients. They found that both needs were significantly positively correlated with liking for practicum students, were positively (though not significantly so) for the senior staff, and were negatively correlated for interns.

Willingness to address hostile client responses was positively correlated with nurturance for senior staff and practicum students; affiliation and approach to hostility were positively correlated for practicum students and interns. Thus, senior staff and practicum students seem to anchor opposite ends of a counselor characteristic continuum and interns fall somewhere in between.

Not enough studies have been conducted to permit formulation of even tentative conclusions about what characteristics contribute to sustained interest in counseling others. The studies in this section do suggest that there is merit in examining patterns of needs since most of the needs are relevant under some circumstances.

PROFESSIONALS IN TRAINING. Most studies of helper characteristics have involved counselors and therapists in training. In examining actual in-counseling counselor behaviors, researchers have been particularly interested in which needs facilitate or inhibit counselors' abilities to deliver the Rogers-Truax-Carkhuff core conditions.

Bergin and Solomon (1963) and Bergin and Jasper (1969) used judges' ratings of the empathy level of counseling and clinical advanced graduate students. In the first study, they found that dominance and change were positively correlated with judged level of counseling empathy; consistency and intraception were negatively related. In the second study, none of those variables were correlated; instead, affiliation and abasement were negatively correlated and achievement was positively correlated. The authors concluded that the obtained correlations represented error or chance fluctuations. Patterson (1962) used a paper-and-pencil measure of empathy in correlation with affiliation, intraception, and nurturance needs. None of the needs were correlated.

Using judges' ratings of work samples of the empathy levels of practicum students in a counselor education program, Jones (1974) found that the abilities to communicate empathic understanding and respect were negatively correlated with the need for order. Rosen (1967) used ratings of interviews of counseling and guidance trainees' initial level of competence and terminal level of competence on the Truax dimensions of accurate empathy, self-congruence, and unconditional positive regard. He found that at the beginning of training, self-congruence was positively correlated with needs for exhibition and affiliation; unconditional positive regard, accurate empathy, and total competency were negatively correlated with the need for aggression. By the end of training, self-congruence and total competency were negatively correlated with abasement and autonomy; unconditional positive regard was negatively correlated with autonomy and endurance and accurate empathy was positively correlated with aggression.

Rosen's (1967) results lead to the speculation that participation in a training program may alter trainees' expressed needs. Danielson (1969) and Apostal and Muro (1970) explored this hypothesis directly. Danielson compared the needs of elementary counselors' in-training to other types of trainees following their participation in a counseling and guidance institute. Following training, the elementary counselor's intraception decreased. Following an entire academic year, their heterosexuality increased while their deference and intraception decreased. Apostal and Muro's (1970) study of male and female teachers who were counselors' in-training as compared to a control group of teachers revealed no changes in needs as a result of participation in group counseling.

Helper behaviors have also been used to examine the relationship between personality needs and trainee's characteristics and/or facilitation of the counseling process. Behaviors have included academic performance as well as counseling process behaviors. In studies of the academic performance of students enrolled in counseling and guidance institutes, McGreevy (1967) and Bernos (1966) identified a number of factors, none of which were replicated across the two studies and few of which correlated with performance criteria such as institute grade point average, faculty ratings of potential success, or test scores. Of passing interest were two predominantly EPPS factors identified by Bernos (1966) for males: need for others (positive loadings: nurturance and affiliation; negative loadings: autonomy, aggression, and order) and need for consistent relationships with others (positive loadings: succorance and abasement; negative loadings: change).

For women only one entirely EPPS factor was identified (and questionably named): striving-cold (positive loadings: achievement; negative loadings: nurturance and affiliation). A second factor, frivolous-unrestraint, consisted of positive loadings for exhibition, change, and autonomy and negative loadings for endurance, order, and deference, Guilford-Zimmerman scales for restraint and thoughtfulness, and Group VII and the interest maturity scales of the Strong Vocational Interest Blank. Entirely EPPS factors identified by McGreevy (1967) were individualism (positive loadings: autonomy and aggression; negative loadings: nurturance and intraception) and not named (positive loadings: aggression and abasement; negative loadings: affiliation).

A sociometric evaluations study was used to compare effective and less effective helpers. Walton (1974) asked graduate student counseling and guidance trainees to select from among their peers the person they would most like to be counseled by. Trainees who were selected most often by their peers at the end of an entry level seminar had high needs for dominance, change, suc-

222 A Practitioner's Guide to the Edwards Personal Preference Schedule

corance, order, nurturance, and achievement, with dominance, change, and succorance accounting for most of the variance.

Rather than noninvolved judges' evaluations of the counseling process, Bare (1967) asked counselors and clients to rate how helpful the counseling had been, how empathic the counselor was, how well the counselor got to know the client, and how well the client got to know the counselor. She correlated their responses with their measured needs. Her results indicated that counselor achievement need was inversely related to both counselors' and clients' perceived helpfulness of the counseling. Counselor achievement need was also inversely related to the counselors' perceptions of their own empathy level and how well they got to know the client. Counselors' ratings of their own empathy were positively correlated with needs for abasement and order and negatively correlated with their achievement and dominance needs. Affiliation and intraception were positively correlated with counselor-perceived helpfulness, intraception was negatively correlated with how well the counselor and client got to know one another, and dominance was positively correlated with how well the counselors felt the clients got to know them. Clients' perceptions of how well the counselor knew them and how well they knew the counselor were negatively correlated with the counselors' needs for order and autonomy, respectively. Her results suggest that outcome(s) as perceived by counselor and client are not necessarily correlated with the same counselor needs.

In-counseling behaviors other than those that derive from a client-centered perspective were investigated by Asa (1967) who found that among graduate students in a counselor education program, accepting leads were negatively correlated with the need for dominance; interpreting was negatively correlated with aggression, but diagnosing was positively correlated with aggression. Maley and Levine's (1968) study of extra-therapy variables, specifically junior-senior high school counselors' willingness to participate in psychological consultation interviews, indicated that participants had greater needs for exhibition and lesser needs for order and abasement.

Trainees' reactions to the training environment were the focus of two studies. Melchiskey and Wittmer (1970) speculated that trainees who chose not to continue their participation in a sensitivity group would differ from those who chose to continue. For his sample, composed of male and female experienced teachers, he found that the rejectors had higher need for achievement whereas continuators had higher need for succorance.

Vander Kolk (1974) divided white and black rehabilitation trainees into groups on the basis of their expectations about supervision. Client-centered dimensions were used to assess expectations. He found no differences on EPPS needs for groups with positive or negative expectations.

Although there are no needs that indisputably appear to be necessary counselor characteristics, a few needs appeared frequently enough across studies to warrant further investigation. Depending somewhat on how one counts them, in order of decreasing frequency, these needs include order, aggression, abasement, affiliation, dominance, intraception, achievement, and autonomy. Interestingly enough, with perhaps the exceptions of order and abasement, it does not appear to matter whether the counselor trainee has high or low scores on the needs mentioned. More important seems to be the kind of counseling criteria, which are of concern to the investigator.

PARAPROFESSIONAL HELPERS. Five studies have involved attempts to discover whether the performance level of students involved in nontherapy helping activities can be predicted from their need levels or patterns. Two of the studies were attempts to identify resident hall advisor characteristics, two were attempts to associate performance of behavior modification program participants with their needs, and the other was an attempt to assess the effects of needs on empathy levels of female volunteers in a mental health hospital companion program. Vesprani (1969) found that change and succorance were negatively correlated with their rated empathy.

Schroeder and Dowse's (1968) comparison of better and poorer female residence hall advisors as determined by head resident and student evaluations indicated no differences on the EPPS needs. However, Holbrook (1972) found that the combination of all fifteen needs and dominance by itself could predict whether male residence hall advisors were highly effective, medium effective, or ineffective according to their supervising counselors' evaluations. However, in support of Schroeder and Dowse's findings, Holbrook found that none of the EPPS needs was effective singly in predicting women resident advisors' performance, although all except intraception, succorance, aggression, and deference were effective in combination.

In his investigation of the performance evaluations and related characteristics of undergraduate trainees for a behavior modification consultation program, Suinn (1974) found that the needs that were important depended on the type of evaluation that was used. When the training staff's evaluations of performance were used, the low performance group was found to have less succorance than the high performance group and the group that had been rejected for training and more endurance than either group. When the consulting agency's evaluations were used, dominance was found to be inversely related to performance.

In the other behavior modification study, Gardiner (1972) studied the effectiveness of ward attendants, who had been exposed to a training program, on retarded inpatients' degree of improvement. He found that achievement and affiliation were positively associated, but intraception was negatively associated with improvement.

The findings from the studies of paraprofessionals have been rather heterogeneous. Perhaps the lack of consistent significant findings can be explained by the diversity of sample characteristics and measures used to study them. Be that as it may, at this time, needs that warrant further investigation are dominance, succorance, and intraception.

Client Characteristics

COMPARATIVE STUDIES. Most studies of client need characteristics have explored some aspect of the vocational counseling process. In two studies, vocational clients were compared to nonclients or other types of clients.

Looking for evidence of needs that might differentiate counseling clients from nonclients, Minge and Bowman (1967) compared scores of vocational-educational clients, personal clients, and nonclients. Vocational clients had higher need for order than the personal clients and nonclients; vocational and personal clients had higher needs for abasement than did nonclients; vocational and personal clients had lower needs for dominance than did nonclients.

Hartsook, Olch, and de Wolf (1976) compared female student volunteer participants in assertiveness groups to vocational counseling clients prior to counseling as well as to the EPPS norms. They found that the assertiveness clients had greater need for succorance and less need for achievement, order, and exhibition than the vocational clients. As compared to the EPPS norms, the assertiveness group members had greater need for aggression, autonomy, heterosexuality and succorance and less need for deference, abasement, order, and exhibition.

The results of the comparative studies may mean that a high need for order is characteristic of vocational clients. Level of abasement or succorance need may distinguish clients from nonclients. Otherwise, there seem to be no replicated consistencies across the two studies.

SELF-KNOWLEDGE. Deficient knowledge about self may be a quality that motivates some people to enter a helping relationship while others do not. Wigent (1974), who investigated the relationship between career choice uncertainty and EPPS needs, found that for a total sample consisting of 58 percent males, students with an average level of uncertainty had lower need for affiliation than students with a high or low level of career uncertainty. For female students, high indecision was associated with a high need for succorance.

Norrell and Grater (1960) asked male sophomore students who had not selected a major to predict their Strong Vocational Interest Blank scores. Their high awareness group as compared to their low awareness group had lower needs for succorance and order; they exhibited a tendency toward higher change and heterosexuality needs.

In a replication study using male veterans' hospital patients, Brown and Pool (1966) found that high aware respondents tended to have higher needs for achievement and lower needs for order, succorance, abasement, heterosexuality, and aggression. With the exception of heterosexuality and aggression, these findings were consistent with Norrell and Grater's predictions regarding the direction of EPPS needs and self-awareness.

Brown and Pool (1966) identified two self-awarenesss clusters, which they called moderately neurotic and character disorder or neurotic adjustment. The first cluster consisted of positive cluster loadings for abasement and succorance and negative loadings for achievement, meaning that a person with high achievement scores and low abasement and succorance scores should demonstrate high self-knowledge as far as vocational interests are concerned. The second cluster consisted of negative loadings on order, aggression, and heterosexuality. The authors suggested that a high score on either one of these scales would be indicative of low vocational self-awareness.

In total, the self-awareness studies present an inverse relationship between succorance, order, or heterosexuality and awareness. In other words, high scores on either of these scales is likely to be associated with relative uncertainty and lack of knowledge about one's self.

OUTCOME STUDIES. Factors related to promoting successful vocational outcome have been at least implicit in three studies. Blum (1961) theorized that college men's need for security might be related to their vocational choice as well as to normal personality characteristics. He found that needs for deference, order, succorance, abasement, and nurturance were positively correlated with need for security whereas needs for achievement, autonomy, dominance, and change were negatively correlated. Security scores were differentially related to students' choice of college major with highest scores being characteristic of teaching majors and lowest scores being characteristic of pre-law majors.

In another study, Pool (1965) looked at the question of whether hospitalized patients who became more realistic in their vocational choices following counseling differed in needs prior to counseling than those who did not. He found that more realistic clients had higher needs for intraception and endurance and lower need for autonomy with a tendency toward lower need for succorance.

Implicit in these first two studies is the possibility that client's level of dependency may influence outcome, a hypothesis explored directly by Heller and Goldstein (1961). Using the sum of the Succorance and Deference scales minus the Autonomy Scale as their measure of client's dependency, they found that dependency and attraction to therapy were positively correlated prior to therapy. Following therapy, clients described themselves as more independent, though their behavior remained dependent. Interestingly, clients, who served as the control group, showed a similar pattern of change though of lesser magnitude.

Heller and Goldstein's (1961) study may be interpreted to mean that clients enter the therapy relationship with a willingness to change, which in turn leads to change perhaps in spite of what the counselor or therapist does. Minge (1966) investigated the idea of *readiness for change* directly. Comparing clients and nonclients who took the EPPS to clients and nonclients who didn't, they found that clients as well as nonclients who took the inventory changed their self-ratings on dimensions similar to those measured by the EPPS more than those who did not take it. Personal clients changed more than did vocational-educational clients.

Minge (1966) contends "that completion of a personality inventory is analogous to a counseling interview" (p. 200) and, as a consequence, similar changes in self-perception can be facilitated by testing. Other authors have investigated aspects of the testing situation for their effect on respondents' perceptions.

Renzaglia et al. (1962) investigated respondents' accuracy in estimating their own scores on the EPPS also. With the exception of deference, estimated and actual scores were significantly correlated. In terms of the comparison of mean levels of needs, subjects as a group were best able to predict their autonomy needs. Gustav (1960) informally used the EPPS plus a sentence completion test to help dentists understand how their own dynamics might influence patient/dentist relationships.

Folds and Gazda (1966) exposed female college students to one of four types of test interpretation conditions: individual, group, written, or a control group. They measured test takers' recall of their test scores four and eight weeks post-test interpretation. None of the groups differed in their ability to recall their scores for needs exhibition, succorance, dominance, abasement, nurturance, or change. Those in the individual interpretation condition as compared to the control group were more accurate in their recall of their achievement, deference, affiliation, intraception, and heterosexuality scores on both occasions. Group interpretation respondents as compared to the control subjects were more accurate in their recall of their affiliation, endurance, and heterosexuality. Test interpretation of any kind seemed to improve the women's knowledge about their measured social needs.

Another interpretation of the Heller and Goldstein (1961) results is that the quality of the counseling relationship contributes to the counseling outcome (at least as perceived by the client). Bare (1967) used counselor and client need similarity as an index of relationship quality and attempted to relate it to counselor and clients' perceptions of outcome. She reported that client nurturance need was positively related to client's perceptions of how helpful the counseling had been. Client deference was negatively related to counselors' perceptions of how well they got to know the client and achievement was positively correlated. Large counselor-client differences in achievement were related to clients' perceptions that counseling tended to be less helpful and that they did not get to know the counselor well. Differences in nurturance led them to conclude that the counselor did not know them well.

Perhaps an indirect indicant of the counseling relationship is the length of time that clients persist in therapy. Van Atta (1968) compared the need levels of combined samples of male and female counseling center clients who stayed in counseling for a minimum of ten sessions to clients who terminated after fewer than ten sessions. He found that stayers had greater needs for exhibition and heterosexuality whereas the leavers had greater needs for order and endurance. Further evidence of the need deviance of the stayers was that they differed from the norms on eleven of the fifteen EPPS needs as compared to three for the leavers.

Though few in number, the studies of the impact of client characteristics on the counseling process suggest that these needs may be related in the following manner: endurance or order may be associated with greater client mental health or realism; nurturance, succorance, or deference possibly predict a need for security, which may carry over into the counseling relationship.

Summary and Discussion

Given that Edwards originally recommended the EPPS for use in counseling as well as research, surprisingly few studies have involved attempts to assess its usefulness in the counseling process. Perhaps, the relative absence of such literature can be explained by practitioners' limited accessibility to professional journals.

Nevertheless, the few studies that do exist are of limited usefulness because as a group they lack a coherent theme and their meaningfulness for the counseling process is not always readily apparent.

In addition, although several topic areas have been examined under the rubric of the counseling process, it is apparent that each of these areas has been fraught with methodological weaknesses: Studies of helper characteristics have infrequently involved experienced helpers. Studies of paraprofessionals have attempted to discover similarities within essentially heterogeneous samples. The main problem with studies of client characteristics is the limited number of such studies. Clearly, more sophisticated studies of the counseling process are needed if we are ever to understand how needs contribute to why people become counselors, seek counseling, and/or do (or do not) benefit from their training and counseling experiences.

References

Apostal, R. A., and Muro, J. J.: Effects of group counseling on self-reports and on self-recognition abilities of counselors in training. *Counselor Education and Supervision, 10*:56-73, 1970.

Asa, L. F.: Interview behavior and counselor personality variables. *Counselor Education and Supervision, 6*:324-331, 1967.

Bare, C. E.: Relationship of counselor personality and counselor-client personality similarity to selected counseling success criteria. *Journal of Counseling Psychology, 14*:419-425, 1967.

Bergin, A. E., and Jasper, A. E.: Correlates of empathy in psychotherapy: A replication. *Journal of Consulting and Clinical Psychology, 74*:474-476, 1969.

Bergin, A. E., and Solomon, S.: Correlates of empathic ability in psychotherapy. *American Psychologist, 18*:393, 1963.

Bernos, E. C.: Factors related to success in fifteen NDEA Counseling and Guidance Institutes. *Counselor Education and Supervision, 5*:94-104, 1966.

Blum, S. H.: The desire for security: An element in the vocational choice of college men. *Journal of Educational Psychology, 52*:317-321, 1961.

Brown, R. A., and Pool, D. A.: Psychological needs and self-awareness. *Journal of Counseling Psychology, 13*:85-88, 1966.

Danielson, H. A.: Personality of prospective elementary school counselors: Implications for preparation. *Counselor Education and Supervision, 8*:99-103, 1969.

Folds, J. H., and Gazda, G. M.: A comparison of the effectiveness and efficiency of three methods of test interpretation. *Journal of Counseling Psychology, 13*:318-324, 1966.

Gardiner, J. M.: Selection of nonprofessionals for behavior modification programs. *American Journal of Mental Deficiency, 76*:680-685, 1972.

Gustav, A.: Use of two tests in brief counseling. *Journal of Counseling Psychology, 7*:228-229, 1960.

Hartsook, J. E., Olch, D. R., and De Wolf, V. A.: Personality characteristics of women's assertiveness training group participants. *Journal of Counseling Psychology, 23*:322-326, 1976.

Heller, K., and Goldstein, A. P.: Client dependency and therapist expectancy as relationship maintaining variables in psychotherapy. *Journal of Consulting Psychology, 25*:371-375, 1961.

Holbrook, R. L.: Student volunteers as helpers in residence halls. *Journal of College Student Personnel, 13*:559-561, 1972.

Jones, L. K.: Toward more adequate selection criteria: Correlates of empathy, genuineness, and respect. *Counselor Education and Supervision, 14*:13-21, 1974.

Maley, R. F., and Levine, D.: Differences between guidance counselors who accept and reject psychological consultation. *Psychological Reports, 22*:332, 1968.

McGreevy, C. P.: Factor analysis of measures used in the selection and evaluation of counselor education candidates. *Journal of Counseling Psychology, 14*:51-56, 1967.

Melchiskey, S., and Wittmer, J.: Some personality characteristics of counselor candidates accepting and rejecting sensitivity training. *Counselor Education and Supervision, 9*:132-134, 1970.

Mills, D. H., and Abeles, N.: Counselor needs for affiliation and nurturance as related to liking for clients and counseling process. *Journal of Counseling Psychology, 12*:353-358, 1965.

Mills, D. H., Chestnut, W. J., and Hartzell, J. P.: The needs of counselors: A component analysis. *Journal of Counseling Psychology, 13*:82-85, 1966.

Minge, M. R.: Counseling readiness as readiness for change. *Journal of College Student Personnel, 7*:197-202, 1966.

Minge, M. R., and Bowman, T. F.: Personality differences among nonclients and vocational-educational and personal counseling clients. *Journal of Counseling Psychology, 14*:137-139, 1967.

Norrell, G., and Grater, H.: Interest awareness as an aspect of self-awareness. *Journal of Counseling Psychology, 7*:289-292, 1960.

Patterson, C. H.: Test characteristics of rehabilitation counselor trainees. *Journal of Rehabilitation, 28*:15-16, 1962.

Pool, D. A.: The relation of personality needs to vocational counseling outcome. *Journal of Counseling Psychology, 12*:23-27, 1965.

Renzaglia, G. A., Henry, D. R., and Rybolt, G. A., Jr.: Estimation and measurement of personality characteristics and correlates of their congruence. *Journal of Counseling Psychology, 9*:71-78, 1962.

Rosen, J.: Multiple-regression analysis of counselor characteristics and competencies. *Psychological Reports, 20*:1003-1008, 1967.

Schroeder, P., and Dowse, E.: Selection, function, and assessment of residence hall counselors. *Personnel and Guidance Journal, 47*:151-156, 1968.

Suinn, R. M.: Traits for selection of para-professionals for behavior-modification consultation training. *Commun Mental Health Journal, 10*:441-449, 1974.

Van Atta, R. E.: Relationship of personality characteristics of persistence in psychotherapy. *Journal of Consulting and Clinical Psychology, 32*:731-733, 1968.

Vander Kolk, C. J.: The relationship of personality, values, and race to anticipation of the supervisory relationship. *Rehabilitation Counseling Bulletin, 18*:41-46, 1974.

Vesprani, G. J.: Personality correlates of accurate empathy in a college companion program. *Journal of Consulting and Clinical Psychology, 33*:722-727, 1969.

Walton, J. M.: Peer perceptions of counselor effectiveness: A multiple regression approach. *Counselor Education and Supervision, 13*:250-255, 1974.

Wigent, P. A.: Personality variables related to career decision-making abilities of community college students. *Journal of College Student Personnel, 15*:105-108, 1974.

SECTION VI

APPENDICES

Appendix A

AN IPSATIVE ANSWER SHEET

Summary of EPPS Test Scores

For: _____ Name _____

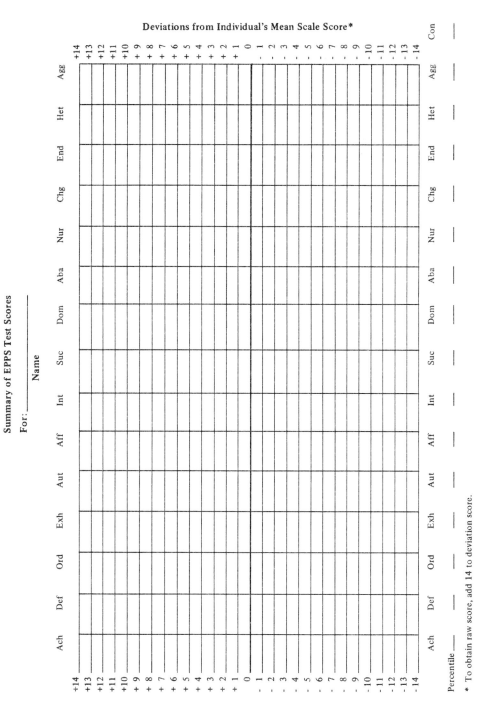

Deviations from Individual's Mean Scale Score*

	Ach	Def	Ord	Exh	Aut	Aff	Int	Suc	Dom	Aba	Nur	Chg	End	Het	Agg	Con

Percentile ___

* To obtain raw score, add 14 to deviation score.

233

A SIMPLE SPSS PROGRAM FOR SCORING EPPS
FROM COMPUTER ANSWER SHEETS

```
Allocate          Transpace = 1500
Run Name          Individual's Scale Scores
Variable List     Item01 to Item225
Input Format      Fixed(10X,70F1.0/10X,70F1.0/10X,70F1.0/
                  10X,15F1.0)
Input Medium      Card
Recode            Item01 to Item70 (Blank=1)
Recode            Item71 to Item141 (Blank=2)
Recode            Item142 to Item210(Blank=1)
Recode            Item211 to Item225 (Blank=2)
Compute           Consis=0
If                (Item01 EQ Item151) Consis=Consis+1
If                (Item07 EQ Item157) Consis=Consis+1
If                (Item13 EQ Item163) Consis=Consis+1
If                (Item19 EQ Item169) Consis=Consis+1
If                (Item25 EQ Item175) Consis=Consis+1
If                (Item26 EQ Item101) Consis=Consis+1
If                (Item32 EQ Item107) Consis=Consis+1
If                (Item38 EQ Item113) Consis=Consis+1
If                (Item44 EQ Item119) Consis=Consis+1
If                (Item50 EQ Item125) Consis=Consis+1
If                (Item51 EQ Item201) Consis=Consis+1
If                (Item57 EQ Item207) Consis=Consis+1
If                (Item63 EQ Item213) Consis=Consis+1
If                (Item69 EQ Item219) Consis=Consis+1
If                (Item75 EQ Item225) Consis=Consis+1
Count             AchR=Item02 to Item05 Item76 to Item80 Item01
                  Item152 to Item155 (2)
Count             AchC=Item06 Item11 Item16 Item21 Item26
                  Item31 Item36 Item41 Item46 Item51 Item56
                  Item61 Item66 Item71 (1)
Compute           Ach=AchC + AchR
Count             DefC=Item06 Item08 to Item10 Item81 to Item85
                  Item56 to Item160 (2)
Count             DefR=Item02 Item12 Item17 Item22 Item27 Item32
                  Item37 Item42 Item47 Item52 Item57 Item62
                  Item67 Item72 (1)
Compute           Def=DefR + DefC
Count             OrdC=Item11 Item12 Item14 Item15 Item86 to
                  Item90 Item161 to Item165 (2)
Count             OrdR=Item03 Item08 Item18 Item23 Item28 Item33
                  Item38 Item43 Item48 Item53 Item58 Item63
                  Item68 Item73 (1)
Compute           Ord=OrdR + OrdC
Count             ExhC=Item16 to Item18 Item20 Item91 to Item95
                  Item166 to Item170 (2)
Count             ExhR=Item04 Item09 Item14 Item24 Item29 Item34
                  Item39 Item44 Item49 Item54 Item59 Item64
                  Item69 Item74 (1)
Compute           Exh=ExhR + ExhC
```

Appendix B (continued)

Count	AutC=Item21 to Item24 Item96 to Item100 Item171 to Item175 (2)
Count	AutR=Item05 Item10 Item15 Item20 Item30 Item35 Item40 Item45 Item50 Item55 Item60 Item65 Item70 Item75 (1)
Compute	Aut=AutR + AutC
Count	AffC=Item26 to Item30 Item102 to Item105 Item176 to Item180 (2)
Count	AffR=Item76 Item81 Item86 Item91 Item96 Item106 Item111 Item116 Item121 Item126 Item131 Item136 Item141 Item146 (1)
Compute	Aff=AffR + AffC
Count	IntC=Item31 to Item35 Item106 Item108 to Item110 Item181 to Item185 (2)
Count	IntR=Item77 Item82 Item87 Item92 Item97 Item102 Item112 Item117 Item122 Item127 Item132 Item137 Item142 Item147 (1)
Compute	Int=IntC + IntR
Count	SucC=Item36 to Item40 Item111 Item112 Item114 Item115 Item186 to Item190 (2)
Count	SucR=Item78 Item83 Item88 Item93 Item98 Item103 Item108 Item118 Item123 Item128 Item133 Item138 Item143 Item148 (1)
Compute	Suc=SucR + SucC
Count	DomC=Item41 to Item45 Item116 to Item118 Item120 Item191 to Item195 (2)
Count	DomR=Item79 Item84 Item89 Item94 Item99 Item104 Item109 Item114 Item124 Item129 Item134 Item139 Item144 Item149 (1)
Compute	Dom=DomC + DomR
Count	AbaC=Item46 to Item50 Item121 to Item124 Item196 to Item200 (2)
Count	AbaR=Item80 Item85 Item90 Item95 Item100 Item105 Item110 Item115 Item120 Item130 Item135 Item140 Item145 Item150 (1)
Count	NurR=Item151 Item156 Item161 Item166 Item171 Item176 Item181 Item186 Item191 Item196 Item206 Item211 Item216 Item221 (1)
Count	NurC=Item51 to Item55 Item126 to Item130 Item202 to Item205 (2)
Compute	Nur =NurR + NurC
Count	ChgR=Item152 Item157 Item162 Item167 Item172 Item177 Item182 Item187 Item192 Item197 Item202 Item212 Item217 Item222 (1)
Count	ChgC=Item56 to Item60 Item131 to Item135 Item206 Item208 to Item210 (2)
Compute	Chg=ChgR + ChgC
Count	EndC=Item61 to Item65 Item136 to Item140 Item211 Item212 Item214 Item215 (2)
Count	EndR=Item153 Item158 Item163 Item168 Item173 Item178 Item183 Item188 Item193 Item198 Item203 Item208 Item218 Item223 (1)
Compute	End=EndC + EndR

Appendix B (continued)

Count	HetR=Item154 Item159 Item164 Item169 Item174 Item179 Item184 Item189 Item194 Item199 Item204 Item209 Item214 Item224 (1)
Count	HetC=Item66 to Item70 Item141 to Item145 Item216 to Item218 Item220 (2)
Compute	Het=HetC + HetR
Count	AggR=Item155 Item160 Item165 Item170 Item175 Item180 Item185 Item190 Item195 Item200 Item205 Item210 Item215 Item220 (1)
Count	AggC=Item71 to Item75 Item146 to Item150 Item221 to Item224 (2)
Compute	Agg=Aggc + AggR
Read Input Data	
(Insert Data)	
End Input Data	
List Cases	Cases=50/Variables=Consis to Aut
List Cases	Cases=50/Variables=Seqnum AffC to Dom
List Cases	Cases=50/Variables=Seqnum AbaC to End
List Cases	Cases=50/Variables=Seqnum HetR to Agg
Finish	

[1]Input format statement should be altered to match the actual format of the computer sheet being used; List cases cards should be changed to indicate the actual number of profiles ("cases") for which scores are being computed.

Because of SPSS space limitations, it may be necessary to use four separate passes through the computer in order to obtain scores for all 16 scales. In that case, the "list cases" cards indicate the scales that should be counted and computed during each run.

Appendix C

TEST LEGENDS

Scale Name	Abbreviation	Code Number

Edwards Personal Preference Schedule (EPPS)

Scale Name	Abbreviation	Code Number
Achievement	Ach	
Deference	Def	
Order	Ord	
Exhibition	Exh	
Autonomy	Aut	
Affiliation	Aff	
Intraception	Int	
Succorance	Suc	
Dominance	Dom	
Abasement	Aba	
Nurturance	Nur	
Change	Chg	
Endurance	End	
Heterosexuality	Het	
Aggression	Agg	
Consistency	Con	

Minnesota Multiphasic Personality Inventory (MMPI)

Scale Name	Abbreviation	Code Number
Cannot Say Score	?	
Lie	L	
Infrequency	F	
Correction	K	
Hypochondriasis	Hs	1
Depression	D	2
Conversion Hysteria	Hy	3
Psychopathic Deviate	Pd	4
Masculinity-Femininity	Mf	5
Paranoia	Pa	6
Psychasthenia	Pt	7
Schizophrenia	Sc	8
Hypomania	Ma	9
Social Introversion	Si	0

Guilford-Zimmerman Temperament Scale (GZTS)

Scale Name	Abbreviation	Code Number
General Activity	G	
Restraint	R	
Ascendance	A	
Sociability	S	
Emotional Stability	E	
Objectivity	O	
Friendliness	F	

Appendix C (continued)

Scale Name	Abbrev-iation	Code Number
Thoughtfulness	T	
Personal Relations	P	
Masculinity	M	

Personality Research Form (PRF)

Abasement	Ab	
Achievement	Ac	
Affiliation	Af	
Aggression	Ag	
Autonomy	Au	
Change	Ch	
Cognitive Structure	Cs	
Dependence	De	
Dominance	Do	
Endurance	En	
Exhibition	Ex	
Harm Avoidance	Ha	
Impulsivity	Im	
Nurturance	Nu	
Order	Or	
Play	Pl	
Sentience	Se	
Social Recognition	Sr	
Succorance	Su	
Understanding	Un	
Infrequency	In	
Desirability	Dy	

Edwards Personality Inventory (EPI)

Responsible
Leader
Sensitive
Anxious
Routine
Plans
Worker
Persistent
Helps
Kind
Independent
Conforms

Sixteen Personality Factor Questionnaire (16PF)

Outgoing-Reserved	A
More Intelligent-Less Intelligent	B

Appendix C (continued)

Scale Name	Abbrev- iation	Code Number
Emotionally Stable- Emotionally Unstable	C	
Assertive-Humble	E	
Happy-go-lucky—sober	F	
Weaker Superego- Stronger Superego	G	
Adventuresome-Sly	H	
Self-reliant-Dependent	I	
Trusting-Suspicious	L	
Imaginative-Practical	M	
Shrewd-Forthright	N	
Apprehensive-Self-assured	O	
Experimental-Conservative	Q1	
Group Dependent-Self- sufficient	Q2	
Undisciplined-Controlled	Q3	
Relaxed-Tense	Q4	

Single Scales

Marlowe-Crowne Social Desirability	MC	
F-Scale Conventionalism	Co	
F-Scale Projectivity	Pro	

SUBJECT INDEX

A

Achievement, 65, 105, 110-111, 180, 185, 203
  ability and, 181-184
  academic, 176, table 177, 179, 181-190, 192-193, 221
  grade point as indicator of, 180-184, 189, 192
  objective measures of, 176, table 177
  patterns of, table 79, 186-187
  projective measures of, 176, table 177
Addictive behavior, 125-126
Adjective Check List, 78, table 79
Alpert-Harber Achievement Test, 105
Anxiety, 22, 67, 104-105, 118, 125, 127, 131
  ego disjunction and, 22-23, 125
  sex differences in, 105

C

California Psychological Inventory, 51, 52-54, 59, 90, table 91, 92, table 93, 95, 96, 176
Cattell's 16 Personality Factors Test, 129, able 130, 132
College majors
  counseling, 220
  education, 15, 31-32, 145-146, table 149, table 160, 166-167, 172, 185, 198, 225
  engineering, 32, 145-146, 180, 181
  liberal arts, table 149, table 160, 163-165, 225
  medicine affiliates, 57, table 149, table 160, 165-167, 180, 226
  nursing, 12, 32, table 149, table 160, 154-163, 172, 180, 181, 204
  physical education, table 149, table 160, 167
Consistency score, 54-57, 73-74, 77, 185
  effects of random responding on, 72-74, table 74
  profile characteristic, 74, 81
  sex differences, 77
Cross-racial/cultural studies, 37-39, 43, 66-67, 113-114, 125
  Asians, 34, 210-211
  blacks, 125, 189-190, 222
  Indians, 182

D

Derived Scales, 18, 24, 205
  dependency ratio, 202, 204, 205

ego disjunction, 18, 22, 23, 107, 125
EPPS components, 18, 19-22

E

Education and training effects, 29-32, 221
Edwards Personality Inventory, 90, 92, table 93, 96

F

Factors analysis, 86, table 91, 97, table 98, 102, 129-132, table 130, 139, 145-146, 165-166, 172, 187-188, 219, 224-225
Faking
  consistency score effects of, 54-58, table 56
  scale elevations and, 51, 57, figure 53
  scale depressions and, 57, figure 55
  scale transparency and, 57
  sex differences and, 37
Family dynamics
  birth order, 113
  cohesion, 113
  disciplinary styles, 114
  educational history, 114-115
  father's success, 114
  marital status, 114
  maternal characteristics, 115-116

G

Guilford-Zimmerman Temperament Survey, table 98, 101, 102, 107, 145, 221

I

Instructions, 16-23, 55, 68
Interpersonal relationships
  attraction, 213, 220
  behavior in, 116-117
  couples, 213, 216
  friendship, 211-213
  groups, 202
  marital discord, 216-217

M

Major, academic (see College majors)
Minnesota Multiphasic Personality Inventory

241

NAME INDEX

A

Abate, M., 210, 217
Abbott, R.D., 90, table 91, 97, tale 98, 103
Abeles, N., 220, 228
Abraham, H.L., 201, 207
Abramson, L.M., 110, 118
Abramson, P.R., 110, 118
Adams, C.K., 111, 119
Adams, H.E., 203, 204, 208
Adams, H.L., 29, 32, 45
Adams, J., 129, 134, table 149, 173
Ager, J., 60, 71
Ahern, E.H., 85, 86, table 87, table 89, 102
Allen, B.V., 171, 174
Allen, L.R., table 149, 173
Allen, R.M., 25, 45, 85, 86, table 87, table 89, table
  91, 97, table 98, 102, 103
Alpert, M.I., 206, 207
Altman, I., 204, 209
Anderson, R.E., table 155, 173
Anzel, A.S., 203, 207
Apostal, R.A., 221, 227
Appley, M.H., 199, 207
Araoz, D.T., 216, 217
Arkoff, A. 37, 45, 56, table 38, 40, 211
Armatas, J.P., 144, 145, 147
Asa, L.F., 222, 227
Asch, S.E., 199, 200, 207
Atkinson, G., 139, 147

B

Bachman, J.B., table 177, 193
Bailey, J.T., table 149, 154, 173
Bailey, K.G., 111, 119
Bailey, R.L., 143-144, 145, 147
Baker, F., table 149, 174
Balazs, E., table 149, 168, 173
Ball, M.F., 127, 136
Bare, C.E., 133, 222, 226, 227
Bartol, G.H., 201, 207
Basset, G.R., table 149, 174
Bates, C., table 155, 174
Becker, G., 191-192, 193, 215, 218
Becker, W.M., 105, 118
Belcastro, F.P., 185, 186, 193
Bendig, A.W., 86, table 91, 102, 134, table 177,

184, 193-194
Bennis, W., 202, 207
Berens, A.E., 187, 194
Bergin, A.E., 220, 227
Berkowitz, W.R., 111, 118
Bernadin, A.C., 199, 205, 207
Bernhardson, C.S., 60, 63, 69, 108, 118
Bernhardt, H.E., Jr., 180, 194
Bernos, E.C., 221, 227
Bernstein, S., 106, 107, 119
Berrien, F.K., 45, 210, 211, 217, 218
Bessmer, M.A., 78, table 79, 80, 81
Bhatnager, R.P., 182-183, 193, 194
Birch, R.W., 25, table 26, 29, 44, 46
Blazer, J.A., 111, 118
Blood, D.F., 29, 32, 45
Blum, H.S., 225, 228
Blumfeld, W.S., 57, 58
Boose, B.J., 25, 37, table 38, table 40, 45
Boose, S.S., 25, table 26, 37, table 38, table 40, 45
Borgatta, E.F., table 14, 102
Borgers, S.B., 108, 118
Borislow, B., 14, 16, 23, table 14, 55, table 56, 57,
  58
Bouchard, T.J., Jr., table 79, table 80, 80, 81
Bowerman, C.E., 212, 218
Bowman, T.F., 224, 228
Brady, J.P., 43, 46, 202, 207
Brazziel, W.F., table 26, table 38, table 40, 45, 189,
  190, 194
Brien, R.L., 108, 118
Brollier, C., 164, 166, 173
Bromer, J.A., tale 155, 173
Brousseau, J.D., table 149, 174
Brown, O.H., 191, 195
Brown, R.A., 224-225, 228
Bruel, I., 108, 120
Bunker, C.S., 170, 173
Burke, R., 202, 207
Burkman, J.H., 132, 135
Burton, D.A., 129, table 130, 131-132, 134
Byers, A.P., 33, 46

C

Caditz, S.B., 132, 134
Cairns, R.B., 116, 118, 201, 203, 205, 207
Camisa, J.M., 126, 135

245